# HOLINESS

# HOLINESS

## Donna Orsuto

New Century Theology

**continuum**

Cover: Detail from the Crucifixtion, Apse Mosaic from the twelfth century. Basillica di San Clemente, Rome. Reproduced by courtsey of the Irish Dominican Fathers.

**CONTINUUM**

The Tower Building,
11 York Road,
London SE1 7NX

80 Maiden Lane
Suite 704
New York NY 10038

www.continuumbooks.com

First published 2006

**British Library Cataloguing-in-Publication Data**
A catalogue record for this book is available from the British Library.

ISBN 0–8264–5398–8

Typeset by Continuum
Printed and bound by MPG Books Ltd, Bodmin, Cornwall

# Contents

# Introduction

Writing a book about holiness in any era has always had its challenges. From a temporal perspective, few things could be less relevant than holiness. Making a living, chasing dreams, tackling goals, dashing to greater conquests and shinier treasures – getting and doing – *these* are sacrosanct to the secular mind, particularly in our age. Holiness, to many, is regarded as a special sort of hybrid hobby for the piously impractical at best, and escapist sissy stuff for the weak at worst. And yet, in the Christian tradition we hold that holiness has a central place in our understanding of who God is and who we are. Holiness for Christians is about union with Christ, who in the Spirit unites us to the Father. It is about abiding in this loving union and letting this relationship flow into our everyday lives. We have received this free gift through baptism, along with the gifts of faith, hope and charity. God's intention in giving us these gifts is that we should maintain and cultivate them, by consciously striving to grow in holiness. Elemental to the responsibility of nurturing these baptismal gifts is the believer's active cultivation and practical application of loving God and loving others.

Holiness as responsibility can be daunting and sometimes seems just a little too vague to live out in the very real flesh-and-blood, cell phone, computer-obsessed, fast-moving world in which we live. This challenge is one reason why the opening words of Donald Nicholl's book *Holiness* resonate with so many of his readers. In 1981, he wrote: 'A certain feeling of absurdity comes over one on being asked to write a book about holiness and then in turn to expect other people to read it after it has been written.'[1] In the early stages of research though, I noted a quotation from C.S. Lewis' *Mere Christianity* that casts this task in a different light. He began his discussion of holiness by considering the meaning behind the imperative: 'Be perfect, therefore, as your heavenly Father is perfect' (Mt. 5:48). Using the analogy of remodelling a house, a 'living' house, he wrote:

Imagine yourself as a living house. God comes in to rebuild that house. At first, perhaps, you understand what He is doing. He is getting the drains right and stopping the leaks in the roof and so on: you knew that those jobs needed doing and so you are not surprised. But presently He starts knocking the house about in a way that hurts abominably and does not seem to make sense. What on earth is He up to? The explanation is that He is building quite a different house from the one you thought of – throwing out a new wing here, putting on an extra floor there, running up towers, making courtyards. You thought you were going to be made into a decent little cottage: but He is building a palace. He intends to come and live in it Himself.

The command *'Be ye perfect'* is ... [not] a command to do the impossible. He is going to make us into creatures that can obey that command. ... If we let Him – for we can prevent Him, if we choose – He will make the feeblest ... of us into ... a dazzling, radiant, immortal creature, pulsating all through with such energy and joy and wisdom and love as we cannot now imagine, a bright stainless mirror which reflects back to God perfectly (though, of course, on a smaller scale) His own boundless power and delight and goodness. The process will be long and in parts very painful, but that is what we are in for. Nothing less. He meant what He said.[2]

Taking our cue from Lewis, let us imagine that *holiness is God's building project*. God is the master builder, the architect. We are subcontractors in a project that is to become God's dwelling. Holiness is not simply about what we do, but about what God is doing in us to facilitate growth by enabling us to become more fully who we are, namely God's holy people. We are being built together like 'living stones ... into a spiritual house' (I Pet. 2:5). 'We' and 'us' are used here purposely because holiness concerns not only the individual, but also the community bound together in God's love. This holiness 'project' is *always* a work in process; it will never be finished in this life, but will find its completion only in the next.

The basic organizational structure of this book hinges on images associated with constructing, remodelling, maintaining, and expanding a house, a house which turns out to be God's 'palace'. The first chapter, 'Laying the Foundations: Insights from the Bible', explores a few of the 'building blocks' that are used for laying a firm foundation for constructing a Christian vision of holiness. It provides the blueprint or drawing-plans that preface the actual building. It supplies a vision that precedes the project and that will see it to completion. This vision is best described as the 'paradox of holiness'. Holiness is intimately intertwined with the notion that God, *the* Holy One, *is* wholly other and invites us to be 'set apart' for him alone, while simultaneously calling us into the intimacy of covenant love. Sacred Scripture shows that holiness is both God's gift and our responsibility. The New Testament focuses on Jesus as the cornerstone for a Christian understanding of holiness (cf. 1 Pet. 2:6, 7). Holiness means being incorporated into Christ, growing in conformity to him, abiding in him and being drawn into union with the Father through him. The vivifying source of Christian holiness is the Holy Spirit and through the Spirit the Church becomes the temple and the household of God.

In the second chapter, 'Many Mansions: Exploring Holiness through the Centuries', we will explore the various ways that holiness has been lived out among God's people. Indeed, there are many mansions – many rooms – in God's ever-expanding palace. The construction of these various 'mansions' is quite diverse and depends on both historical context and cultural circumstances. God has an intricate set of drawings for this great dwelling. These include structural, architectural, mechanical, plumbing, and electrical dimensions. God also takes into account the landscape, the soil, the adjacent buildings, the weather conditions and how they will affect the building, the cultural environment and the special use of the building. He even knows the time frame in which the project needs to be completed. A glance at the tradition allows us to catch a glimpse of the sheer wonder of God's architectural skill and originality. By exploring the various writings from those considered exemplars or saints, we can appreciate the breadth and depth of Christian holiness. Among the selected models are the experiences of martyrs, desert dwellers, monks, mendicants, married couples, contemplatives, and even someone considered on the threshold of the Church. The goal here is to show the diverse ways of living out holiness while recognizing certain common characteristics. This chapter concludes with a reflection on Mary and the beauty of holiness.

'Ordinary Maintenance for an Extraordinary Dwelling', the third chapter, maps out the ordinary means for living out the call to holiness. Although this chapter is written from a Roman Catholic perspective, it is hoped that other Christians will identify with much that is developed here. To clarify and establish a common ground for this chapter's terminology, the reader is asked to keep in mind that if one believes that sacraments effect what they signify, they are vehicles of God's transforming presence and power in our lives. They are an ordinary means of growth towards union with God in Christ. Living the sacramental life to the full also affects in a profound way one's actions in the midst of the world. The foundations are the sacraments of baptism, confirmation and Eucharist. Plunged into Christ's death and resurrection, anointed by the Holy Spirit and nourished by the body and blood of Christ, we participate in God's life. The sacraments of reconciliation and healing, as well as the vocational sacraments of marriage and ordination, are in and of themselves vehicles of growth in holiness. This understanding is not limited merely to the actual celebrating of the sacraments once and for all. Rather, it expands to include the living out of the practical implications of the sacraments in everyday life. Besides focusing on the sacraments, this chapter examines the place of prayer, reflection on the Word of God, the virtues, and the gifts of the Spirit as traditional ways of being open to the Holy One. It also explores the place of sacramentals – the various forms of popular piety such as blessings, the rosary, pilgrimages – that have always been a part of the Roman Catholic paths towards holiness. These are some of the ordinary means, or the tools, that God uses to maintain his dwelling.

In the fourth chapter, 'Beyond Basic Floor Plans: Towards a Contemporary Understanding of Holiness', we will seek to explore what holiness means especially since the Second Vatican Council (1962–65). For Roman Catholics, the Second Vatican Council, its consequent conciliar documents, and post-conciliar statements are a benchmark for understanding holiness today. Here we will consider the insights suggested by the Magisterium regarding a do-able, liveable holiness for our times.

The purpose of the concluding chapter, 'The Expansion Project: Holiness in the twenty-first century', is to focus on what it means to live holy lives in today's tightly wound, complicated world. Application is fundamental. Critical to our discussion is the point that God is always calling us out of our well-established *status quo* and into the ever beyond. This is the challenge that C.S. Lewis recognized when he wrote that '[God] is building quite a different house from the one you thought of'. Here we will explore new rooms or understandings of holiness that are emerging in our time. We are already standing on the 'footers' of a new excavation site in God's ever-expanding palace. By broadening our vision and cultivating a contemplative gaze, God's expanding building project will become more recognizable. This is the preparation necessary for exploring the new rooms or understandings of holiness that are unfolding in the twenty-first century. Two such 'footers' are the challenges of understanding and living holiness in the context of globalization and interreligious dialogue. These lead us to reflect on holiness and its effect on our social responsibilities including caring for the more vulnerable members of our society and considering the implications of holiness with an informed regard for our environment.

The call to holiness is an invitation to godly effectiveness. It means being open to the power of the Spirit so that we can follow in the footsteps of Jesus and give glory to God in our lives. It implies humbly accepting the limits and amazing potential of our humanity, and recognizing the presence of love's redeeming work in us as individuals, in our church, our society and in our world. *Holiness is God's building project, stone by stone, brick by brick, grace and effort, effort and grace.* Sometimes we are amazed, other times we are perplexed at the edifice that is being constructed around us. Sometimes, the building project is nothing but disciplined drudgery, and other times the effort and progress are exhilarating. And always, it is good to recall that we are working together in a great communion of saints, and in our working we find ourselves being curiously built into 'the holy temple' of the Lord. Eph. 2:20 offers a glimpse of this vision: 'You are fellow citizens with the saints and members of the household of God built upon the foundation of the apostles and prophets, Christ Jesus himself being the cornerstone, in whom the whole structure is joined together and grows into a holy temple in the Lord, in whom you are also built into it for a dwelling place of God in the Spirit.'

Writing this book has also been a sort of extended 'building project' and I would like to express my gratitude to those who supported me in its 'construction'. I am grateful to the administration of the Gregorian University for granting me a six-month sabbatical which allowed me to finish this project, and to Riekie Van Velzen, David Dawson-Vásquez, the staff and students at the Lay Centre at Foyer Unitas as well as James and Sandra Keating and Jean Chiswell. Nothing would have been accomplished without their generous and gracious assistance and support. I am also indebted to the Woodstock Theological Center at Georgetown University, under the leadership of Gasper LoBiondo, S. J., for welcoming me for three months into their International Fellows

Program, to Leon Hooper, S. J., librarian, and the staff of the Woodstock Library. Warmest appreciation and gratitude goes to the Sisters of Georgetown Visitation for their cordial hospitality and to Nancy Eisold Lindsay for all the many ways she helped and encouraged me during my stay in Washington, D.C.

I spent the second part of my sabbatical in Jerusalem, living at the Pontifical Biblical Institute while teaching a course at the Hebrew University, and I am grateful to all who enriched my visit there. A special note of thanks goes to Hubert and Aldegonde Brenninkmeijer-Werhahn for sponsoring the exchange of professors between the Hebrew University and the Gregorian University. Numerous friends have either read parts of the chapters in this book or have given invaluable advice. To Mary Popio; Christopher O'Donnell; O. Carm.; Francis Sullivan, S. J.; Francesco Rossi de Gasperis, S. J.; Anthony McSweeney, S. S. S.; Gerald O'Collins, S. J.; Kevin O'Neil, C. Ss. R; Stephen Rehrauer, C. Ss. R.; James and Sandra Keating; Michelle Mueller; and Jon O'Brien, S. J., I express my heartfelt thanks. I am also grateful to the Prior of San Clemente in Rome, John Cunningham, O. P., for providing the splendid prints of that basilica's twelfth-century mosaic. To Robin Baird-Smith, Andrew Walby and Anya Wilson at Continuum for their patience and gracious assistance in seeing this book through to publication, I am grateful. Finally, to my brother, George and my two sisters, Jean and Arlene, my deepest gratitude for all of their love and support. I dedicate this work to my sister, Arlene Jacobs, who during a prolonged illness has taught me much about holiness in these last few years.

Rome

Feast of All Saints

1 November 2005

## Notes

1 Donald Nicholl, *Holiness* (London: Mahwah: Paulist Press, 1987). This was first published in England by Darton, Longman and Todd, LDT in 1981. Other more recent books on the topic include John Webster, *Holiness* (London: SCM Press; Grand Rapids: Eerdmans, 2003), a Trinitarian dogmatics of holiness written from a Barthian perspective. For John Endean's review of this, see *The Way* (July 2004), pp.152; for Elizabeth Dreyer's review, see 'Shorter Notices', *Theological Studies* 66 (June 2005), p.501. Cf. also John Haughey, *Housing Heaven's Fire*: *The Challenge of Holiness* (Chicago: Loyola

Press, 2002) and Stephen G. Barton (ed.), *Holiness Past and Present*, (London: T&T Clark, 2003).

2 Clive Staples Lewis, *Mere Christianity* (revised and amplified edn; San Francisco: HarperSanFrancisco, 2001), pp.205–6. This was first published in 1952.

*'Abide in me as I abide in you. Just as the branch cannot bear fruit by itself unless it abides in the vine, neither can you unless you abide in me. I am the vine and you are the branches. Those who abide in me and I in them bear much fruit, because apart from me you can do nothing.'* (John 15: 4–5)

Basilica of Saint Clement, Rome
Apse and Triumphal Arch
12th-century mosaic
Reproduced by courtesy of the Irish Domincan Fathers

# 1
# Laying the Foundations: Insights from the Bible

'A human being is holy not because he or she triumphs by will-power over chaos and guilt and leads a flawless life, but because that life shows the victory of God's faithfulness in the midst of disorder and imperfection ... Humanly speaking, holiness is always like this: God's endurance in the midst of our refusal of him, his capacity to meet every refusal with the gift of himself.'

Rowan Williams
*Open to Judgment: Sermons and Addresses*
(London: Longman and Todd, 1994), p.136.

*'The only tragedy in life is not to be a saint.'*
Raïssa Maritain
*Les grandes amitiés*
(Paris: Desclée de Brouwer, 1949, p.117.)

*'Our progress in holiness depends on God and ourselves – on God's grace and on our will to be holy. We must have a real living determination to reach holiness. 'I will be a saint' means I will despoil myself of all that is not God.'*

Mother Teresa of Calcutta
*A Gift for God*
(New York and London: Harper and Row, 1975, p.78.)

## Introduction

Holiness as God's big and complex building project is meant to lead us into a practical and simple participation of Christ's way of being and acting in our everyday lives. It involves you and me, the people we meet on the street, as well as the huge celestial choirs we see on Christmas

cards. For Christians there is no better place to find the building blocks
and the underlying girders for this call than in the Bible. It is here, in
sacred Scripture, that we find God's plan for us called yet often under-
developed saints.[1] The purpose of this chapter is to focus on some key
passages from the Bible and ask what they mean for contemporary
Christians in their search for holiness.

Scripture passages such as 'Be holy as God is holy' (Lev. 19: 2)[2] or 'Be
perfect as your heavenly Father is perfect' (M. 5:48) can sometimes lead
to feelings of guilt and inadequacy. If these imperatives are understood
as a call to meticulously follow prescribed rules, then the feelings of guilt
could lead to despair. People ask, 'How can I ever live up to the expectations placed before me by God?' Life brings its own challenges, without
adding God's demand for perfection or holiness.[3] Perhaps this is one of
the reasons why holiness has been neatly severed from our everyday
vocabulary. Rarely does it find its way in to a homily.[4] An exception to
this reticence is found in the words and actions of the late John Paul II.
His entire pastoral plan for the new millennium focused on the universal call to holiness. In fact, during World Youth Day celebrations in Rome
in the year 2000, banners appeared around the city with the words, 'Do
not be afraid to be saints of the new millennium.'[5] In August 2005,
Benedict XVI continued this theme with his words to the young people
gathered in Cologne, where he proposed the saints as models of sanctity.
The message is that everyone, without exception, is called to holiness.

In order to live out this holiness with all of its challenges in contemporary society, we can turn to the Bible for insight and inspiration.
Though at times the various books of the Bible are marked by theological diversity, together as part of the Christian canon, they reflect an over-
arching continuity that can be characterized as the 'paradox of holiness':
*God, the majestic and transcendent One, reaches out to men and women
in mercy and draws them into a relationship of covenant love. This
dialectic of majesty and availability in God characterizes a Scriptural
understanding of holiness.*[6] Holiness brings its demands and responsibilities, but these must be seen in the context of a God who graciously
embraces humankind with mercy and love. To speak of holiness in the
context of covenant love reminds us of the solemn agreement between
God and Israel. In biblical terminology, two people enter into a covenant
when there is a sworn agreement between them to do or not to do something. Similarly, Israel's relation with Yhwh is couched in language of
relationship, of mutual commitment. This is the background from

which we can begin to understand the exhortation to live holy lives, to live a life worthy of our calling.[7]

Holiness in the Bible refers to that which is separated or set apart. Above all *God is holy*, meaning that God is wholly other. People, places and objects are considered holy when they are set apart for the worship of God. Holiness means that some people or things are separated *from* the common to be consecrated *for* the divine. Thus holiness is about being possessed by God and responding to this call through offering all that one (whether individually or communally) is to God. The first part of this chapter will focus on select books of the Hebrew Scriptures and show how this paradox of holiness is played out. The second part, on the New Testament, considers Jesus as the cornerstone for a Christian understanding of holiness. He, at one and the same time, shows us who God is in whose image we have been made, and who we are to be as people created in that image. Jesus is the one who lived a life of love without compromise and who calls us to do the same. Through abiding in Jesus and taking on his way of being and acting, Christians together can respond to this call in the power of the Spirit to the glory of the Father.

**Old Testament Building Blocks**

To delve comprehensively into the concept of holiness as presented in the Old Testament would be beyond the scope of this book. It is, however, important to note that the primary Hebrew root used to denote holiness, qdŝ, occurs no less than 850 times in the Bible. Subsequent discussions regarding the idea and its ramifications are extremely rich.[8] In sacred Scripture, right from the beginning, holiness is a vitally important concept as applied both to God and his people. Here the teachings on holiness are two-fold: they tell us something about the innermost nature of God, and about our own obligation. Holiness is both the response to the God who is calling and the standard for living our vocation. The statement 'God is holy ... touches on that which constitutes the deepest and innermost nature of the God of the Old Testament'.[9] Underlying this reading of the Bible is the reverberating question: how can a fresh sense of the holiness of God through a deeper appreciation of the Hebrew Scriptures surface in our time?[10] Though what follows is a Christian re-reading of the Hebrew Scriptures it is important to remember the perennial value that the Old Testament concepts about holiness and models of holiness still have for all believers in God.[11]

*Holy God, Holy Time*

The first five books of the Bible – Genesis, Exodus, Leviticus, Numbers and Deuteronomy – constitute the Law or Torah. Basically they explain the will of God for Israel by recounting the story of human rebellion and divine redemption. They bring us to the origins of the Judao-Christian tradition[12] and to the heart of the distinctive call to holiness. These teachings are about a Holy God who makes time, things and people holy through drawing them into his presence.

The first five books of the Bible are from various sources: the two that concern us most are from a priestly hand, and another which is marked by the divine name *yhwh*. It is the priestly author who uses the word 'holy' for the first time in the Bible, at the end of the first narrative of creation: 'And God blessed the seventh day and made it holy' (Gen. 2:3). In *The Sabbath*, Abraham J. Heschel notes that all that God created was declared 'good', but only the Sabbath was specifically declared 'holy'. This Sabbath holiness is highly significant for Jewish spirituality. As Heschel writes, 'The meaning of the Sabbath is to celebrate time rather than space. Six days a week we live under the tyranny of things of space; on the Sabbath we try to become attuned to *holiness in time*. It is the day on which we are called upon to share what is eternal in time, to turn from the results of creation to the mystery of creation; from the world of creation to the creation of the world.'[13] The Sabbath is holy because God the Creator is holy.[14] God is the One who is set apart, the transcendent one and on the Sabbath, the Israelites are called to worship him, and him alone. Here, holiness is linked with the separation and the consecration of time. The keeping of the Sabbath is a symbolic way for Israel to remember the source of holiness. When Exod. 31:12-17 links the creation story with the Sinai revelation, the Sabbath becomes a sign of an 'everlasting covenant':

> Between myself and the Israelites, this is a sign for ever, for in six days Yahweh made heaven and earth, but on the seventh day he rested and drew breath. (Exod. 31:17)

Remembering the Sabbath by keeping it holy is a way to celebrate both creation and 'the Beyond in our Midst'.[15] It is a sign to remind the Israelites for all generations 'that you may know that Yawwh am the one who sanctifies you' (Exod. 31:13).[16]

*The mystery of the holy: Moses before the burning bush*

Though the theme of holiness occurs in the Genesis creation story with reference to the Sabbath, the introduction of holiness in Israel's history has its origins in the call of Moses at the burning bush.[17] The experience of Moses evokes, in the words of Rudolf Otto, both dread and fascination before God who is 'wholly other". According to Otto's *The Idea of the Holy (Das Heilige)*,[18] every religion deals with mystery, which is specifically 'feelings of the non-rational and numinous' or the 'sheer absolute wondrousness that transcends thought'. Otto identifies this mystery as 'the numinous' (from the Latin *numen*, 'divine spirit or power').[19] The two key human responses to the holy are dread (*tremendum*) and fascination (*fascinans*). In the holy, there is power and energy that is truly 'aweful' and overpowering, invoking dread. The holy is a force with an ardor and vitality similar to that of a fire.[20]

In the biblical presentation, it is clear that Moses, a powerful leader who knew both success and disappointment, experienced in his life the special providence of God. A pivotal point for him occurred in his encounter with the Holy One at the burning bush. The story is a familiar one: while tending sheep at Mount Horeb, Moses saw a burning bush that was not consumed and from it he hears the divine voice saying, 'Come no closer! Remove the sandals from your feet, for the place on which you are standing is holy ground' (Exod. 3:5). The ground is holy because God is present. Moses responds by hiding his face, 'for he was afraid to look at God' (Exod. 3: 6). Simultaneously with this theophany, God call's to Moses to set the Israelites free from the Egyptians and makes promise of divine closeness ('I will be with you', Exod. 3:12). Moses embraced the call, but with the understanding that he wanted to know who was doing the sending. The response was 'I AM WHO I AM … Thus you shall say to the Israelites, "I AM has sent me to you".' The passage continues, 'Thus you shall say to the Israelites, 'The Lord, the God of your ancestors, the God of Abraham, the God of Isaac, and the God of Jacob, has sent me to you".' (Exod. 3:14-16 *passim*). God manifests his holiness to Moses and communicates his divine purpose.

Here, the holiness of God implies not merely separation or distance but also intimacy – the Holy One becomes accessible to Moses and the Israelites. This holiness is manifest concretely in deeds, as in the deliverance of the Israelites from the Egyptians. An early poem, possibly written around the eleventh century BCE, expresses this idea succinctly.

Who is like you, O Lord, among the gods?
Who is like you, majestic in holiness,
awesome in splendor, doing wonders? (Exod. 15:11)

Sung by Moses and the Israelites after the deliverance from Pharaoh and
the Egyptians, this song of victory is another example of how holiness is
linked with the covenant love of God.[21] Holiness will mean henceforth
not only separation from the profane, but also belonging to Another. At the
same time, one must always remember that God is unique, unlike anyone or anything, and Israel can approach God only with great reverence.

Another revealing moment in Israel's journey of faith occurs at the
first theophany on Sinai, when Yhwh enters into a covenant with them
and places holiness at the centre of Israel's self-understanding.

Then Moses went up to God; the Lord called to him from the mountain, saying, "Thus you shall say to the house of Jacob, and tell the
Israelites: You have seen what I did to the Egyptians, and how I
bore you on eagles' wings and brought you to myself. Now therefore, if you obey my voice and keep my covenant, you shall be my
treasured possession out of all the peoples. Indeed, the whole earth
is mine, but you shall be for me a priestly kingdom and a holy
nation. These are the words that you shall speak to the
Israelites."' (Exod. 19:3-6)

Taken in the context of covenant, it becomes clear that holiness touches
not only Israel's relationship with God, but also their lifestyles and relationships with each other. 'Because they have been declared holy, so
they must live in a particular way, by the careful keeping of the Torah.
Holiness affects the lifestyle of every individual in Israel; the Torah
touches on every aspect of life.'[22]

The consequences of holy living are manifest specifically in Moses'
life. Led to great intimacy with God, Moses speaks to God 'face to face',
and his own countenance reflects the glory of the Lord. After forty days
and nights alone with Yhwh on the mountain, Moses descended: 'When
Aaron and all the people of Israel saw Moses, the skin of his face was
shining, and they were afraid to come near him' (Exod. 34: 30). Jo
Bailey Wells notes, 'God's glory is reflected through a human face,
through the person who is loyal to Yhwh's side; in a word, through the
person who is holy. God's purpose in making a covenant with Israel is

that the whole nation becomes holy (Exod. 19:6) and reflects the presence and character of Yhwh in the way that their leader does.'[23]

As the people of Israel journeyed through the desert, God's holiness and glory were manifest in an accompanying cloud. Eventually, when Moses set up the tabernacle in the tent of meeting, the glory of the Lord descended upon the Tent and filled the tabernacle so that Moses could not enter it. The glory of the Lord, the overpowering presence of holiness, was among the people of Israel. Indeed, the holy God had come to dwell among his chosen people, a people who had been called into a special association with him. In this relationship with Yhwh, these wandering, desert people had become a priestly people enfolded in covenant love. The cultic and ethical implications of the call to 'be holy because I, Yhwh am holy' became a constant theme throughout the remainder of the Torah.[24]

### The making of a holy people

God's plan is to make Moses, as well as the people of Israel holy, to create a 'kingdom of priests, a nation' (Exod. 19:6). God's people, both individually and collectively, are set apart. The Israelites are to be moulded into God's people through knowing and keeping the commandments and through celebrating in their assemblies the good deeds that God has done. Thus, holiness is a response to God's covenant love. It is a response that is equally a moral responsibility and a liturgical expression.[25]

Israel is both declared and called to be holy in four ways. First, Israel is a holy nation, because of its association with God and his presence. Second, the Israelites recognize God as their creator and sustainer. The third dimension of this call is that Israel has been called to live for God, to obey God's commands and to keep the covenant. Finally, this nation is called into a relationship with other peoples.[26]

> Yhwh's special relationship with Israel does not preclude his relating to other people. Being 'holy' does not infer a separation in terms of isolation; rather it allows for a broadness and a generosity of outlook. Indeed ... it even *demands* a relationship with others, for if Israel is invested with God's presence, then it may represent it and mediate it to others.[27]

It is important to keep in mind that Israel's distinctiveness is a reflection of the otherness of its God just as a beautiful building is a reflection of a good master architect or builder. This is why the ground surrounding the burning bush is holy in a way that other places are not. The same can be said of Bethel, where Jacob wrestled with the angel (Gen. 28:10–22). For the Israelites, a place becomes holy because of its association with God's presence or revelation. This is why Mount Sinai, where God revealed himself to Moses (Exod. 19:3), where the covenant was ratified and where the leaders ate a communal meal (24:9–11) is holy. Also Mount Zion in Jerusalem, the setting for the sanctuary of the Lord, was considered a holy place of encounter with the living God. In his study of this theme, Allen Ross notes, 'For Israel what made these mountains truly holy was the presence of the living God, first at Sinai in making the covenant, and then on Zion in taking up residence among his people. To his holy mountain the people went to worship with sacrifices and offerings; and at that holy hill they saw evidence of his power and glory ... '.[28]

Nowhere more are the degrees of holiness more evident than in the Temple, the place of God's presence (*shekinah*) par excellence. Pilgrims drew near to the Temple to be purified and made holy through their contact with God in this holy place. They came into the courtyards to make sacrifices while the priests entered the holy place in the tent for intercession. Only the high priest went into the holy of holies on the Day of Atonement. It was there that God's glory dwelt, covered by the tent and veiled by curtains.[29] God made his people holy through these rituals associated with temple life.

### Standing in the presence of the Holy

Having focused on the forming of God's holy and priestly people in the book of Exodus, we now turn to the book of Leviticus, which is based on a fundamental belief that if the Israelites make a tabernacle, God would dwell in their midst (cf. Exod. 25:8). God chooses to draw near to the Israelites, but a question surfaces: Who can stand in God's holy presence?[30]

The book of Leviticus is best understood in the context of the covenant at Sinai. Leviticus teaches the Israelites how they could approach God through elaborate rituals (Lev. 1–7); how these rituals are mediated through a consecrated priesthood (Lev. 8–10); how they could regulate their lives in light of God's presence through cleansing and purification of all that contaminates them (Lev. 11–16), and how they were called to holiness in every aspect of their life for they were to be set apart as God's covenant people (Lev. 17–26).[31] The book of Leviticus develops the theme of divine holiness as it draws out its practical and ritualistic implications.[32] Everyone and everything that is incompatible with God's holiness, because of sin, impurity or imperfection, has to be purified through elaborate rituals before they can be placed in the presence of the eternal and living God. The holiness of God is the standard by which all of life in its detail is to be judged.

The book of Leviticus, especially chapters 17–26, the so called 'Holiness Code', thunders repeatedly with the phrase, 'Be holy, as I am holy'. Holiness is a quality that belongs to God alone, but creatures or things become holy as they draw near to the Holy One. Thus, the tabernacle is holy because God dwells there; and sacrifices, utensils and priests are holy because they are related to the service of the holy God. There are grades of holiness, or rings which radiate outwards. Holiness is most intense at the centre or in the holy of holies where the tabernacle is present.[33] It decreases as one moves away.

As previously mentioned, holiness has two dimensions.[34] Its negative aspect requires that the people of God are separated from other nations so that they can live in a special relationship with God. In Lev. 18:2–4, clear boundaries are set up between Israel and other nations. Distinctions are made between 'insiders' and "outsiders'. The positive side is that this 'separation from' enables the Israelites to be 'separated for' service to God. This service includes not only fulfilling cultic acts, but also practising justice. Above all, however, holiness is ultimately measured by one's love for God and neighbour (Lev. 19:18). [35]

> The holiness of Yahweh is understood . . . as the careful management of the mystery of access, which in turn opens the mystery of life. At the center of this preoccupation is Yahweh, who is in Israel the undoubted source of life, but who cannot be lightly or directly or easily apprehended, except with utmost care not to offend or violate.[36]

In Exodus the Israelites are declared a holy and priestly people, while Leviticus instructs these people with a rubric for holy living. There are challenges to living out the declaration of holiness, specifically with respect to impurity and sin that thwart contact with the Holy One.

Similarly, the book of Numbers focuses on the seriousness of observing these principles. Like all Torah literature, the book of Numbers endeavors to provide a foundation for the Israelites in defining the 'self' in contrast to the 'other', which, as we have seen, is at the root of its teaching on holiness. This is nowhere more evident than in Numbers 22–24 which recounts the dramatic confrontation between the Moabites and the Israelites.[37] Eventually this contrast is recognized not only by Balaam, but also by his donkey!

The context is important: faced with the crisis of how to deal with a large number of Israelites gathered on the Moabite border, the king of Moab, Balek, sends for the diviner Balaam. In a medley of narratives and poems, Numbers 22–24 recounts Balaam's persistent reluctance to use his divining powers to curse the Israelites. His first oracle recognizes that the Israelites are a people who dwell apart (Num. 23:9). His second oracle acknowledges that 'the Lord their God is with them, acclaimed as a king among them' (Num. 23:21). Despite the outrage of Balek, Balaam continues in his third and fourth oracle to refuse to curse the Israelites, whom he recognizes as God's people.

Wedged within these narratives and poems is the perplexing fable of Balaam and his donkey (Num. 22:22–35). Literary analysis suggests that this ironic fable, most likely from a later date than the rest of the book, was probably written by someone who wanted to humiliate Balaam by lampooning him. When Balaam's donkey attempts to bring Balaam to join the officials of Moab who are on their way to curse the Israelites, she finds herself hemmed in and blocked. Three times, Balaam uses force to try to coax the donkey to move, and three times she is blocked by an angel of the Lord. The thoroughly frustrated Balaam then finds himself in a conversation with his donkey who at this point is lying under him. In the ensuing dialogue, as the Jewish Midrash (i.e. rabbinic commentaries) of this passage accentuates, the clairvoyant diviner seems dumber than his donkey, who clearly sees the angel of the Lord blocking the way.[38] Certainly one point of the fable is to show the separateness of the Israelites. The presence of the angel of the Lord blocking the path is a way of saying that Israel is off-limits to the Moabites. Because God dwells with the Israelites, they must be set apart from other people. Whether Balaam emerges as a saint or a sinner is not a question for us to explore here: rather, what is important is that the separateness and the protection of God's holy people is recognized even by a donkey.

## A theology of divine possession

The book of Deuteronomy stresses that separateness leads to possession. Though Deuteronomy never actually declares that God is holy, it does show some of the qualities of this holy God and it exhorts the Israelites to remember that 'the Lord your God has chosen you out of all the peoples on earth to be his people, his treasured possession' (Deut. 7:6; 14:2).[39] This last book of the Pentateuch with its diverse authors and long history of formation spans the pre-exilic to postexilic period. It offers, especially in chapters 4–30, a complex and impressive theology of holiness, despite the fact that the word 'holy' is rarely used.[40] Holiness is linked with loyalty to the God who calls his people into a relationship, not because they are more numerous (Deut. 7:7) or more righteous (9:4–5) than others, but because of his love (7:8). This loyalty is expressed by the Israelites through living in absolute dependence upon God, obedience to God's commandments, and trusting not in their own righteousness, but in God alone. Above all, in Deuteronomy, Moses declares that the Israelites are called to be a holy people (Deut. 14:2, 21). 'God sanctified Israel and chose them from among the nations to be his, to be the place for his name to dwell. It is on the basis of this declaration that they are expected and urged continually to keep the commandments that they may be "set high above the nations that he has made, in praise and in fame and in honour" (26:19)'.[41] This covenant faithfulness links God's blessing with obedience to the law:

> If you will only obey the Lord your God, by diligently observing all his commandments that I am commanding you today, the Lord your God will set you high above all the nations of the earth; all these blessings shall come upon you and overtake you, if you obey the Lord your God … The Lord will establish you as his holy people, as he has sworn to you, if you keep the commandments of the Lord your God and walk in his ways. (Deut. 28:1–9)

More than merely following minutely the letter of the law, obedience to the covenant is a matter of responding to the embrace of God's love.[42]

### A prophetic understanding of holiness

The Old Testament prophetic writings developed out of and sometimes reacted to the priestly and cultic conceptions of holiness.[43]Among the prophetic writers, Isaiah is *the* prophet of holiness.[44] In fact, the adjective 'holy' with reference to God is used more often in Isaiah (34 times) than in the rest of the Old Testament together (26 times). The controlling or unifying theme of the Book of Isaiah is holiness, despite the fact its three parts were composed in different centuries by various authors for diverse reasons.[45] The holiness of God is revealed first to Isaiah, then through the prophet to Israel, and finally through Israel to the world. Within this movement, holiness is revealed to be 'paradoxical' in that the God who is transcendent and 'wholly other', reaches out in self-giving love to the wayward Israelites. The God who reveals also conceals. The God who reveals himself to the prophet is also the hidden God (*Deus absconditus*).[46] It is this complex vision that constitutes the book of Isaiah's distinctive contribution to the idea of holiness.[47]

The first manifestation of divine holiness occurs in a cultic setting, in Jerusalem, in the year of the death of King Uzziah (742 BCE), when Isaiah has a vision of 'the Lord sitting on a throne high and lofty; and the hem of his robe filled the temple' (Isa. 6:1). In this inaugural vision (Isa. 6:1–13), Isaiah comes to a deeper understanding of his own call only after he experiences something of God's holiness and majesty, whose glory abides not only in Jerusalem, but fills the whole earth. When the prophet Isaiah sees the Lord sitting on a throne surrounded by seraphs who called to one another 'Holy, holy, holy is the Lord of Hosts, the whole earth is full of his glory', Isaiah responds by saying, 'Woe is me! I am lost, for I am a man of unclean lips, and I live among a people of unclean lips; yet my eyes have seen the King, the Lord of Hosts!' It was then that the seraph touches Isaiah's mouth with a glowing coal and purifies him from sin. Afterwards, in response to the question from the Lord, 'Whom shall I send, and who will go for us?' Isaiah responded, 'Here am I; send me!'

Isaiah accentuates, first of all, the lordship and majesty of yhwh through the attitude of the seraphs. In contrast to Egyptian iconography where the winged cobra, who occupied the same position as Isaiah's seraphs, places its wings over the deity in a protective gesture, Isaiah's seraphs cover their faces for God's glorious presence is so awesome that even they cannot look at him and live. According to Isaiah's vision, Yhwh has no need for protection. There can be no rival to Yhwh, he alone is Lord, the Holy One of Israel.[48]

Secondly, God's holiness exposes all that is defiled and unclean. In this vision, Isaiah is confronted not only with his own personal sin, but also with that of the people. As Isaiah recognized the absoluteness of God who is the Holy One of Israel, he also comes to know that he and his people are lost and sinful. To be lost and sinful are synonymous for Isaiah.[49] The holiness of God confronts Isaiah with an understanding of

how far away he is from God and how it is God who brings the necessary purification so that he and his people can respond fully to his call.
When the seraph touches his lips with burning coals, he is purified of his
moral or psychological guilt and his sins are forgiven. Only then is he
given the challenging mission to speak the prophetic word of judgment
to the house of Israel.

A third consideration in the book of Isaiah is that Yhwh is the Holy
One not in some abstract way, but because he is specifically the Holy
One *of Israel*. As J. B. Wells notes,

> Israel, in Isaiah, is most commonly a religious term, used in par-
> allel with 'my people' (cf. 1.3) and invested with all the theological
> implications of the elect. It is only loosely used as a geographical
> referent. Belonging to 'Israel' does not denote a political identity
> so much as a familial identity with respect to God (cf. 1.2) and thus
> a responsibility to bear good grapes – of justice and righteousness
> – in his vineyard (cf. 5:1-7). The Holy One of Israel demands a just
> people of Israel; this is the outworking of holiness (cf. 5:16). Thus
> 'Israel' denotes the vocation as well as the people of God.[50]

This is an 'astonishing theological maneuver' because by linking the
two it means that 'the completely separated One is the characteristically
related One'.[51] Because 'God the Holy One has displayed his holiness by
his justice' (Is. 5:16), God deals with the Israelites with a 'transparent
sanctity' that embraces both gentle love and justice.[52] Oppression of the
poor and other acts of injustice and unrighteousness are an affront to
God's holiness and this explains the explicit connection in this book
between social justice and holiness (1:10-17; 3:13-15; 5:1-10, 20-23;
10:1-4).[53]

Ritual cleansing is not enough to purify the Israelites and bring
about holiness. This final point is of utmost importance: holiness is
linked to justice, to 'doing' justice in a very real and active way. The
blunt words of the opening chapter of Isaiah make this connection
abundantly clear:

> 'When you come to appear before me,
>     who asked this from your hand?
> Trample my courts no more;
>     Bringing offerings is futile;

incense is an abomination to me.
New moon and Sabbath and calling of convocation –
    I cannot endure solemn assemblies with iniquity.
Your new moons and your appointed festivals
    my soul hates;
They have become a burden to me,
    I am weary of bearing them.
When you stretch out your hands,
    I will hide my eyes from you;
Even though you make many prayers,
    I will not listen ...

Wash yourselves; make yourselves clean;
    Remove the evil of your doings from before my eyes
Cease to do evil,
    Learn to do good;
Seek justice,
    Rescue the oppressed,
Defend the orphan,
    Plead for the widow.
(Isa. 1:12-17 *passim*)

Thus, holiness is no mere cultic devotion to Yhwh. To recognize the holiness of God also means to live justly in relation to others.

What are the practical implications for us as we read the prophet Isaiah? One point is that God's holiness was revealed in a cultic context. Although doxology and worship are crucial for us to encounter the holiness of God, worshipping God through devotion is not enough. It is a starting point. A truly authentic encounter with the Holy One always brings about repentance and conversion. That which is defiled must be cleansed out of necessity for communion with a holy God, for God is indeed perfect in goodness and righteous, utterly holy. Thus, true, comprehensive holiness embraces an ethical dimension. Finally, holiness is not merely a relationship between God and us; it is also intimately intertwined with our relationship with others. John Haughey offers an important insight into this dimension of holiness:

God's plan initially involves a separation from the unholy but with the intention of leaving no one outside of the ambit of this holy field of force. One can now see that there is a dialectic between the separation-from-the-profane note being played in the priestly account of holiness and the universal inclusion-of-the-separated note in the prophetic account of Isaiah. The first keeps holiness from becoming sloppy and presumptuous while the second keeps holiness from becoming exclusionary and sectarian. The first without the second would leave holiness prone to a vertical, pious religiosity. And the second without the first would leave holiness prone to activism and under the control of human agency. Doxology sanitizes social justice, and social justice tethers piety to the social condition in which people live.[54]

Most scholars recognize that both Second Isaiah (chapters 40–55) and Third Isaiah (chapters 56–66), were written later than chapters 1–39. Coming from the exilic (597/586–539 BCE) and postexilic periods respectively, they build upon this basic vision of holiness that has been presented. In Second Isaiah, the universal dimension is accentuated. In Third Isaiah, this holiness is extended to the marginalized.[55] In a passage that echoes the inaugural vision of Isaiah 6, Isa. 57:14-16 states:

> Build up, build up, prepare the way,
>> remove every obstruction from my people's way.
> For thus says the high and lofty one
>> who inhabits eternity, whose name is Holy:
> I dwell in the high and holy place,
>> and also with those who are contrite and humble in spirit,
> to revive the spirit of the humble,
>> and to revive the heart of the contrite.

Paradoxically, Yhwh, who is the 'High and Exalted One,' dwells with the contrite and humble. For Third Isaiah, the high and holy place is with the lowly. The problem with Israel, as expressed earlier for example in Isa. 5:15, is that they placed a barrier between themselves and Yhwh through their prideful, haughty and self-deceptive behavior.[56] Here the message is that God chooses those who are despised and humble to reveal his holiness.

*Holiness and a broken and contrite heart*
In the Psalms, the link between holiness and the predilection of God for the humble is nowhere more evident than in Psalm 51, a psalm that

finds its way not only into Jewish and Christian penitential liturgies, but is also often part of the personal prayer of many. For example, the twentieth-century desert-dweller, Charles de Foucauld, called it the daily prayer of the Christian. The pertinent passages for our focus are verses 10 and 16–17.

> Create in me a clean heart, O God,
>     And put a new and right spirit within me.

> For you have no delight in sacrifices;
> if I were to give you burnt offerings, you would not be pleased.
> The sacrifice acceptable to God is a broken spirit;
> a broken contrite heart, O God, you will not despise.

The full impact of these startling statements becomes evident when one realizes that instead of presenting a burnt offering, the psalmist gives himself, his broken and contrite heart, as the victim of sacrifice.[57] The immediate context is the confession of sin and a resulting awareness of God's saving mercy and steadfast love.

One of the important dimensions of this psalm is to recognize that only God can create a new heart. In fact, in the Hebrew Bible, the verb *bara'*, 'to create', is predicated only of God. No one else can accomplish this new creation. Granted, this requires 'a shattering' of the old, but what is shattered is not lost; the old is in the new.[58] Surrendering to God's call to holiness allows this shattering to happen both on a personal and communal level.

What is striking is the 'concreteness' of this image. Commenting on this Psalm, Walter Brueggemann notes that

> The very lips which diminished the self are now able to exalt God [for the psalmist prays 'O Lord, open my lips, and my mouth will declare your praise'(v. 15)]. This verse is frequently used as a liturgical prayer. As in so many such uses, it may be intuitively correct. But when taken out of context, its force is greatly weakened. The full psalm shows that one cannot ask for lips to praise until one has engaged in a profound yielding and emptying. This is because the God of the psalms wants no religious conventions (the kind often given after the liturgical prayer) but only a dismantled self.

> The dismantled self, characterized in verse 17, requires a shatter-
> ing of one's spirit, a brokenness of one's heart (cf. Isa 57.15). *True*
> *worship and new living require a yielding of self to begin again on*
> *God's terms. But the brokenness may not be a psychological dis-*
> *mantling. It may as well be an economic unburdening, a political*
> *risking, a stepping away from whatever form of power we have*
> *used by which to secure ourselves.*[59]

Clearly, this is not the only time in the Hebrew Scriptures that there is
reference to brokenness of heart. The reasons for this heart-break are
varied: suffering, persecution and sorrow. The occasion for a contrite
and broken heart can also be a recognition of God's judgment on one's
own sins or the sins of others.[60]

In Psalm 147:2–3, the psalmist employs the language of healing the
broken-hearted to celebrate God's saving action towards the postexilic
community in their struggle against political opposition and economic
adversity. This 'rending,' or 'breaking' makes a new life possible. It is 'the
raw, terrible tearing that opens up healing and makes new'.[61] A broken-
hearted person contrasts with the hard-hearted one. The key difference is
that when confronted with sin, the former repents. 'The brokenness of their
natural confidence in life and self points to a condition of frightful anguish
and despair vis-à-vis God. But such bottomless despair mysteriously conceals within itself the miracle of nearness to God.'[62] To summarize, the
broken-hearted person is pleasing to God not simply because he or she
lacks arrogance and is humble, but above all because this experience leads
one to trust no longer in one's own resources but in God's mercy and
steadfast love, the God who is the creator of a new heart. So, through a
broken heart, God enters. From a broken heart, God's love flows out to
others. Self-emptying and openness to God's healing love are essential
elements for growth in holiness. The theme of brokenness emphasizes
what will be clearer in the New Testament, namely that holiness is a work
of God. It is God who must put his law within the Israelites and write it
on their hearts (see Jer. 31:33). The idea is also expressed in Ezekiel:

> I will give them one heart, and put a new spirit within them; I will
> remove the heart of stone from their flesh and give them a heart
> of flesh, so that they may follow my statutes and keep my ordi-
> nances and obey them. Then they shall be my people and I will be
> their God. (Ezek. 11:19–21)

By the sixth century BCE the people realized that keeping the covenant
had proved beyond them and that a decisive work of God was needed for
the ideal of holiness that would constitute the ideal relationship
between God and his people.

### Personal integrity and holiness

So far we have seen how the *priestly* understanding of holiness emphasized separation, purity and segregation. Furthermore, using Isaiah as
an example of the *prophetic* understanding of holiness, we have reflected
on the relationship between worship, social justice and conversion of
heart. Then, in the analysis of Psalm 51, we have seen the connection
between broken-heartedness, humility and holiness. We can conclude
this brief reflection on the Old Testament by showing how *sapiential*
holiness is concerned with individual integrity. While these various
strands are not watertight categories, they do bring out both the com-
plexity and unity of the holiness theme found in the Hebrew
Scriptures.[63]

Despite the inevitable diversity resulting from the long history of the
Wisdom literature, with some of the earliest proverbs (10:1–22:16) perhaps predating Solomon and the latest works written in Greek (the
Wisdom of Solomon probably comes from between 100 BCE and 38 CE),
three fundamental themes emerge consistently throughout. In Proverbs
10:1–22:16:

> (1) There is a fascination and sense of mystery with respect to the
> divine omniscience (*mysterium et fascinans*). (2) There is a strong
> conviction that the fear of the Lord (*tremendum*) leads to life. (3)
> It is also affirmed that the all-knowing divine majesty (*majestas*)
> requires purity of heart and inner integrity.[64]

These early sages were convinced that God's holiness is linked to divine
omniscience. Nothing is hidden from God (Prov. 15:3), least of all the
thoughts of the human heart (Prov. 15:11). The fear of the Lord, a
theme presupposed in these wisdom traditions, leads to long life (Prov.
10:27; 14:27; 19:23), honour (Prov. 15:33: 22:4), avoidance of evil (Prov.
16:6), humility (Prov. 15:33) and riches (Prov. 22:4).[65] Finally, there is a
relationship between holiness and purity. Though there is an insistence
that nobody is without defilement – 'Who can say, "I have made my
heart pure, I am clean from sin?" '(Prov. 20:9) – the Wisdom literature,

like the Holiness Code in Leviticus is concerned with ethical norms by which people show love and respect for one another and follow God's plan for the benefit of humankind: 'The one who will love purity of heart and whose speech is gracious, will have the king as his friend' (Prov. 22:11).

The sapiental literature is a good introduction to Jesus, the Holy One of God, who through his life, death on the cross, and resurrection shows us what holiness means for Christians both yesterday and today. Like the Israelites, his life was lived among the people; he knew he was set apart for God alone. His prophetic words and deeds brought freedom to captives and good news to the poor. His personal integrity also became an example for those who would follow him. The various dimensions of holiness in the Old Testament are important in their own right; they are also found in the life and ministry of Jesus, who came to fulfill the law and bring it to perfection (see Matt. 5:17–18). Thus they take on a particular significance for Christians, a significance that while respecting the Hebrew Scriptures, cannot be underestimated.[66]

## New Testament building blocks

We have seen something of God's plan for the holiness of the people. The Old Testament already makes it clear that holiness is what pertains to God and that the people share in that holiness and are to live according to it. The New Testament builds upon this foundation and shows how God's plan of salvation is revealed in the life, death and resurrection of Jesus.

The word 'holy' is used 42 times in the Gospels and 191 times in the rest of the New Testament. The Acts of the Apostles (53), Romans (20), Ephesians (15) and Revelation (25) have the most frequent number of references. Many of these refer specifically to the Holy Spirit, particularly in the case of the Acts of the Apostles.[67] The Spirit who was active in the life of Jesus is also, after his death and resurrection, at work in God's people, expressing God's holiness to the world.

Like the Old Testament, the New Testament reflects the paradox of holiness. As Clarence T. Craig wrote more than a half century ago, 'Believers have been sanctified, yet they must be exhorted to be holy. Their sanctification is entirely the work of God, yet holiness, like love and peace, are objectives towards which the saints should strive. What is the relationship between gift and endeavor, between what is received and what is achieved?'[68] In response to this question a New Testament vision of holiness is required. Here holiness is best understood as a journey, a continually on-going dynamic process by which God's life takes root in the believer and in the Christian community.

Holiness is God's building project, but the building is much different than what one would imagine. In one sense the 'building' is the people of God, who are declared holy, primarily because of their special relationship with God who is the Holy One. At the same time, they are also called to become holy. This is the standard they are to strive for in their lives. Ultimately they are called to become who they are and this implies a journey towards holiness.[69]

*Jesus, the Holy One of God*

Jesus is explicitly called 'the Holy One of God' only three times in the Gospels: twice by a demon (Mk 1:24: Lk. 4:34) and once by Peter (Jn 6:69). One could add a fourth, if we include the angel Gabriel's proclamation to the Virgin Mary that 'the child will be holy and will be called the Son of God' (Lk. 1:35). Though these explicit references are few, the whole of Jesus's life and teaching, death and resurrection is a paradigm for what it means to be holy. In fact, the whole of the New Testament understanding of holiness hinges on the fact that 'God was in Christ' (2 Cor. 5:19).[70]

*Incarnation: a hint of God's dealing with humanity*

The door to a Christian understanding of holiness is Christ. Jesus's vision of holiness must not be confused with a nostalgic longing for order. Holiness is more than appearances.[71] Salvation depends on our participation in the paschal mystery, in being conformed to Christ's death so that we can share in his resurrection. Holiness involves our acceptance of the self-offering of Jesus Christ on the Cross, in which even our alienation and brokenness are used for God's purpose.[72]

The incarnation shatters any illusions that holiness simply means mere legal rectitude or even mere wholesomeness. Both Matthew's and Luke's Gospels portray the birth of Jesus as taking place under less than respectable circumstances. Matthew's Gospel begins with a lengthy genealogy of Jesus. Glancing at this cast of characters, most of us would probably avoid such a beginning if we wanted to share the good news of Jesus Christ with others. Yet, Matthew's Gospel wisely starts here for this genealogy contains the essential theology of the Bible in miniature. It provides a context for exploring a Christian understanding of holiness. The three sets of 'fourteen generations', from Abraham to David, from David to the Babylonian Exile, and from the Exile to Christ, contain an assortment of saints and sinners. What emerges from these lists is that 'God does not necessarily choose the best or the noble to carry out his plan of salvation. He is not controlled by human merit but manifests his own unpredictable graciousness.'[73] Raymond Brown notes, among the kings there is an 'odd assortment of idolaters, murderers, incompetents, power-seekers and harem-wastrels.'[74] Those mentioned in the genealogy between the exile and birth of Jesus are largely unknown. Furthermore, all of the women named in the genealogy have a marital history that contains elements of scandal or scorn, yet God uses all these men and women, the virtuous and the villainous, to continue the sacred line of the Messiah.

Why bring up the genealogy when speaking about holiness? Simply because it is a reminder of how God operates. God does not search out exclusively the best of characters to carry out his plan of salvation. Again, drawing from the work of Raymond Brown, we note that 'the God who wrote the beginning (of the genealogy of Jesus Christ) with crooked lines also writes the sequence with crooked lines, and some of those lines are our lives and witness. A God who did not hesitate to use the scheming as well as the noble, the impure as well as the pure, men to whom the world hearkened and women upon whom the world frowned – this God continues to work through the same mélange.'[75]

Luke's more poetic and artistic presentation of the events surrounding Jesus's birth are no less startling. Here Jesus's birth is surrounded by a surprising situation. The angel appears to the Virgin, Mary. The child is born in poverty, and placed in a feeding trough. Jesus is indeed the Holy One of God, but his birth gives us the first hint of what holiness really means. It is not about appearances. It is about God breaking into our lives in the most unexpected circumstances. It is about God's gracious love that can write straight with crooked lines. It is about God manifesting his power in human weakness, in the most unlikely and unpredictable circumstances. It is about God using unlikely folk, and including the occasional shady character, to change the course of human history. It is about God using you and me in his plan of salvation. The Incarnation is crucial in developing a proper understanding of Christian holiness. According to M. Cathleen Kaveny, 'Holiness is a response to the reality of embodied life. Wholesomeness, in contrast, is fundamentally an effort to sustain an illusion of what we would like to be.'[76]

*Jesus's public ministry and teaching*

In his teaching, Jesus does not directly instruct his disciples *about* holiness. Indirectly, through both his words and deeds, he communicates its essential nature. To the Pharisees, the most righteous of their time, Jesus linked holiness with mercy and the fulfilment of God's will, and not simply with legal rectitude (cf. Lk. 10:29-37; 18:10–14; Mt 21:28–31). Holiness is manifest more in interior attitudes than exclusively in external actions (cf. Matthew 23, Luke 11). He also questions the motives for which others pursue holiness – if they are focused exclusively on concern for survival, for example, acting only for the preservation of Israel, then it does not represent his vision of holiness (Matt. 5:13–15; Matt. 25:14-20; Lk. 13:6–9).[77]

The Pharisees are often seen too exclusively in negative terms by readers of the New Testament, and this is a mistake. They were strict observers of the law and as such dedicated to serving God. Their code of holiness though was not without problems: they condemned those who were not as strict as themselves (see Lk. 18:9–14), and they often focused on an outward show of religion (see Mt. 6:1–18). The law as interpreted at the time of Jesus was a great burden. There were 365 negative and 248 positive precepts. Jesus came with a lighter burden and easier yoke (see Mt. 11:28–39). Later Paul could say that he observed the law to perfection, but he came to see this extraordinary achievement as loss or rubbish (see Phil. 3:6-8). In the controversy about the law and the gospel, Paul insists that it is by gift and by faith that we come into justification and holiness (see Gal. 2:15–3:5; Rom. 8:29–30).

When the *Catechism of the Catholic Church* considers the call to holiness, it cites Matt. 5:48: 'Be perfect as your heavenly Father is perfect.' The Greek *teleios* means the goal towards which one is moving. Thus one translation that might render this more clearly is: 'Be perfected as your heavenly Father is perfect'.[78] This translation points to a process. Understanding holiness as a process frees us from complacency or any sense that we have arrived. The Christian vocation is a call to be always in the process of being perfected or made holy in Christ. The initiative belongs to Christ: 'I consecrate myself for them, so that they may also be consecrated in truth' (Jn 17:19).[79]

*Holiness as abiding in Jesus*

Holiness finds its greatest manifestation in the death and resurrection of Jesus. To the extent that Christians share deeply in the mystery of

Jesus's dying and rising, they participate in his holiness. In the fare-well discourse of John's Gospel, Jesus says, 'I am the vine, you are the branches. Whoever remains in me, with me in him, bears fruit in plenty; for apart from me you can do nothing' (Jn. 15:5). Though the word 'holiness' is not mentioned here explicitly, this passage sums up the Christian understanding of holiness. Holiness means abiding with Jesus, it means being grafted into his life and letting his life flow into the life of the believer and the community.

On the cover of this book is a reproduction of a twelfth-century mosaic found in the apse of the Church of St Clement in Rome. It depicts the cross as a tree of life and out of it is a vine stretching out throughout the entire apse and, in a way, reaching out to embrace men and women everywhere. In fact, encircling the mosaic are the words: 'We have likened the Church to this vine: the law made it wither but the cross causes it to bloom.'

The cross is the great centerpiece of the whole mosaic. The crucified one is surrounded by Mary his mother and John the beloved disciple. From the foot of the cross, the vine spreads out in bold and graceful curves. One message of the mosaic is that Christ's life touches us in our daily life. Our ordinary lives become extraordinary because they are nourished by the life giving power that flows from Christ. The bright green branches of the vine completely fill the apse, as if to reach out to all people at all times and in all places. The living union with Christ is actually brought about as the faithful take part in the Eucharist cele-brated at the altar.[80] Embracing all who respond to the call to holiness is the living vine of life-giving holiness.

Across the centuries, all of us regardless of geographic location or social status are caught up in this Christ vine. Perhaps, if the mosaic were done today, it would include people commuting to work on the tube, someone working at her computer, perhaps an elderly man taking care of his wife, or a mother nursing her child. It would embrace each of us in the activities of everyday life. The vine image is important because it reminds us that we are in communion with both Christ and one another.

*In Christ* (en Christō) *and in the Spirit, according to Paul*
Like the Johannine theme of abiding, St. Paul emphasizes that Christian holiness is not merely about sheer imitation of Christ's way of being and acting: instead, we are invited to participate in his life. We are invited to find ourselves 'in Christ', to discover ourselves in the edifice where he is

the cornerstone. This happens only through the working of the Holy Spirit. On St. Paul's understanding of holiness, Raymond Corriveau summarizes the implications of this call.

> Briefly we can say that for St. Paul the holiness of the Christian is a participation of the holiness of God through the presence of his Spirit (cf. Rom 15:16; 1 Cor 6;11) and through consecration in Christ (1 Cor 1:2; Phil 1:1). Having been brought into the divine sphere by their baptismal consecration all Christians can be called 'saints' (Rom 1:7, 15: 25; 1 Cor 16:1). They have something of the holiness which belongs to a temple and as such are consecrated to God's service and worship. This has the effect of rendering Christians priests in Christ (Rom 12:1, 15:16), able to offer up their bodies as living sacrifices (Rom 12:1; 15:16) and to engage in the liturgy of Christian life (Phil 2:17).[81]

To be 'in Christ' is to enter into his experience of God as 'Abba', to be brought into an intimacy with the One whose name is 'hallowed'. Entering into this relationship comes as a gift for we can call God 'Father' only though the power of the Spirit that has been given to us (Gal. 4:4-6). As Lawrence Cunningham says so well, 'Jesus is the catalyst for a new form of living that puts us in contact with him and with Abba. Jesus, in short, is the agent of our holiness. In this the experience of the earliest Christian assemblies is paramount. Jesus, according to the most ancient profession of Christian faith, died for our sins and was raised up as the "firstborn" of all who would come after him and believe in him (see 1 Cor. 15).'[82]

St. Paul emphasizes the Christian community's vocation to holiness in many of the greetings of his letters. For example, Christians in Rome 'are called … to be holy' (Rom. 1:7). Similarly the congregation addressed in 2 Corinthians are greeted as well as 'all the holy ones throughout Achaia' (1:1). The 'holy ones' are mentioned also at the beginning of the letters to the Colossians (1:2), the Philippians (1:1) and the Ephesians (1:1).[83] On one level, the saints or holy ones are simply believers in Christ. This greeting is more than a friendly title for it embraces a deep insight into the Christian vocation, because to be holy means to live in Christ (*en Christō*, in Greek).[84]

St. Paul uses an extensive range of words, to describe life in Christ. They often have a prefix, *syn* (with), which indicates various ways of being in Christ, sharing daily in the death and resurrection of Christ: suffering with Christ (Rom. 8:17), being configured to his crucifixion (Gal. 2:19), configured to his death, (Phil. 3:10); dying a death like his (Rom 6:5), dying with him (2 Tim. 2:11), being buried with him (Rom. 6:4), rising with him (Eph. 2:6). It also means being brought to life with Christ (Eph. 2:5), and being glorified with Christ (Rom. 8:17), who transfigures our bodies into the mould of his glorious body. Finally it means reigning with Christ (2 Tim 2:12). Quite simply, according to Paul, holiness is incorporation or conformity to Christ that is made possible by the working of the Holy Spirit in us. The implications of this are profoundly expressed in 2 Corinthians 6: 16–7:1, specifically verse 16:

> For we are the temples of the living God. We have God's word for it: *I will live in them and move among them and I will be their God and they will be my people.* (2 Cor. 6:16)

This passage repeats the holiness theme found in the prophets and applies it to the Christian community. On the one hand, the Church is God's dwelling, like the temple of old, and because of that it should be set apart for divine purpose. On the other hand, and on a much deeper level, Paul implies that God's presence in the Church is much more than the divine dwelling in the old sanctuary. What Paul is saying is that 'God not only dwells *with* his people in a sanctuary which they make for him; he dwells *in* them and *they* are his temple.'[85] In the New Testament, holiness is presented as a dynamic process. Christians are called to become who they truly are in Christ. Baptism leads both to a new life in Christ and to freedom from the slavery of sin; being freed from sin and enslaved to God gives sanctification (see Rom. 6:1–23, especially 22). This is a growing process that is especially emphasized in Galatians and Ephesians.

### The Spirit in us: the vivifying source of Christian holiness

The temple is significant in any consideration of holiness in the Old or New Testament. The temple belongs to God who dwells there and is worshipped there. In the New Testament, God is seen to dwell and to be worshipped in Christ Jesus (see Jn 2:21), who is the temple par excellence. Reflecting on holiness after his experience of receiving the gift of the Spirit, St Paul suggests that the Christian community has become that dwelling place for God's presence: 'Do you not realize that you are a temple of God with the Spirit of God living in you? If anybody should destroy the temple of God, God will destroy that person, because God's temple is holy and you are that temple' (1 Cor. 3:16–17). Both the Christian community as a whole and its individual members are considered by Paul to be temples of God. To the Christians of Corinth who were dealing with a case of sexual immorality, Paul writes, 'Do you not realize that your body is the temple of the Holy Spirit, who is in you and whom you received from God? You are not your own property, then; you have been bought at a price.' These passages emphasize what we are through the gift of the Spirit and our new life in Christ.

The only point of departure into a correct understanding of a working definition of holiness is to grasp that holiness is a work that God is doing in us. In reflecting on Romans 12:1–2, Joseph Fitzmyer comments that ' ... it is by God's mercy that this new Christian life is lived. It is not we who bring it about that the gospel transforms our lives, but God's mercy that transforms our lives. "It depends not on human willing or effort, but on God's mercy."(9:16)'.[86] We are called to respond to this mercy by lives offered to God.

> I urge you then, brothers, by God's mercy to offer your bodies as living sacrifices, holy and acceptable to God, as a cult suited to your rational nature. Do not conform yourselves to this present world, but be transformed by a renewal of your whole way of thinking so that you may discern what is God's will, what is good, acceptable to him, and perfect.[87]

In this passage, Christians are compared with the slaughtered animals in Jewish and pagan cults, but there is one crucial difference. Paul adds the word 'living' to sacrifice when speaking about the Christian call. Christians are not called to offer dead animals to God; nor are they called to offer the dead stuff of their own lives, but rather they are to invited to 'give a cultic or sacrificial sense to their lives, as they offer themselves and their conduct to ... [God]'.[88]

*Christ the Cornerstone*
Another important image that focuses on the centrality of Christ for a Christian understanding of holiness is that of the foundation, cornerstone or keystone. The foundation stone in most modern buildings is usually inscribed with a dedication that tells when the building was

constructed and who paid for it. Scripture scholars offer different interpretations on the location and purpose of this stone in the New
Testament period. A more traditional interpretation is that this stone
was laid probably at a corner of a building to hold the walls together.[89]
According to Near Eastern mythology, the foundation stone was placed
at the centre of the universe at the creation of the world. From this hub,
the chaotic waters were capped and creation was sustained. This
mythology underlies Isaiah 28:16, a passage cited by 1 Peter 2:6. Mount
Zion is the site of this cosmic cornerstone and it is upon this unshakable
foundation that Jerusalem and its temple are built.[90] R. J. McKelvey
notes that 'the harmony and the welfare of the physical order were
dependent upon it, just as the divine and the human were conjoined into
one organic whole by it'.[91] In this context, there is a parallel between the
historical stone in Jerusalem and Christ, who has become the cornerstone of this spiritual building. Christ not only harmonizes and unifies
it through creating and sustaining it, he also determines its shape and
growth.[92]

Other scholars would suggest that the stone was not at the foundation
of the building, but was at the top, the capstone. For example, in her commentary on *Ephesians*, Pheme Perkins recognizes that various texts about
the cornerstone in Zion were applied to Jesus (Isa. 8:14; Lk. 2:34; Rom.
9:32; 1 Pet. 2:8). She also suggests though, that especially in light of the focus
on the exaltation of Christ (Eph. 4:16), cornerstone can also be understood
as the capstone, at the top of the walls, that holds the building together.[93]
In reflecting on this passage, think of how Roman arches are constructed.
In a Roman arch, the keystone has a different shape from the other
stones – those perfectly shaped bricks or stones that are placed one upon
the other. At the very centre of the arch, the keystone, often carved from a
rejected piece of stone; fuses the two parts together. If the keystone is
removed, the arch crumbles. In the same way, in the household of God,
Jesus is the cornerstone, capstone or keystone who keeps the whole edifice
together.

### 'You also are living stones'

Both Ephesians 2:19–22 and 1 Peter 2:4–8 refer to the Christian community as being built into a spiritual dwelling for God. The Ephesian
passage emphasizes the communal dimension of the church, showing
that even Gentiles are called to be part of God's people.

So then you are no longer strangers and aliens, but you are citizens with the saints and also members of the household of God, built upon the foundation of the apostles and prophets, with Christ Jesus himself as the cornerstone. In him the whole structure is joined together and grows into a holy temple in the Lord; in whom you also are built together spiritually into a dwelling place for God. (Eph. 2:19–22)

The Letter to the Ephesians, with its image of both a building and the temple, brings out the idea of growth. In the first letter to the Corinthians, Christ was presented as the foundation; in Ephesians, Christ is described as the cornerstone. Ephesians brings out the dynamic element of growth – the building temple is in the process of becoming.

Similarly the first Letter to Peter focuses on the community's relationship with Jesus, but adds that he is the living stone that has been rejected by humankind.

Come to him, a living stone, though rejected by mortals yet chosen and precious in God's sight, and like living stones, let yourselves be built into a spiritual house, to be a holy priesthood, to offer spiritual sacrifices acceptable to God through Jesus Christ. (1 Pet. 2:4)

Further on, the writer shows the impact of this call especially on Christian Gentiles:

But you are a chosen race, a royal priesthood, a holy nation, God's own people, in order that you may proclaim the mighty acts of him who called you out of darkness into his marvellous light.
Once you were not a people,
    but now you are God's people;
Once you had not received mercy,
    but now you have received mercy. (1 Pet. 2:9–10)

This passage utilizes an assortment of Old Testament passages in order to present the gospel of Jesus Christ in light of the Hebrew Scriptures.[94] While respecting the authority of the Hebrew Canon, the author of 1 Peter re-writes these in the context of an early Christian community's identity and vocation to a life of holiness in the midst of the world. Taken in the context of the whole letter, this passage is a culmination of various previous statements that explain who the Christian community is in Christ. Furthermore, the letter offers practical ways to help this community to live up to their calling, thus 'to become who they are'.[95] Above all, 1 Peter reminds us that 'he who called you is holy, be holy yourselves in all your conduct; for it is written, "You shall be holy, for I am holy"'. In repeating Leviticus 19:2, we see a continuity between the Old and New Testament call to holiness.

This passage is a pivotal point in the letter: the first half builds up to it and the second flows from it. The Christian community is depicted as a house composed of living stones founded in Christ who himself is a living stone, rejected by men but chosen by God and precious to him. The house is a spiritual one because it is a work of the Holy Spirit (1 Pet. 4:14). The Christian community is the place that God has chosen to dwell, where he can be worshipped and revered through true sacrifice. In Christ, the people have become a holy priesthood, called to draw near to God and serve him through a life of commitment, surrendering themselves to do his will.

In this context, holiness means to be set aside for God alone – it implies a strong sense of belonging to God. This belonging is not based on biological or historical foundations, but on belief in Jesus Christ that implies conversion from one's former way of life. Thus a new vision of who we are affects our distinctive behavior in the world.

> Christians are given a clear call to live according to their election – to *be* holy given that they *are* holy – and to do this as aliens in the face of the world, even when it is hostile. It is not that they are challenged to cross the divide between private devotion and public witness; it is that there is no divide. Holiness is not a matter of personal faithfulness; it is a community identity which necessarily involves standing out and being different, because it *is* their difference. At root, this difference is that Christians belong to God, and so they must act as such.[96]

Bonded with Christ, the cornerstone, the Christian community becomes, in the words of John H. Elliott, 'a home for the homeless, an *oikos* for *paroikoi*'. (1 Peter)[97] It is likely that 1 Peter was written for resident aliens living on the fringes of society in Asia Minor. These exiles of the diaspora, far from 'home', are invited to recognize that, even now, they are being built up into God's dwelling. Peter clearly emphasizes that this spiritual dwelling is still under construction, it is 'being built up'.[98]

In quoting the prophet Hosea, 'once you had not received mercy but now you have received mercy', or as some translators say, 'once you were outside his pity now you have received pity', the author completes his medley of images to describe the Church consisting not only of Jewish Christians, but also Gentiles. As Donald Senior remarks in describing this final image:

> Once the Christian community were [sic] 'no people' caught in a dizzy merry-go-round of self-seeking (cf. 1:14, 18, 21, 43–4). But now they are caught up in God's embrace and have become his people. Once they had experienced 'no mercy' – lives out of touch with God, lives without hope. But now they have tasted God's goodness.
>
> The Hosea text injects the right hue into 1 Peter's portrait of the church. This is neither a community of angels nor some doe-eyed band of innocents. They are a people who have come home after a long and troubled absence. They are a sadder-but-wiser church, more likely to look with compassion on a broken world because they have been there themselves.[99]

*The Letter to the Hebrews: 'Seek peace ... and holiness'*[100]

Similar to the texts we have just examined, the Letter to the Hebrews emphasizes that holiness is not an optional extra for Christians, but a necessity for those who wish to see the Lord:[101] 'Seek peace with all people, and the holiness without which no one can ever see the Lord' (Heb. 12:14). When understood within the context of the entire letter, the holiness which is to be sought is understood as both a gift and a responsibility.[102] It is gift because Jesus Christ the great high priest has offered himself as a sacrifice once and for all to purify God's people (2:11, 10:10). As the one mediator of a new covenant between God and humanity (Heb. 9:13-15), he obediently accepted the Father's will '[a]nd this *will* was for us to be made holy by the *offering* of the *body* of Jesus Christ made once and for all' (Heb. 10:10). Jesus's sacrificial death unleashes new possibilities for us because as we now approach the Father through Christ, we are drawn towards sanctification and perfection (completion).[103] Though the gift of holiness has been given through the death of Jesus, it is also a responsibility to be lived out in a practical ways.

The radical nature of Christ's gift of holiness to us becomes clear when comparing the notion of holiness in Hebrews with that of the Levitical practice. Craig R. Koester explains this in his commentary:

Sanctification means setting something apart *from* what is common (9:13) *for* God (13:12). In Levitical practice, a priest was set apart from the common people in order to minister in the sanctuary, which was holy. God is holy, and his holiness is a numinous power. Nothing common was to be brought into the presence of God ... (Num. 3:4; 26:61). Since a sanctuary or holy place *(ta hagia)* was set apart for God, one needed to be sanctified *(hagiazein)* or set apart before entering it. Everything holy had to be clean, but just because something was clean did not mean that it was holy ... Lay people, for example, were normally considered clean unless they became unclean through skin disease, a discharge, or contact with something unclean. Purification would cleanse them, but would not make them holy.[104]

The good news according to the Letter to the Hebrews is that Christ is both the high priest and sacrifice. He gave himself once and for all, and through this gift he both sanctifies and purifies. We cannot make ourselves holy, but we can be made holy in Christ.[105] Paradoxically, though believers are declared holy, they are also called to pursue holiness 'in daily life by seeking peace with other people and by guarding against immorality and godlessness' (Heb. 12:14–16; cf. 12:28–13:6).[106]

The Letter to the Hebrews demonstrates a deep conviction about the awesome holiness of God,[107] and it also shows that through Christ, believers can *now* freely approach God. To the early Christians who first received this letter and to us, the author shows the efficacy of the new covenant wrought in Jesus Christ. 'But what you have come to is Mount Zion and the city of the living God, the heavenly Jerusalem where the millions of angels have gathered for the festival, with the whole Church of first-born sons, enrolled as citizens of heaven. You have come to God himself, the supreme Judge, and to the spirits of the upright who have been made perfect; and to Jesus, the mediator of a new covenant' (Heb. 12:22–24 *New Jeruslaem Bible*). We can approach this heavenly Jerusalem to some extent even now, as we glimpse its glory with reverence and awe, with trust and love in God's mercy.[108]

**Conclusion**

In this chapter we have considered some important themes in sacred Scripture with the purpose of providing a biblical foundation for a Christian understanding of holiness. This chapter began with three somewhat paradoxical or even slightly contradictory quotations – each illustrating a particular aspect of what sacred Scripture teaches about holiness.

First, the Archbishop of Canterbury, Rowan Williams says that 'A human being is holy not because he or she triumphs by will-power over chaos and guilt and leads a flawless life, but because that life shows the victory of God's faithfulness *in the midst* of disorder and imperfection ... Humanly speaking, holiness is always like this: God's endurance in the midst of our refusal of him, his capacity to meet every refusal with the gift of himself.'[109] A constant theme in this chapter has been the faithfulness of God's covenant love, which embraces a sinful people and calls them to a life of holiness. The emphasis is on holiness as primarily a gift given by a gracious God.

Raïssa Maritain's shocking link between tragedy and saintliness resonate with Bible teaching as well. Saint Paul equates holiness with being 'in Christ' and possessed by the Spirit. To be a 'saint' is to live through the power of the Spirit a life of profound union with Christ, to let Christ's life flow into our own and to respond to God's call both as individuals and as a people. Raïssa Maritain is correct: 'The only tragedy in life is not to be a saint.'[110] This is a personal call to each one of us and to the Christian community as a whole.

The words of Blessed Mother Teresa of Calcutta also capture a dimension of the good news: 'Our progress in holiness depends on God and ourselves – on God's grace and on our will to be holy. We must have a real living determination to reach holiness. "I will be a saint" means I will despoil myself of all that is not God ...'[111] We have seen in this chapter that the demands intrinsic to holiness abide with God's invitation to open ourselves to grace. Holiness is above all God's gracious embrace, but it does call for our response. What the Bible teaches is that holiness is gift, response and responsibility. We are called to accept the gift that has been given and to let it transform our lives. We are called to become who we are: *God's holy people.* These are the basic building blocks for the edifice that God is building. The different ways of living this out day by day are the theme of the next chapter. While using the same building blocks, we shall see that there are different ways, or many mansions, each of which are authentic expressions of God's building project.

## Notes

1 See Jacques Guillet, 'Sainteté', in *Dictionnaire de spiritualité*, vol 14, cols 184–92; Aimé Solgnac, 'Sainteté – sanctification de l'homme', *DSpir*, vol. 14, cols 192–94; Thomas Spidlik *et al.*, 'Saints' *DS*, vol. 14, pp.195–230; Lawrence Cunningham, 'Holiness,' *New Dictionary of Catholic Spirituality* (Collegeville: Liturgical Press, 1993), p. 480.

2 For an interpretation of this passage see Massimo Grilli, ' "Siate Santi perché io sono santo" Lv 19,2 La santità nell'Antico Testamento: Separazione o appartenenza', in *La santità* (Naples: Cirico, 2001), p.15.

3 Pheme Perkins, *First and Second Peter, James and Jude. Interpretation, A Commentary for Teaching and Preaching* (Louisville: John Knox Press, 1995) p.36.

4 Tim Vivian, 'Witness to Holiness: Abba Daniel of Scetis', *Coptic Church Review* 24 (Spring/Summer 2003) pp.2–52. (Especially p.2).

5 See the thoughtful article by David V. Meconi, 'On the Fear of Sanctity', *New Oxford Review* 69 (2002) pp.33–5.

6 Samuel Terrien uses this phrase specifically to refer to the prophets Hosea and Isaiah: 'The paradox of holiness which Hosea perceived in the power of love also dominated the thinking of his southern disciple, Isaiah of Jerusalem.' I think 'the paradox of holiness' can be applied to much of the Old Testament teaching. See Samuel Terrien, *The Elusive Presence: The Heart of Biblical Theology* (San Francisco: Harper and Row, 1978), p.254. For a discussion of the paradox of holiness in the New Testament, see Clarence T. Craig, 'Paradox of Holiness: the New Testament Doctrine of Sanctification', *Interpretation* 6 (1952) pp.147–61. See the preface by Walter Brueggemann of John G. Gammie, *Holiness in Israel* (Minneapolis: Fortress Press, 1989), pp.x.

7 Perkins, *First and Second Peter*, p.40.

8 It is beyond the scope of this chapter to offer an exhaustive and in depth exegetical understanding of holiness in the Bible. There are some excellent full-length studies that can be consulted for more detail: J. G. Gammie, *Holiness in Israel* (Minneapolis: Fortress Press, 1989); David T. Wright, 'Holiness (OT)', *The Anchor Bible Dictionary,* (ed. David Noel Freedman *et al,* New York: Doubleday, 1992) pp.237–49. Jo Bailey Wells, *God's Holy People: A Theme in Biblical Theology*, Journal for the Study of the Old Testament Supplement 305 (Sheffield: Sheffield Academic Press, 2000); see the ample bibliography on pp.247ff. for other references.

Furthermore, this chapter cannot enter into the debates among Scripture scholars surrounding the correct approach to Old Testament Theology. For a helpful and scholarly overview of former and more recent issues see Walter Brueggemann, *Theology of the Old Testament: Testimony, Dispute, Advocacy* (Minneapolis: Fortress Press, 1997) and Bernhard W. Anderson with the assistance of Steven Bishop, *Contours of Old Testament Theology* (Minneapolis: Fortress Press, 1999).

9 Ernst Sellin, *Theologie des Alten Testaments* (Leipzig: Quelle & Meyer, 1936) p.19 as quoted both in Gammie, *Holiness in Israel*, p.3 and Anderson, *Contours of Old Testament Theology*, p.41. See also the comment of Walter Eichrodt, *Theology of the Old Testament*, (trans. J. A. Baker, London: SCM Press, 1961), vol. 1, p.270 where he notes that 'it has been possible to characterize the whole religion of the Old Testament as a "religion of holiness" (Hänel).' See also Theodore C. Vriezen, *An Outline of Old Testament Theology* (2nd edn, Oxford: Oxford University Press, 1970, original published in Dutch, 1949): 'The Holiness of God is the central idea of the Old Testament faith in God' (p.151). Vriezen's exposition on holiness is found on pp.149–62.

10 Gammie raises this question at the end of *Holiness in Israel* (p.198), where he says, 'Nowhere in this volume has the attempt been made to spell out how a sense of the holiness of God might be regained in our day. That is, I have not explicitly attempted to show how spirituality might be enhanced. However, many clues are to be found in the simple rehearsal of how holiness was discerned in Israel. Job 31 and Psalm 51 illustrate most profoundly that whenever a person has been led to honest self-examination, that person has already begun to enter into the presence of holiness. Insofar as a recovery of a sense of holiness may be affected by human initiative, I have suggested that there is no one, single way. Whatever the way, it will include an attempt to keep the Sabbath holy, a wholehearted pursuit of justice, and some attention to individual moral attitudes and acts.'

11 As the Pontifical Biblical Commission has noted, 'The Old Testament in itself has great value as the Word of God.' See Pontifical Biblical Commission, *The Jewish People and Their Sacred Scriptures in the Christian Bible* (Vatican City: Casa Editrice Vaticana, 2002), para. 6.

12 See Roland E. Murphy, 'Introduction to the Pentateuch', *New Jerome Biblical Commentary* (ed. Raymond E. Brown, Joseph A. Fitzmyer and Roland E. Murphy, New Jersey: Prentice Hall, 1990), pp.3–7.

13 Abraham J. Heschel, *The Sabbath: Its Meaning for Modern Man* (New York: Farrar, Straus and Giroux, 1951, 12th printing 1986); p.10. See John C. Haughey, *Housing Heaven's Fire: The challenge of Holiness* (Chicago: Loyola Press, 2002), pp.37–8.

14 For a more chronological approach to the Hebrew notion of holiness, see Haughey, pp.35–63.

15 Dietrich Bonhoeffer, *Letters and Papers from Prison* (ed. Eberhard Bethge, trans. Reginald Fuller, *et al.*, New York: Macmillian, 1962), p.182.

16 Gammie, *Holiness in Israel*, p.21. This is his translation of Exodus 31:13.

17 Jo Bailey Wells, *God's Holy People*, p.13. According to both Jewish and Christian tradition, Moses' long life was divided into three forty-year periods. The first, his time in Egypt, was marked by his experience under Pharaoh. The second includes his visit to his brothers, who totally misunderstand his intentions to bring about their liberation, and ends with his flight into the desert. The third forty years begins with the burning bush and culminates with his death.

18 Rudolf Otto, *The Idea of the Holy* (trans. John W. Harvey, Oxford/New York: Oxford University Press, 1950, 2nd edition). This was first published in German as *Das Heilige* in 1917. See John L. McKenzie, 'Aspects of Old Testament Thought', *New Jerome Biblical Commentary*, p.1285.

19 Rudolf Otto, *Idea of the Holy*, p.72. See Melissa Raphael, *Rudolf Otto and the Concept of Holiness* (Oxford: Oxford University Press, 1997). A contemporary rereading of Otto is the concise article by Colin Crowder, 'Rudolf Otto's *The Idea of the Holy* Revisited', in Stephen C. Barton, *Holiness Past and Present* (London: T&T Clark, 2003), pp.22–47.

20 See Gammie, *Holiness in Israel*, pp.5–6.

21 See Anderson, *Contours of Old Testament Theology*, p.41.

22 Wells, *God's Holy People*, p.70.

23 *Ibid.* pp.76–7.

24 *Ibid.* p.240.

25 Haughey, *Housing Heaven's Fire*, pp.40–1.

26 Wells, *God's Holy People*, pp.56–7.

27 *Ibid.* pp.56–7.

28 Allen P. Ross, *Holiness to the Lord: A Guide to the Exposition of the Book of Leviticus* (Grand Rapids, MI: Baker Academic, 2002), pp.23–4.

29 Philip P. Jenson, *Graded Holiness: A Key to the Priestly Conception of the World,* Journal for the Study of the Old Testament Supplement 106 (Sheffield: Sheffield Academic Press, 1992), p.89 ff.

30 Anderson, *Contours of Old Testament Theology*, p.117.

31 Ross, *Holiness to the Lord*, p.21. There are other ways of looking at the book, for example by dividing it into two parts: Leveticus 1–15 and Leveticus 16–26, but the unifying theme is still the holiness of God (p.20, n.11).

32 *Ibid*. p.44.

33 See Gammie's excellent reflection on the tabernacle as symbol of the Holy God who cannot be confined to one place (*Holiness in Israel*, pp.14–19).

34 See Jenson, *Graded Holiness*, pp.47–8. '[H]oliness (and its opposite, the profane) represent the divine relation to the ordered world, and the clean (with its opposite, the unclean) embraces the normal state of human existence in the earthly realm. The holy–profane pair represent (positively and negatively) the divine sphere, and this may be distinguished from the human sphere (which is marked by the opposite between clean and unclean). The presence of a holy God and a holy sanctuary in the midst of Israel ensure that these two points of view overlap in a complex way.'

35 Anderson, *Contours of Old Testament Theology*, pp.124–8.

36 Walter Brueggermann, *Theology of the Old Testament: Testimony, Dispute, Advocacy* (Minneapolis: Fortress, 1997) p.289

37 Most scholars recognize the 'Balaam pericope' as an independent unit within the Book of Numbers. See Baruch Levine, *Numbers 21–36* (New York: Doubleday, 2000), p.41ff.38; Jacob Milgrom, *The JPC Torah Commentary. Numbers* (Philadelphia: The Jewish Publication Society, 1990), p.469.

39 Wells, *God's Holy People*, p.96.

40 See Gammie, *Holiness in Israel*, pp.106–7; Wells, *God's Holy People*, p.94.

41 Wells, *God's Holy People*, p.94.

42 Haughey, *Housing Heaven's Fire*, p.43.

43 Gammie, *Holiness in Israel*, p.71.

44 See Wells, *God's Holy People*, p.130, where she cites various scholars who lean in this direction. Of particular interest is the statement by Martin Buber in *The Prophetic Faith* (trans. C. Witton-Davies, New York: Harper and Brothers, 1960, first English edition: 1948), p.129. Buber suggests that in one generation, three basic conceptions of God emerge in the prophets: 'righteousness' with Amos, 'loving-kindness' with Hosea and 'holiness' with Isaiah. See also Gammie, *Holiness in Israel*, p.74.

45 See J. Barton, *Isaiah 1–9* (OTG, Sheffield: Sheffield Academic Press, 1995), p.112; P. R. Ackroyd, 'Isaiah 1–12: Presentation of a Prophet'.

46 This is developed by Samuel Terrien, *The Elusive Presence*, pp.246–52; see Gammie, *Holiness in Israel*, p.77.

47 Wells, *God's Holy People*, p.130.

48 J. J. M. Roberts, 'Isaiah in Old Testament Theology', *Interpretation* 36 (1982), pp.130–43 and reprinted in J. L. Mays and P. J. Achtemeier (eds) *Interpreting the Prophets* (Philadelphia: Fortress Press, 1987), pp.62–74, as quoted in Wells, *God's Holy People*, p.149. Roberts notes: 'If there is any one concept central to the whole Book of Isaiah, it is the vision of Yhwh as the Holy One of Israel. Israel's inaugural vision of the awesome majesty of Yhwh with the seraphs' thundering, three-fold proclamation of Yhwh's holiness, left a lasting impression on the eighth-century prophet's whole ministry' ('Isaiah', p.63.) See also Joseph Blenkinsopp, *Isaiah 1–39* (The Anchor Bible, New York: Doubleday, 2000), pp.222–6; T. C. Vriezen, 'Essentials of the Theology of Isaiah', in *Israel's Prophetic Heritage. Essays in honor of James Muilenburg* (ed Bernhard W. Anderson and Walter Harrelson, London: SCM, 1962) pp.128–46.

49 Vriezen, 'Essentials of the Theology of Isaiah', p.133.

50 Wells, *God's Holy People*, p.137.

51 Brueggemann, *Theology of the Old Testament,* p.289.

52 Joseph Jensen and William H. Irwin, 'Isaiah 1–39', *The New Jerome Biblical Commentary* (Student edition: editors Raymond E. Brown, Joseph A. Fitzmyer and Roland Murphy, London: Geoffrey Chapman, 1993), see on Isaiah 5:16, note f.

53 Brueggemann, *Theology of the Old Testament,* p.230.

54 Haughey, *Housing Heaven's Fire*, p.56,

55 *Ibid.* pp.56–7.

56 Wells, *God's Holy People*, p.154. This theme is beautifully illustrated in other parts of the Old Testament, for example Isaiah 57:15; 66:1-2, Ezekial 17:24, and of course in the New Testament in Luke 1:51-53 where the God who is wholly other is *especially* with the humble [*she-falim*]. For example, Psalms 113: 5-8 says:

Who is like the Lord our God, who is seated on high, who looks far down on the heavens and the earth? He raises the poor from the dust, and lifts the needy from the ash heap.

See Antonella Carfagna and Francesco Rossi De Gasperis, *Terra Santa e Libro Santo: Una lectio divina* (Bologna: Centro Editoriale Dehoniano, 2000), p.19.

57 Roland Murphy, *The Gift of the Psalms* (Peabody, MA: Hendrickson Publishers, 2000), p.99. See also Gianfranco Ravasi, 'Contro di te, contro te solo ho peccato! (Salmo 51,6)', *La Confessione, Rivista internazionale di teologia e cultura*, 194 (March–April 2004, pp.8–14.

58 Irene Nowell, 'The Concept of Purity in the Old Testament', in *Purity of Heart in Early Ascetic and Monastic Literature. Essays in Honor of Juana Raasch, O.S.B.* (Harriet A. Luckman and Linda Kulzer, Collegeville: The Liturgical Press, 1999), pp.26–7.

59 Walter Brueggemann, *The Message of the Psalms: A Theological Commentary.* (Minneapolis: Augsburg Publishing House, 1984), see especially p.101 (emphasis mine).

60 See the following examples: suffering, persecution, sorrow (Job 17:1; Pss. 34:18; 69:20; 109:16; 147:3; Prov. 15:18; Isa. 61:1; 65:14). It can also result from recognition of God's judgment on the sins of others (Jer. 23:9; Ezek. 21:6). Confessions of brokenness occur in the immediate context of petitions for or confessions of faith in God's rescue (Pss. 34: 17–18, 69:16–20; 109:16–32). This openness awakens God's compassion and moves him to bind up the broken-hearted (Isa. 61:1).

61 See Walter Brueggemann, *Israel's Praise: Doxology against Idolatry and Ideology* (Philadelphia: Fortress Press, 1988), pp.129–30.

62 Hans-Joachim Kraus, *Psalms 1-59: A Commentary* Hilton C. Oswald, (Minneapolis: Augsburg Publishing House, 1988), p.507.

63 See Lawrence Cunningham, 'Holiness', p.480, who neatly summarizes the three strands of holiness. I have added the reflection on Psalm 51.

64 Gammie, *Holiness in Israel*, p.126.

65 Ibid. p.127.

66 See Pontifical Biblical Commission, *The Jewish People and Their Sacred Scriptures,* (Vatican City: Libreria Editrice Vaticana, 2001).

67 Wells, *God's Holy People*, p.236, n.122. See Robert Hodgson, Jr. 'Holiness (NT)', *The Anchor Bible Dictionary*, pp.249–54; David Peterson, *Possessed by God: A New Testament Theology of Sanctification and Holiness* (Grand Rapids: William B. Eerdmans, 1995).

68 Craig, 'The Paradox of Holiness: The New testament Doctrine of Sanctification', *Interpretation* 6 (1952) p.153.

69 Wells, *God's Holy People*, pp.243–4.

70 See Stephen C. Barton, 'Dislocating and Relocating Holiness: A New Testament Study', in Barton, *Holiness Past and Present*, p.197.

71 M. Cathleen Kaveny, 'Wholesomeness, Holiness and Hairspray', *America* (3 March 2003), pp.15–18.

72 James Fenegan, *Invitation to Holiness* (San Francisco: Harper and Row, 1984), p.5.

73 Raymond E. Brown, *A Coming Christ in Advent: Essays on the Gospel Narratives Preparing for the Birth of the Messiah* (Collegeville: The Liturgical Press, 1988), pp.16–26.

74 Ibid. p.21.

75 Ibid. p.25.

76 Kaveney, 'Wholesomeness', p17.

77 Wells, *God's Holy People*, p. 234.

78 Ronald D. Witherup, *Matthew: God With Us* (Hyde Park: New City Press, 2000) p.60.

79 Cunningham, 'Holiness', p.481.

80 See *Mosaico di San Clemente* (Rome: Collegio di San Clemente, 1980).

81 Raymond Corriveau, *The Liturgy of Life: A Study of the Ethical Thought of St. Paul in His Letters to the Early Christian Communities* (Brussels: Desclée de Brouwer, 1970), p.231.

82 Cunningham, 'Holiness', p.485.

83 Ibid. p481.

84 The phrase 'in Christ (Jesus)' is used twenty-nine times in Paul's letter to the Romans. As Joseph Fitzmyer notes, 'The phrases are used with different connotations, depending on the context. Sometimes they express the instrumentality of Christ's activity (3:24, 8:39); sometimes they express the intimate relation of Christians and Christ, who live a sort of symbiosis (6:11); sometimes they are a mere synonym for the Christian name (16:7). Modern commentators have variously explained the nature of this symbiosis, understanding it in a local, spatial sense ... in a mystical sense ... or in other dynamic, eschatological, or metaphysical senses. No one sense appears adequate.' *Romans* (The Anchor Bible; New York: Doubleday, 1993), p.141.

85 R. J. McKelvey, *The New Temple: The Church in the New Testament* (Oxford: Oxford University Press, 1969) p.95.

86 Fitzmyer, *Romans*, p.639.

87 The translation here is from Fitzmyer, *Romans*, p.640.

88 Fitzmyer, *Romans*, p. 640. Commenting on the phrase 'Offer your bodies', Ernst Käsemann says, 'Naturally, that implies the surrender

of the whole man. But the Pauline conception of the body is not a matter exclusively or primarily of the personality of man but, at least in the passages of the greatest theological significance, of his capacity for communication and the reality of his incorporation within a world which limits him. God lays claim to our corporeality because he is no longer leaving the world to itself, and our bodily obedience expresses the fact that, in and with us, he has recalled to his service the world of which we are a part. Ernst Käsemann, *New Testament Questions of Today* (Philadelphia: Fortress Press, 1969), p.191.

89 R. J. McKelvey, 'Christ the Cornerstone', *New Testament Studies* 8 (1962), pp.352–59. See especially the conclusion on p.359. McKelvey argues that, based on philological analysis and the reading of various Jewish sources, the New Testament authors were probably referring to a stone at the foundation of the building instead of a copestone or keystone. As McKelvey points out, arches of this sort were not common in Semitic architecture, and none of the Old or New Testament passages suggests that keystone was what was in mind (see pp.353–4).

90 Donald Senior, *1&2 Peter* (2nd edition, Wilmington, DE: Michael Glazier, 1987), p.28.

91 McKelvey, *'Christ the Cornerstone'*, p.358.

92 McKelvey, *'Christ the Cornerstone'*, p.359.

93 Pheme Perkins, *Ephesians* Abingdon New Testament Commentaries (Nashville: Abingdon, 1997), p.76.

94 Wells shows how this passage is influenced by the Hebrew Scriptures (*God's Holy People*, p.209). She explicitly cites six passages: Exodus 19:5-6 'you shall be my own possession among all peoples; for all the earth is mine, and you shall be to me a kingdom of priests and a holy nation'; Isaiah 43: 20–21: 'For I give water in the wilderness, rivers in the desert, to give drink to my chosen people, the people whom I formed for myself that they might declare my praise'; Hosiah 1:6: 'And Yhwh said to him "Call her name Not pitied, for I will no more have pity on the house of Israel, to forgive them at all" '; Hosiah 1:9 'And Yhwh said, "Call his name Not my people, for you are not my people and I am not your God" '; Hosiah 2:1: 'Say to your brother, "My people", and to your sister, "She has obtained pity"'; Hosiah 2:23: 'And I will have pity on Not pitied, and I will say to Not my people, "You are my people"; and he shall say, "Thou art my God".'

95 Wells, *God's Holy People*, p.212.

96 Wells, *God's Holy People*, p.229.

97 John H. Elliott, *A Home for the Homeless. A Sociological Exegesis of 1 Peter, Its Situation and Strategy* (Philadelphia: Fortress Press, 1981), p.181.

98 Senior, *1 and 2 Peter*, (New testament Message 20, A Biblical-Theological Commentary), (Wilmington and Micholl Glazier, 1980), p.32. p.32.

99 Ibid. p.38. See also the most recent commentary, Donald P. Senior and Daniel J. Harrington, *1 Peter, Jude and 2 Peter, (Sacra Pagina* 15, (Collegeville: The Liturgical Press, 2003) pp.39–42.

100 See especially David Peterson, *Hebrews and Perfection* (Cambridge: Cambridge University Press, 1982); Barnabas Lindars, *The Theology of the Letter to the Hebrews* (Cambridge: Cambridge University Press, 1991), especially pp.42–7 and 98ff.; Allen Wikgren, 'Patterns of Perfection in the Epistle to the Hebrews', *New Testament Studies* 6 (1960), pp.159–67.

101 F. F. Bruce, *The Epistle to the Hebrews*, The New International Commentary of the New Testament (Grand Rapids, MI: William B. Eerdmans Publishing Company, 1990), p.348. See also Donald. Hagner, *Encountering the Book of Hebrews* (Grand Rapids: Baker Academic, 2002), p.161.

102 For the structure of Hebrews see Albert Vanhoye, *Structure and Message of the Epistle to the Hebrews* (Rome: Pontifical Biblical Institute, 1989).

103 Lindars, *Letter to the Hebrews* pp.98–9.

104 Craig R. Koester, *Hebrews: A New Translation with Introduction and Commentary* (New York: Doubleday, 2001) pp.120–1.

105 Ibid. p.121.

106 Ibid. p.236–7.

107 This point is emphasized particularly by Bruce, *The Epistle to the Hebrews*, p.265.

108 Ibid. p.366.

109 Rowan Williams, *Open to Judgement: Sermons and Addresses* (London: Longmand and Todd, 1994), p.136.

110 Raissa Maritain, *Les grandes amitiés* (Paris: Desclée de Brouwer, 1949), p.117.

111 Mother Teresa of Calcutta, *A Gift for God* (New York and London: Harper and Row, 1975), p.78.

'The lower edge of the mosaic consists of a a series of scenes from everyday life: a woman feeding ... [chickens], various serfs with flocks and herds. Busy at their occupations beneath the Vine and its brilliant gold background, these workers typify the Christian faithful who live their day-to-day life under the friendly fostering shelter of the Vine.'
*Mosaico di San Clemente* (Rome: Collegio S. Clemente, 1988), p.5.

Basilica of Saint Clement, Rome
Apse Mosaic, 12th century
Woman feeding chickens
Reproduced courtesy of the Irish Dominican Fathers.

# 2
# Many Mansions: Exploring holiness Through the Centuries

*Holiness, whether ascribed to popes well-known to history or to humble lay and religious figures, from one continent to another of the globe, has emerged more clearly as the dimension which expresses best the mystery of the Church. Holiness, a message that convinces without the need for words, is the living reflection of the face of Christ.*

John Paul II, Apostolic Letter *Novo millennio ineunte*
to the Bishops Clergy and Lay Faithful at the Close of the Great
Jubilee of the Year 2000 (Vatican City: Case Editrice Vaticana, 2000), n.7

*We are all called to holiness ... the call to personal conversion and transformation ... is to be heeded by all Christians, not just spiritual athletes. Moreover, every canonization reminds us (or should) that the communion of saints is real, that we are all implicated in each other's response to God's grace.*

Kenneth Woodward, 'Slow up on saint-making',
*The Tablet* 253 (13 November 1999) p.1539.

*Don't call me a saint – I don't want to be dismissed that easily!*

A comment by Dorothy Day made to a journalist
as quoted in Jim Forest, 'The Trouble with Saint Day',
*U.S. Catholic* 62 (November 1997) p. 18

Holiness has been lived out in various ways through the centuries. If these paths are perceived as different mansions or rooms built by God, then it can be said that though the same basic building materials are used for each, the designs are often quite diverse. As history shows, many of these dwellings have been constructed in surprising ways under extraordinary circumstances. Some are under construction even now, for every age will have its particular contribution to make with regard to how holiness is lived out. Reviewing some of these different ways gives a small glimpse of the sheer wonder of God's architectural skill and originality. Exploring the lives and writings of holy women and men through the ages encourages us to take seriously the divine imperative to cultivate holiness in our lives, in our time.

Holy people are often identified as saints, either formally or informally. For example, long before Mother Teresa's holiness was recognized officially by the Roman Catholic Church through her beatification on 19 October 2003, Christians and non-Christians alike acknowledged her sanctity. The process of beatification, followed in many cases by canonization in the Roman Catholic Church, is a way of celebrating this holiness[1] and in recent years, the number of beatifications and canonizations has increased greatly. For example, during the pontificate of John Paul II (1978–2005), 483 people were canonized (of whom 411 are martyrs) and 1338 were beatified (of which 1030 were martyrs). Among these 1338, 50 (28 of these were martyrs) were subsequently canonized.[2] Since promoting models of lay sanctity, especially married couples, was a priority of his pontificate, it is no surprise that more than half of those canonized were lay people.[3] The beatifications and canonizations on different continents was a way to celebrate the different cultural expressions of holiness. Though some have complained about the 'inflation' of saints, the proliferation of these newly beatified and canonized saints in recent years in the Roman Catholic Church is a reminder that the call to holiness is for everyone, without exception.[4]

Informally, others are considered 'holy' by their contemporaries because the lives of these men and women manifest characteristics found in a Christian understanding of holiness. In both the canonized and un-canonized 'saints', these characteristics include signs of union with and conformity to Christ through a life of self-giving love, in solidarity and service of others. In every celebration of the sanctity of an individual, whether through a formal canonization process or informally, we are reminded 'there are no *ordinary* people. You have never talked to a mere mortal. Nations, cultures, arts, civilizations – these are mortal, and their life is to ours as the life of a gnat', says C. S. Lewis. 'But it is immortals whom we joke with, work with, marry, snub, and exploit . . . Next to the Blessed Sacrament itself, your neighbour is the holiest object presented to your senses. If he is your Christian neighbour he is holy in almost the same way, for in him also Christ ... the glorifier and the glorified, Glory himself, is truly hidden.'[5]

Above all, the saints, who are our companions, models and intercessors, encourage us to reflect on our dignity as people who mirror God's image. With their lives, they show us that we too are recipients of God's redeeming, restoring love. As we consider God's work in their lives, we can gain an insight into the meaning of holiness because their actions say more than words; they are truly a *locus theologicus*, a source for theological reflection.[6] This chapter explores some different paths to holiness. Included among the holy men and women studied here are desert and city dwellers, monastics, mendicants and cloistered nuns, married people, and an individual that eludes labelling.[7] It concludes with a reflection on the Blessed Virgin Mary, first among this great cloud of witnesses, who exemplifies the beauty of holiness.

Presenting models of Christian sanctity has both a positive and negative dimension. Positively, in the words of Robert Maloney, models:

> 'give a clear, brief (even if incomplete) insight into the concrete realities of holiness and make us aware of what commitment to it involves. They are like 'icons' of the Gospel, symbols of Christian self-giving. Models do not exhaust the reality; they are partial representations of it. They complement rather than exclude each other, even as each places a particular emphasis on what it means to be holy. As symbols, they arouse an affective response within us, drawing us towards the goal of holiness.[8]

Negatively, individuals accentuate the personal dimension of the call to holiness and 'in an age in which we emphasize the role of community in the quest for holiness (we are baptized into *the church*; we celebrate the liturgy as a *community*) ... they leave something to be desired'.[9] If however, following the image that underlies this book, models are representative of different rooms or mansions of the great palace that God is building, then the unity within diversity becomes more evident.

### Martyrdom: Holiness exemplified

In the Christian tradition, we have always held up the martyrs – those who have witnessed to Christ to the point of death – as the paradigm of holiness. They witness in an exemplary way to the gift God has given them: to lay down their life for their faith. Martyrs, in every era, both men and women, through the grace of God, dared to stand up for their beliefs, without compromise, in the face of extreme opposition. Their example encourages us to speak clearly and to live the gospel boldly and with conviction. In recent years, an explicit parallel has been made between the persecutions of the first century and the martyrs of modern times. As the late Pope John Paul II said, 'The Church of the first millennium was born of the blood of the martyrs: *Sanguis martyrum – semen christianorum ... At the end of the second millennium, the Church has once again become a Church of martyrs.'* [10]

The Church considers martyrdom to be the 'highest gift' (*donum eximium*) and 'supreme test of love' (*suprema probatio caritatis*: *Lumen Gentium* 42). [11] This gift, given only to a few, is considered the summit of holiness, for there is no greater love than to lay down one's life for Christ and for others (cf. 1 3:16, Jn 15:13). Since Jesus's love was manifest most clearly in the laying down of his life for us, those who embrace his example by laying down their life for Christ and for others manifest holiness in a particularly poignant way.

In the primitive church, numerous men and women died as martyrs in the many waves of persecution that broke out in the Roman Empire. Justin, the first significant Christian philosopher, was martyred in Rome around 165. He sought to establish a dialogue between faith and philosophy, between Christians and Jews, between the East and the West. Though born in Samaria of Greek parents, he studied philosophy in Ephesus and Alexandria. After becoming a Christian around 130CE, he led an important school of philosophy in Rome with numerous disciples. He freely debated with Jews, Gnostics, and those who worshipped Roman gods, and wrote an apology in defence of the Christian faith directed to pagans. When arrested during the reign of Marcus Aurelius, he openly confessed his Christian faith and refused to sacrifice to the gods. He was martyred along with six of his disciples. [12]

Another example of a courageous martyrdom in the early Church comes from Carthage, probably around 203. Based partially on the prison diary of Perpetua, a married woman with a new-born child, it recounts her experience, along with that of her companions, as they were interrogated in prison and waited for their death for confessing their faith. This first extant writing of a female Christian was completed by a narrator and editor, possibly Tertullian, who notes that Perpetua 'went along (to her death) with shining countenance and calm step as the beloved of God'. During her time in prison, Perpetua affirmed her faith despite the lack of comprehension not only from her persecutors, but from her family. In her account, she describes two painful encounters with her father. [13] In the first, her father tries to shake her resolution.

Her reply was adamant:

> 'Father,' said I, 'do you see this vase here, for example, or water
> pot or whatever?'
> 'Yes, I do,' said he.
> And I told him: 'Could it be called by any other name than what it
> is?'
> And he said: 'No?'
> 'Well, so too I cannot be called anything other than what I am, a
> Christian.'[14]

At the second encounter, when she appeared before the governor
Hilarianus, her original response again remained firm. Even though she
was well aware that confessing her core convictions would bring about
great suffering for her aged father, her baby son and for herself personally, she could not recant her basic Christian beliefs.

> ... Then, when it came my turn, my father appeared with my son,
> dragged me from the step and said, 'Perform the sacrifice – have
> pity on your baby!'
> Hilarianus the governor ... said to me 'Have pity on your father's
> grey head; have pity on your infant son. Offer the sacrifice for the
> welfare of the emperors!'
> 'I will not,' I retorted.
> 'Are you a Christian?' said Hilarianus.
> And I said: 'Yes, I am.'
> When my father persisted in trying to dissuade me, Hilarianus
> ordered him to be thrown to the ground and beaten with a rod. I
> felt sorry for my father, just as if I myself had been beaten. I felt
> sorry for his pathetic old age.
> Then Hilarianus passed sentence on us all. We were condemned to
> the beasts and we returned to prison in high spirits.[15]

Not only in the early Church, but throughout the centuries and most
particularly in the twentieth century, numerous Christians have died
for their faith.[16] During the Jubilee Year 2000, in a moving ecumenical
celebration organized by the Roman Catholic Church, various Christian
churches and ecclesial communions participated in a prayer service,
'Witness of Faith in the Twentieth Century', that took place in the

Colosseum on 7 May 2000.[17] In this public 'witness' the following words were proclaimed, emphasizing that ours is an age where the blood of martyrs continues to flow:

> *In our own century the martyrs have returned,* many of them nameless, *'unknown soldiers'* as it were of God's *great cause.* As far as possible, their witness should not be lost to the Church ... Perhaps the most convincing form of ecumenism is *the ecumenism of the saints* and of the martyrs. The *communio sanctorum* speaks louder than the things which divide us. The *martyrologium* of the first centuries was the basis of the veneration of the saints. By proclaiming and venerating the holiness of her sons and daughters, the Church gave supreme honour to God himself; in the martyrs she venerated Christ, who was at the origin of their martyrdom and their holiness.[18]

In the 1995 encyclical letter *Ut unum sint* ('That they may be one'), the ecumenical implications of this communion of saints are stated even more explicitly:

> In a theocentric vision, we Christians already have a common martyrology. This also includes the martyrs of the present century, more common than one might think, and it shows, at a profound level, that God preserves communion among the baptized in the supreme demand of faith, manifested in the sacrifice of life itself.[19]

The martyrs express through the ages and into our own era the price of holiness. Through their very lives, they accentuate the durable, do-able nature of a living sanctity. One recent saint, proclaimed a martyr by the Catholic Church, is Edith Stein. Her life spanned the years from 1891 to 1942. Although a meticulous and respected scholar, she is best remembered as a Carmelite nun who died a martyr's death in Auschwitz. Her biographical background helps us to understand her insights into holiness. Edith Stein had very little contact with Christianity while growing up in a Jewish household. Though surrounded by a devout Jewish family, she considered herself an atheist at the age of fourteen. This brilliant, questioning young girl quickly rose through the ranks of academia to become a gifted philosopher, lecturer and writer. One day, when she was just over thirty years old, while visiting a friend's house, she picked up the *Autobiography* of Teresa of Avila. Having read it in one sitting, she put it down declaring, 'This is the truth,' and began her journey into Christianity. In 1922 she was baptized and in 1936, she became a Carmelite until her death in 1942.

What does Edith Stein (St. Teresa Benedicta of the Cross as she is now known) teach us about holiness? The life and witness of Edith Stein teaches us that the foundation of her courage is rooted in her response to the call to holiness by cultivating a relationship with God each day. She explains this in a small pamphlet, *The Mystery of Christmas*:

> To be a child of God means to go hand-in-hand with God, to do his will, not one's own; to place all our hopes and cares in his hands and no longer be concerned about one's self or future. Thereupon rest the freedom and the good cheer of the child of God ... Trust in God will remain unshakably firm only if it is willing to accept from the Father's hand anything and everything. He is the only one who knows what is good for us ... If this can be done, then one can freely live on in the present and the future.[20]

This trust in God was to regulate the day from morning to evening and led Stein to cling to God in her darkest hour, when she was most aware of the tremendous power of evil in the world. A witness who spoke with her in the concentration camp to which they were deported recalls that she said, 'I never knew people could actually be like this ... and I honestly had no idea of how my sisters and brothers were being made to suffer.' In the horrors of the concentration camp, 'she went among the other women comforting, helping and consoling them. Many of the women were on the brink of insanity ... [and gave] little thought to their children. Edith Stein immediately set about taking care of the little ones.'[21] In the final days of her life, her daily trust in God and identification with Christ sustained her. While she deplored the evil around her, she was animated through her relationship with God to act compassionately towards others. Her attitude towards the end of her life was the summit of her obedience to God in daily life. What we see in St. Teresa Benedicta of the Cross and in other twentieth-century martyrs is that their deaths are the result of living out a commitment to God in solidarity with others.

Another moving testimony from the twentieth century comes from the witness of a Trappist community murdered in Algeria. Though not officially recognized as martyrs in the Roman Catholic Church, the seven Trappists were kidnapped from the Monastery of Notre Dame de l'Atlas by armed terrorists on the night of 26 March 1996 and killed on 21 May 1996. They are certainly witnesses of a Christian faith lived to the utmost. The testimony of the prior of the community, Dom Christian de Chergé, brings us to the heart of holiness lived in daily life with the immediate threat of martyrdom looming. In his *Spiritual Testament*, he writes:

> If it should happen one day – and it could also be today – that I become a victim of terrorism, which now seems ready to engulf all foreigners living in Algeria, I would like my community, my Church, and my family to remember that my life was GIVEN to God and to this country.[22]

It is important to note that Dom Christian's life belongs to *another*; it is not his own. This is the first sign of holiness: that one lives one's life as a gift for God in solidarity with others. Dom Christian himself put special emphasis on the word 'given' in his *Testament*. Significantly, it is capitalized in the original. Dom Christian's life has been surrendered not only to God, but to a specific country, Algeria. He saw himself as one among many who had given their life to God. At one point in his testimony, he noted that his life has no more value than that of anyone else's. Further, he did not desire martyrdom because that would imply that someone whom he loves should be accused of murder: 'It would be too high a price to pay, to owe what might be called "the grace of martyrdom" to an Algerian, whoever he may be, especially if he says he is acting in fidelity to what he believes to be Islam.'[23]

The Trappists who lived at Notre Dame de l'Atlas considered themselves to be a typical monastic community. Though they were encouraged to go to a safer location, they wanted to stay where they were so that they could be in solidarity with the people to whom they were dedicated. When the Abbot General met with Dom Christian in 1994, he said that the order did not need martyrs, but monks. After listening to this, Dom Christian was silent and then said, 'there is no contradiction'.[24]

To live for God in solidarity with others is a fruit of holiness. Whether done in the routine of monastic work and prayer or as a martyr, the call to holiness is to be embraced with gratitude as gift. This point is movingly made by Dom Christian:

For this life lost, totally mine and totally theirs, I thank God, who seems to have willed it entirely for the sake of that JOY in everything and in spite of everything. In this THANK YOU, which is said for everything in my life from now on, I certainly include you, friends of yesterday and today, and you, my friends of this place ... And also you, my last-minute friend, who will not have known what you were doing: Yes I want this THANK YOU and this 'A DIEU' to be for you, too because in God's face I see yours [*en-vis-agé de toi*].[25]

In this reflection on martyrdom, the focus has been on those who have died for their faith in times of persecution. Without underestimating the value of this unique witness, there also must be a sense in which martyrdom is a universal vocation. Here one can make a distinction between physical and moral martyrdom. If martyrdom literally means witnessing to Christ by taking up one's cross – voluntarily accepting the suffering that comes our way and living a life of self-gift in solidarity with others to the point of death – then there is a sense in which it is a call to every Christian. This 'inner or moral martyrdom', recognized by the early Christian community, is succinctly summarized by Paul's phrase, 'I die, every day' (1 Cor. 15:31). In the early Church, especially through the writings of St Cyprian of Carthage, a distinction was made between 'red' martyrdom through the shedding of blood in times of persecution and 'white' martyrdom, self-sacrificing acts of compassion and charity in times of peace.[26] With that in mind, it is important to consider that taking care of a well-loved child dying of cancer or living charitably with a psychologically frail community or family member are very real examples of the daily martyrdom of self-sacrificing love.

*Holiness in the desert*
When the persecutions of the early Church ceased and the peace of Constantine brought stability to the cities, many men and women went into the desert seeking holiness. One example is Antony of Egypt, who is considered the father of desert monasticism. According to the *Life of Antony*, written by St. Athanasius (c. 296–373), when Antony's parents, rich Christian landowners, died, he, who at that time was between 18 and 20 years old, was left with the responsibility for his sister. Upon hearing the words (probably in 270–271), 'If you would be perfect, go, sell what you possess and give to the poor, and you will have treasure in

heaven' (Matt. 19:21), he arranged for the care of his sister and eventually sold his possessions so that he could become an ascetic. He lived a life of intense prayer and fasting, first in his own neighbourhood and then in the Egyptian desert. After spending twenty years in solitude fighting demons within and without, his friends and admirers came along and, according to Athanasius, 'forcefully removed the fortress door' of his cell. Antony emerged as an exemplar of holiness who encouraged others to 'prefer nothing above the love of Christ'.[27] It would be hard to underestimate the immense impact he has had on the monastic tradition which would follow. As William Clebsch wrote, 'In the lore surrounding the Egyptian desert fathers that was transmitted throughout the Medieval and Byzantine churches, the name of Antony retained its lustre. He was Egypt's most famous example of the quest for individual perfection and of the power given to those submissive to the "bloodless martyrdom." The Antonian ideal formed a central part of the bold definition of holy living that won converts to Christianity.'[28] In fact, even during his lifetime, Athanasius reminds us that Antony 'persuaded many to take up the solitary life' and that the 'desert was made a city by monks'.[29]

Both Antony's seven extant letters and Athanasius's *Life of Anthony* emphasize that his experience of desert-dwelling included a profound renunciation of self and an interior detachment that eventually led him to cling to God alone. For Antony, the desert was a place of conversion where he faced his compulsive self and allowed himself to be transformed by grace into a new self conformed to Christ. In all of Antony's struggles, Athanasius reminds us that 'working with Antony was the Lord, who bore flesh for us, and gave to the body victory over the devil, so that each of those who truly struggle can say, *It is not I, but the grace of God in me*' (1 Cor. 15:10).[30] The solitude of the desert and of his cell were the places where he faced his vulnerable and broken self and where he allowed God's transforming power to take root in his life.

The *Life of Antony*, along with other writings from the desert fathers and mothers, highlights that the search for holiness was shaped by the images of the desert and the cell. The desert was considered both a fearful and a sacred place. It elicited fear because it was a fierce wasteland where, in the starkness of the terrain, one came to grips with a radical life of renunciation. Quite simply, the desert meant death and abandonment – death to self and abandonment of all the supports that kept one from facing his or her true self. At the same time, the desert was sacred because it was a place of encounter: the radical break from the main-stream of society was seen as a way of opening oneself up for an encounter with the living God. Like the desert, the cell was also under-stood as the place where one faced oneself, one's demons and fears, in solitude. The key to desert spirituality is to remain in silence and soli-tude so that the work of holiness can begin. 'A brother came to Scetis to visit Abba Moses and asked him for a word. The old man said to him: "Go, sit in your cell, and your cell will teach you everything." '[31] Learning to sit in silence in one's cell was not then, nor is it now, always easy. For example, Abba Agathon learned how to embrace silence by liv-ing with a stone in his mouth for three years. This was a drastic solu-tion to his problem, but apparently it worked.[32]

The withdrawal into the desert or into one's cell was not seen as a way of escaping from others, but rather as a way of growing in the Lord and in love of one's neighbour. As Antony said, 'Our life and our death is with our neighbour. If we gain our brother we have gained God, but if we scandalize our brother, we have sinned against Christ.'[33] The cell was a place of rounding off one's rough edges in order to live more peacefully with others. 'He who dwells with his brethren must not be square, but round', according to Abba Mateos, 'so as to turn himself towards all.'[34] Rough edges were also smoothed through meditating on the Word of God. As Abba Poemen said, 'The nature of water is soft, that of stone is hard; but if a bottle is hung above the stone, allowing the water to fall drop by drop, it wears away the stone. So it is with the word of God; it is soft and our heart is hard, but the man who hears the word of God often opens his heart to the fear of God.'[35]

A sign of holiness for the desert dwellers was a sense of total detach-ment or freedom from material things. This is marvellously illustrated in the various robber stories told by the desert fathers. For example, upon returning to his cell, Abba Macarius; once encountered a thief and helped him load up his booty and saw him off in 'complete tranquillity'.[36] As Douglas Burton-Christie points out, when commenting on this pas-sage, 'the manner of Macarius's behavior is ... significant. He sees the thief off "in complete tranquillity," a sign that his actions flow from a pure heart and a deep appropriation of the meaning of renunciation.'[37]

What do the desert dwellers say to contemporary Christians seeking holiness? Though we may not have the opportunity to go physically to the desert, the fact is that often the desert comes to us. The desert can come to us in forms of loneliness, emotional, physical or social breakdown, dryness and emptiness in prayer, discouragement or depression. We might experience it in personal illness or in seeing the suffering and death of someone we love. We encounter the desert in the city when we see the overwhelming poverty of street people or when we are aware of the very real fear that many have, for example, of terrorist attacks. The desert dwellers assure us that as we face the fearful uncertainties of our own wastelands – in silence, solitude and trust in the Word of God, we will come to experience God's transforming and redeeming love shaping our lives. The desert dwellers encourage us courageously to face the darkness with an obstinate trust that our places of personal discomfort are exactly where the Living God wants to meet us.

### *The monastic way*

The stark solitude of an ascetic life personified by Antony was complemented eventually by a more communal or cenobitic form of monasticism. The main characteristic of this type of monasticism is that those seeking holiness gathered together in monasteries under the guidance of an abbot. Though this cenobitic lifestyle existed for more than two centuries before Benedict of Nursia wrote his *Rule*, it was he who gathered and distilled with brevity and simplicity the monastic wisdom that preceded him. This is particularly evident when comparing the *Rule of the Master*, an earlier monastic rule, and Benedict's *Rule*. Benedict was neither an innovator nor an original thinker, but a person who assimilated the tradition that came before him in such a way that it would become the norm for future monasticism in the West. For this reason, though there are diverse ways of living monastic spirituality, it seems appropriate to focus on Benedict and his *Rule* as representative of the 'monastic mansion'.

What little we know about Benedict comes from Book Two of Pope St. Gregory the Great's *Dialogues*.[38] For Gregory (540–604), Benedict was a model of holiness whose life was characterized by a constant search for God. Born around 480 in Nursia (Norcia today), which is north-east of Rome, Benedict eventually studied in Rome, where he experienced a religious conversion. Frustrated and disgusted with the academic scene in the Eternal City, he finally renounced the world and went to live first in Afile outside of Rome and then as a hermit for three years in Subiaco. Other monks eventually joined him in this search for God at Vicovaro, though this first monastic community experience turned out to be a disaster – especially when the monks, who considered him too severe, rebelled and tried to poison him. Eventually at Subiaco, Benedict's monastic community flourished. During his lifetime, he established twelve monasteries of twelve people each, the last of which was at Monte Cassino. He died in the middle of the sixth century.

Gregory presents Benedict as a man of God who progressed in holiness over the years. As Benedict overcame one temptation after another, he radiated God's presence in his life and became an exemplar of holiness for others. As Timothy Fry observed, 'Benedict is an example who shows forth the workings of God in ... [human] life. He illustrates the law of paradox: genuine fruitfulness comes from what at first light seems sterile; life comes forth from death; the ... [one] who concentrates upon his [or her] own sanctification becomes an apostle, an instrument of God for the good of others. Through Benedict, Gregory teaches his readers the stages through which ... [one] advances towards God.'[39] Gregory's message to his readers was that whatever obstacles they may face, God is always at work in their lives and they too can grow in holiness.

If Benedictine monasticism is representative of one of the many mansions in the Christian tradition, then the *Rule of Benedict* offers an insight into the building plan of this particular mansion. Quite simply, Benedict's path to holiness is a life-long process of learning to live in the presence of the Lord through a balanced rhythm of life characterized by listening to the Word of God, especially through *lectio divina* (a prayerful reflective reading of sacred Scripture which will be discussed in Chapter 3), reciting the psalms, interior prayer, work and being a responsible member of the community,[40] all sought under the guidance of an abbot. Attentiveness to God in the ebb and flow of everyday life is the key for understanding the Benedictine way of holiness. Ever the realist, Benedict recognized that growth in holiness does not happen overnight and therefore he exhorted his monks: 'Do not aspire to be called holy before you really are, but first be holy that you may more truly be called so' (4:62).

Benedict offers the Church a modest rule for beginners that he calls a 'school for the Lord's service' (Prologue 45). In the prologue, St. Benedict says, 'Listen carefully, my son, to the master's instructions, and attend to them with the ear of your heart.'[41] First, there is an invitation to 'listen carefully' (*obsculta*), and second to listen to the other with 'the ear of your heart' (*inclina aurem cordis tui*). This intense listening needs to be cultivated and Benedict was convinced that the monastery was an ideal environment which this could happen.

Divided into two parts, the *Rule* consists of a prologue and seven
chapters on spiritual doctrine (Prologue, 1–7) and then sixty-six chapters
of monastic regulations (8–73). Benedict was certain that stability as
a life-long commitment to one house or monastery, prayer and *lectio
divina* are at the heart of this intense listening. The combination of
communal prayer and personal prayer, which takes about four hours a
day in all (43:3), marks the rhythm of each day. Prayer (*ora*) was intricately balanced with work (*labora*), which was not considered a secondary or mundane activity; both were to be done with attentiveness.
Objects like monastic utensils and other monastic goods were treated
with the same care and reverence as sacred vessels (31:10). This care
and reverence was not only reserved for objects, but also, and most especially, for guests, particularly the poor. 'All guests who present themselves are to be welcomed as Christ, for he himself will say: *I was a
stranger and you welcomed me*' (Matt. 25:35, 53:2). The attractiveness
of Benedict's path to holiness is its capacity to integrate every dimension of life in its sheer everyday ordinariness. It offers a simple and balanced way to seek the Holy One in the routine and rhythms of everyday
life and seasons.

In recent years, many lay people have come to appreciate the wisdom
of St. Benedict's *Rule* and have applied it to their own lives. One example
of this application is given by Esther de Waal's most recent commentary
on the rule, *A Life Giving Way: A Commentary on the Rule of St.
Benedict*. There, she remarks:

> When I first read the Rule, I found that it gave me much practical
> wisdom about how to cope with the demands of daily life and to
> make them a way to God. I learned about the handling of people
> and of material things, about how to impose some sort of rhythm
> and structure on my day so that there was time and space for God.
> All this was immensely wise and useful, and it made enormous
> sense in a busy life, with a large household to run, family to look
> after, a part-time time job, and all the other many multifarious
> demands that meant I was continually living under considerable
> pressure.[42]

While living with her family in what had been the former prior's lodge
of a large Benedictine Community in Canterbury, this Anglican woman
discovered that the *Rule of Benedict* offered her practical insights into

how to respond to God's call to holiness in her daily life. The monastic tradition has much to offer lay people in everyday life. After all, originally it was a 'lay movement'. Perhaps in the years since the Second Vatican Council, in our zeal to promote a specifically 'lay spirituality', we have failed to plumb the depths of the monastic tradition. Certainly, the monastic way is a particular charism or gift in the Church – one mansion among many (and the Benedictine way is just one example of how to live this). Benedict's *Rule* or way of life is an invitation to seek a greater consciousness of God's presence in our daily life – an awareness of God in our work, prayer, and leisure – and as such it has practical applications for every Christian in their search for holiness.

## *Mendicants*

Mendicants join the martyrs, desert dwellers and monastics as witnesses to holiness. These groups began to flourish in the in the late twelfth and early thirteenth century. Called mendicants because early on they literally begged for food, they lived evangelical poverty and manifested in their lives an apostolic zeal to spread the gospel. They include, first of all, the Order of Preachers that was founded by Dominic Guzman (1170–1221) with the mission to preach and to work for the salvation of others.[43] Secondly, the Carmelites, who began as hermits in the Holy Land, as witnessed by their *Formula of Life* (1206–14) approved by Albert, patriarch of Jerusalem, eventually became mendicants when they emmigrated to Europe around 1238 (with a *Rule* approved in 1247 by Innocent IV).[44] The Augustinians, yet another mendicant order, emerged out of various Italian communities of hermits in the twelfth and thirteenth century.[45] Finally, the Order of Friars Minor was founded by Francis of Assisi (1182–1226), whose spirituality has been lived over the centuries by the Franciscan Friars, the Poor Clare nuns, and 'Third Order' laity and religious.[46]

Francis of Assisi is one of the best known mendicants and religious figures of all time. When a 1992 survey by *Time* magazine considered the ten most influential people in the last thousand years, this poor man of Assisi found a place among the artists, scientists, statesmen, explorers, musicians and religious figures mentioned.[47] Even today, people continue to flock to Assisi to reflect on the life of this *poverello*, this poor man, who chose radically to follow the poor Christ. For example, Jews, Muslims, Buddhists, Hindus, Christians and leaders of other religions have come to Assisi over the years for large gatherings and smaller unnoticed occasions. Two of the most memorable events were the October 1986 and the January 2002 meetings of religious leaders with Pope John Paul II. One reason other believers and even people far removed from religion are drawn to Francis is because they recognize qualities of holiness in him:[48] specifically, his joyful love for and obedience to God's will, his simplicity of life, and his service to and solidarity with the poor attract others.

Francis was born in 1181 or 1182 into a merchant-class family. His father, Pietro da Bernadone, a cloth dealer, and his mother Pica had Francis baptized as 'Giovanni' (John): however his nickname, 'Francesco' stuck with him throughout his life. When one reads the various legends concerning his life, it becomes clear that he lived somewhat dissolutely in his early years. Sifting through these various accounts, Lawrence Cunningham sums up this period best: 'Francis seems to have been a typical indulged, wealthy, spoiled, and thrill-seeking adolescent who was indulged by a family who could afford to look with a benevolent eye on the peccadilloes of his youth ... Francis seems to have done all the things that adults deplore in the youth of today: waste time and money; be preoccupied with fancy clothes which had to be in the latest mode; run around with the wrong crowd, chase after women; and take an interest in subversive music – in his case, the love songs (*chansons*) introduced from France.'[49]

Francis's call to holiness was experienced through a series of deepening conversions. The first hint of conversion from this worldly life seems to have occurred when Francis was convalescing after a brief stint in a war between Perugia and Assisi in 1202. At this point, he had decided to become a knight, though it seems that something happened on his journey to southern Italy to join the militia of Pope Innocent III that caused him to change his mind. Francis himself describes his first steps towards conversion with these simple and unpretentious words at the beginning of his *Testament*, written in 1226, just a few months before he died:

> The Lord gave me, Brother Francis, thus to begin doing penance in this way: for when I was in sin, it seemed too bitter for me to see lepers. And the Lord himself led me among them and I showed mercy to them. And when I left them, what had seemed bitter to me was turned into sweetness of soul and body. And afterwards I delayed a little and left the world.[50]

Notice that he says, 'The Lord gave me,' 'the Lord himself led me'. Francis remembers this turning away from self and turning towards God as a gift that he received. This gift also had practical implications in his changed attitude and behaviour towards lepers. Some of the early legends tell of Francis, while riding a horse, encountering a leper and instead of avoiding him, gaving alms. Whether this really happened or not, it is clear that Francis' conversion led him eventually to serve the most despised and isolated members of society. The lepers were the 'poorest of the poor'; the *minores* of society and service to them was literally a way for him and his followers to imitate Christ.[51]

The early biographers also focus on the confrontation with his father as another moment of conversion. Francis had sold some of his father's cloth and had given the money to the poor. The father–son conflict came to a head in the presence of Giudo, bishop of Assisi. As depicted in both Saint Bonaventure's *Major Legend of St. Francis*[52] and in the painting in the upper Church of St Francis in Assisi, Pietro Bernadone holds the clothes of Francis as the bishop covers the naked Francis with his mantle. This scene captures an essential element of Francis' way to holiness: radical abandonment to God, symbolized by the stripping off of his clothes (representing his former way of life) and following Christ in complete poverty and naked trust. His one desire was to live without anything of his own, which was in direct contrast to his father's expectations and the norms of what constituted twelfth-century success. Francis' choice can be summarized with the classical formulation attributed to St Jerome: 'to nakedly follow the naked Christ' (*nudus nudum Christum sequi*).[53] Embracing Christ's poverty, manifest both in the incarnation and in the passion, meant a dispossession of all worldly wealth.

What exactly Francis was to do with his life once he 'left the world' was not particularly clear to him. An early prayer (1205/06) which Francis prayed before the crucifix in the Church of San Damiano beautifully captures the spirit of Francis in these early years:

Most High,
Glorious God,
Enlighten the darkness of my heart
and give me
true faith,
certain hope,
and perfect charity,

sense and knowledge,
Lord,
That I may carry out
Your holy and true command.[54]

Francis was filled with a great desire to serve God, but he needed light
to know what to do next. He began by simply serving lepers, spending
time in prayer and repairing abandoned churches in the area, including
San Damiano. As he repaired these building, he came to understand the
importance of churches as places set apart for praise and reverence of
God. He also began to grasp the real meaning of his own life: to rebuild
and to support the living Church through his life of service, prayer and
poverty.[55]

More clarity came when he heard Matt. 11:7–10 read at mass on the
feast of St. Matthias. When the passage about Christ's invitation to
carry nothing on the journey and to go forth and proclaim the good news
was reread to him by the priest after mass, he realized this was his vocation. According to his first biographer Thomas of Celano, he said, "'This
is what I want. This is what I seek; this is what I desire with my whole
heart." With these words, he removed his shoes, took on a simple cord
as a belt, and then signed his tunic with a cross. This poor man in a
"very rough," "very poor and plain" tunic 'wanted to carry out [the gospel]
to the letter.'"[56] Eventually a fraternity formed around him – men who
were bound together by a common way of life. The main characteristic
of this early fraternity is that they did not possess anything. They supported themselves by working with their hands or by begging for alms.

Francis' idea of holiness needs to be understood in the context of two
key themes in his spirituality, namely, his focus on the crib and the
cross.[57] The focus on the crib refers to his concentration on the incarnation that was symbolized by his celebration of Christmas at Greccio.
On Christmas Eve in 1223, he gathered with his friars in a poor stable
with a manger, where a mass was celebrated. This event, described brilliantly by Thomas of Celano, suggests that Greccio may have become an
annual event because for Francis:

There simplicity is given a place of honour,
Poverty is exalted,
Humility is commended,
and out of Greccio is made a new Bethlehem.[58]

For Francis, the belief that the 'Word became flesh' (Jn 1:14) meant that in becoming man Christ lived a life of humility, extreme poverty and simplicity. Francis stayed at Greccio probably at least until Easter 1224. He eventually went to Mount La Verna in Arezzo, in October 1224, where during a period of fasting and prayer, he received the stigmata which was a confirmation of his desire to live a life conformed to Christ crucified. Lawrence Cunningham offers a summary of these two pivotal moments of Francis' life:

> In a sense those two moments at Greccio and La Verna were two parentheses that summed up the evangelical vision of Francis. If the later Franciscans were to enter into sterile debates about the meaning of poverty, that all-too-human fact stands in contrast to how Francis saw poverty: as a self-emptying whose meaning had to be anchored in the reality of the gospel message whose center is the cross. That self-emptying began, of course, when the Word became flesh, when the Son of God was born of Mary in a simple stable in Bethlehem. The seal of the stigmata is crucial as a counterweight to any attempt to romanticize Francis as a medieval Doctor Doolittle who innocently hymned the cosmos and its inhabitants in a constant state of felicity.[59]

Just after his experience at Mount La Verna, Francis went to Assisi where, as a truly poor man, he composed his famous *Canticle of Brother Sun*. In stark contrast with the romantic and sentimental image of him romping around the Umbrian countryside talking to the birds, the *Canticle* was written in the eventide of his life when Francis, exhausted by fasting and illness, was nearly blind and was also suffering from severe abdominal pain. In this context, he gathered his brothers and recited for them this celebrated hymn to the Most High, who is praised in and through the elements of creation. One of the two verses which he added later, praised 'Sister Death' 'from whose embrace no mortal can escape'. Francis was not threatened by death, but saw it as a fraternal encounter with the inevitable and something to be celebrated. This *Canticle* verse can be seen as an expression of his radical holiness, a self-stripping or self-dispossession that recognizes that all is gift. Holiness, for Francis, was a participation in Christ's self-emptying as described in Phillippians 2: 1–11. In one of his letters, Francis told his brothers, 'Hold back nothing of yourselves for yourselves, that He Who gives

Himself totally to you may receive you totally'.[60] Francis died on the eve
of 3 October 1226, a poor man in his little *portiuncula*, the church of St.
Mary of the Angels, a man who had given his all to God.

## Married models of holiness

Martyrs, desert dwellers, monks and mendicants have no monopoly on
holiness. We also find within the Christian tradition models of marital
sanctity. The fact that this has not always been accentuated is illustrated by a story once told by John Paul I about Frédéric Ozanam, a married man of the nineteenth century who was eventually beatifiedin Paris
on 22 August 1997, by John Paul II:

> In the last century in France lived Frédèric Ozanam. He was a
> famous professor who taught at the Sorbonne; he was so eloquent
> and so great! His friend, Lacordaire said of him: 'He is so talented,
> so good, he could become a priest, this man could become a great
> bishop.' No! he met a fine woman and they got married.
> Lacordaire was sad and said, 'Poor Ozanam! Also he has fallen into
> the trap!' But two years later, Lacordaire went to Rome and had
> an audience with Pius IX, who said 'Come, come Father, I always
> thought that Jesus had instituted seven sacraments. Now you
> arrive and change everything. You tell me that he instituted six
> sacraments and a trap! No, Father, marriage is not a trap, but a
> great sacrament.'[61]

In the history of spirituality there were times when marriage was considered more a trap than a sacrament; yet, within the Christian tradition, we have consistently recognized the presence of married saints.
For example, the first missionary couple, Priscilla and Aquila, who made
tents and spread the gospel with St. Paul, have always been considered
saints. The Orthodox tradition honours emperor and empress, Saint
Justinian (482–565) and Saint Theodora. Saint Stephen and Blessed
Gisela (eleventh century) were the first king and queen of Hungary. The
farmer Saint Isidore of Madrid was canonized in 1622 in good company
with Ignatius of Loyola, Francis Xavier, Teresa of Avila and Philip Neri.
Isidore's wife Maria de la Cabeza is considered blessed.[62]

Though models of marital sanctity have been proposed over the
years,[63] it is not always clear that their marital status was seen as an
integral part of their journey towards holiness. One problem is that

marriage has not always been presented by the Christian tradition in a positive light. The ascetic and monastic life, with its positive and valid emphasis on virginity, often became in the post-Constantine Church *the* model of Christian perfection. Consequently, marriage was sometimes undervalued as a way to sanctity. Furthermore, the suspicion of genital sex as somehow sinful clouded any healthy view of marriage for many centuries.

Still another problem is that some of the examples of marital holiness upheld in the Christian tradition have been inappropriate to the reality of the married state. Already in the seventeenth century, the Flemish Jesuit, Andreas de Boeye (1571–1650), aware that most of the literature dealing with sanctity at the end of the Tridentine reform was focused mainly on popes, bishops, priests, and nuns, wrote a book on married people who led saintly lives. De Boeye was quite realistic when presenting some of these figures, particularly those who did not want to get married in the first place and who convinced their spouse to make a solemn vow not to have sexual relations. Aware of his married readers, he wrote in the margins, 'Wonderful, but not to be imitated!'[64]

One example of such a married saint is Nicholas de Flüe (1417–87), the Swiss ascetic and hermit. He was canonized not so much for the twenty years that he lived as a farmer together with his faithful wife and ten children, but for the eremitic life he led after he left his family. We know from historical evidence that his wife sustained him in his vocation to become a hermit. Together they passed many nights in prayer before coming to this decision. Without a doubt, his life as a hermit bore much fruit, and this was officially acknowledged in his 1947 canonization. Nicholas said that he was grateful to God for the three graces of being able to live without food for eighteen years, of having a wife who supported him in his vocation, and for the gift of never being tempted to return to his family. There can be little doubt what Father de Boeye's response would be to this saint: Nicholas is a marvellous Swiss saint and though he can and should be honoured for other reasons, he cannot be proposed as a model of marital sanctity.

In more recent years, more 'ordinary' married Christians have been proposed for beatification and canonization. The most recently canonized married person in the Roman Catholic Church was the Italian Gianna Beretta Molla, physician, wife and mother. Her canonization took place in May 2004 in the presence of her ninety-two year-old husband and children. In the articles and books written about her, she is consistently presented as a saint of everyday life. Her greatness, in the words of Cardinal Carlo Maria Martini, consists in the fact that she 'walked day after day in our footsteps, she had our problems and difficulties, showing us that in the ordinary activities of life, we can grow in holiness'.[65]

Gianna Beretta Molla was born on 4 October 1922, in Magenta near Milan, Italy, into a large Catholic family where Christian values were fostered. Many of her brothers and sisters committed themselves to lives of service; two of her brothers became priests, one of whom was a missionary in Brazil, and another became an engineer and helped build a hospital in that same country. A sister became a physician and pharmacist and another sister, following her graduation from medical school, became a Canossian missionary in India. Gianna, also a physician by training, wrestled with the decsision whether to marry or to become a missionary. After prayer and reflection, Gianna concluded that her vocation lay in marriage. She eventually married Pietro Molla.

Her letters to Pietro demonstrate that she viewed marriage as a genuine vocational choice.[66] Their married life mirrored a reciprocal happiness and profound love. They eventually had three children, Pierluigi (1956), Marialina (1957) and Laura (1959). Throughout this period, Gianna continued her profession as a physician. The key to her discipleship was a sense of vocation. In a notebook written sometime between 1944 and 1948, she explains:

> One thing is certain, that we have been the object of predilection from all eternity ... Everything happens for an established end ... To each of us God has given us a life, a vocation: beyond the physical life, a life of grace.
>
> Faced with the problem of what will come: it isn't necessary to resolve it at the age of fifteen, but it is important to focus all of our life towards the life to which the Lord calls us. Our ... happiness depends upon following well our vocation ... it is a gift from God, thus it comes from God. If it is a gift from God, our concern must be to know the will of God. We must enter into the path first if God wills ... second when God wills, third, as God wills ... There are many difficulties, but with the help of God we must walk always without fear. If in the struggle of our vocation, we must die, then that will be the most beautiful day in our life.[67]

She lived her discipleship in the rough and tumble, joys and grief, of everyday life. She was typically preoccupied with her husband and his profession, she also suffered from complicated pregnancies – two of which ended in miscarriage – and juggled the tasks of raising children with her professional responsibilities as a medical doctor. She lived her call to holiness not through exceptional fasts or great acts of penance, but through an asceticism of daily life.[68] Hers was not a dour, grim life of a misdefined holiness; her life was filled with joy. Photographs exist of her with her husband and children – pictures of the family on skiing holidays in the Alps and family photos taken at home. She was a woman who knew how to enjoy the good gifts of living and the goodness of God in her ordinary life. 'With simplicity and equilibrium she harmonized the demands of mother, wife, doctor and her passion for life', is how one writer put it.[69]

In September 1961, towards the second month of pregnancy, her physicians discovered a fibroma in her uterus and decided to operate immediately. Gianna was firm in saying that under no circumstances should the life of the child be put in jeopardy. Though the operation was a success, she continued the pregnancy with great risk to her personal health. Gianna died on 28 April 1962, just one week after her daughter, Gianna Emanuela, was born.

A deep faith, nurtured over the years through a life of prayer and a sense of vocation, was the foundation of her peace in the last months of her life. She lived the call to discipleship in a radical way throughout her life and this sustained her during her final suffering. The final act of her life shows the depths of her discipleship: for there is no greater expression of conformity to Christ than to lay down one's life for another. Father Paolino Rossi, the postulator of her cause, discourages us from excessive emphasis on the manner of her death: 'It is an error to reduce her sainthood and her example to the last extreme gesture. It was the culmination of a life lived with great intensity and a profound love of God and her fellow man.'[70]

The first time in the Roman Catholic Church that a couple were beatified together was on 21 October 2001. The beatification of Luigi Beltrame Quattrocchi (1880–1951) and Maria Corsini (1884–1965) is one more sign that marriage is a genuine means towards holiness. Many people question the clarity of this sign, given the fact that the couple seemed to live a 'quasi religious life' that included, in their later years, a commitment to celibacy within marriage. At the same time, it ought

to be noted that a consistent theme in the literature associated with
their cause was the fact that they lived an ordinary life with extraordinary love. In the words of Bruno Forte:

> They tell us above all that Grace passes through human values
> and affection, through at times even the most banal or even humblest
> of daily tasks, where everyday there is a gift to discover, a response
> to be given, a grace to be embraced ... What the little, big story of
> these *borghesi* shows us is that it is possible ... to live holiness in
> the ordinariness of everyday life.[71]

Perhaps in the future, Forte's insight will lead to an even greater recognition within the Church that ordinary married life – ordinary in every
sense of the word – is a normative path to holiness. Marriage is, in fact,
the path of the vast majority of Christians and it is important to find
examples who reflect the real experience of most married couples, in
their intimacy with one another, in their family commitments, and in
their professional lives. Much needs to be done to find such models. As
John Paul II said at the end of the last millennium, 'In particular, there
is a need to foster the recognition of the heroic virtues of men and
women who have lived their Christian vocation *in marriage*. Precisely
because we are convinced of the abundant fruits of holiness in the married state, we need to find the most appropriate means for discerning
them and proposing them to the whole Church as a model and encouragement for other Christian spouses.'[72]

### A cloistered call to holiness

Though all Christians are invited to seek holiness, those who embrace
an enclosed or cloistered life have a distinct vocation to cultivate this
gift. One example is Thérèse of Lisieux (1873–97), whose teaching on
holiness extends beyond Carmel to the world. The depth of her thought
is not easily grasped at first sight. This was the case for Cardinal Basil
Hume (1923–99), the former Archbishop of Westminster and one of the
most respected spiritual leaders of our time. A few years prior to his death,
he gave a conference in which he spoke of Thérèse as 'the Millennium
Doctor'. He prefaced his remarks with a personal experience:

> I used to find her almost impossible to read – not almost, but
> impossible. It just wasn't me, but happily now at the age of 74 I
> have discovered her – I discovered her some years ago. I was invited

to go and preside at a celebration of 100 years of her entry into Carmel. I said I would do so on one condition: that my fee was to spend a half an hour alone in her cell. When you are a Cardinal one of the nice things is that you can barge in anywhere! It was a lovely half hour. Then I saw what I knew existed on the side of her cell. She had scratched into the woodwork in French, *'Jésus est mon unique amour'*, 'Jesus is my only love'. When she was beatified in 1925 they covered it up because you couldn't have a *beata* indulging in graffiti. Now it is uncovered, and you can see it just scribbled. The interpretation is that she went through the dark night of the soul, a very great trial and when she was experiencing this trial she had to express what she really wanted to feel or perhaps what she actually felt just to reassure herself. This is what I stand for: *'Jésus est mon unique amour.'* Jesus is my only love.[73]

Love is the key to unlocking Thérèse's understanding of holiness. It is significant that she was introduced as a doctor of the Church in 1997 with these words: *Divini amoris scientia*, 'The Science of Divine Love'. In her *Autobiography*, commonly called *The Story of a Soul*, Thérèse describes how these words came to her at the end of a silent and arid period of prayer: *'Here is the teacher whom I am giving you; he will teach you everything that you must do. I want to make you read in the book of life, wherein is contained the science of LOVE.* The science of Love, ah, yes, this word resounds sweetly in the ear of my soul, and I desire only this science.'[74] The *'science of divine love'* brings us to the centre of the paradoxically simple, yet profound call to holiness that Thérèse lived and communicated in the heart of the Church.

Born in Alençon, France on 2 January 1873, Thérèse Martin was the youngest of nine children, four of whom had died before her birth. Her parents, Louis and Zélie, were devout Catholics who strongly encouraged their children to fully embrace the sacramental life of the Church at a time when Jansenism, a severe and harsh spirituality, was prevalent. The family was generous in extending their love to one another and to those who were in need. Thus, in her early years, Thérèse experienced God's love through the strong family bonds with which she was surrounded. In 1877, when she was four years old, her mother died and it was shortly thereafter that her family moved to Lisieux. This period in her life included eight years of religious scrupulosity and hypersensitivity.

An important change in her life took place after the Christmas Eve mass in 1886 when, after a moment of crisis, she felt both charity enter her heart and the need to forget herself for the sake of others. A few days later, while praying before a statue of Christ crucified, she committed herself to stand before the cross and gather Christ's blood for others. She had a strong desire, 'a thirst', to work for the salvation of humanity. This desire for the spiritual care and salvation of others showed itself in deeds, such as when she prayed incessantly for the unrepentant murderer, Henri Pranzini. She was convinced that through her prayers he had been converted just before his execution.

At the age of fourteen, she wanted to enter Carmel to pray for sinners, but she was told to wait until she was twenty-one. She and her father petitioned the local bishop for special permission and on a pilgrimage to Rome she personally asked Pope Leo XIII to intervene. He responded, 'If it is God's will, you will enter.' On 9 April 1888 at the age of fifteen, Thérèse entered the local Carmel, becoming Sr Thérèse of the Infant Jesus and of the Holy Name. The name captures the mystery of her life in Christ, alternating between the crib and the cross, between hope and suffering.[75]

For the next ten years, until her death from tuberculosis, she lived an intense and simple life unwaveringly focused on Christ and the dedicated practice of practical holiness in the Lisieux Carmel, which is not to imply that her life was one of ease and consolations. Through the report from a member of Lisieux Carmel, we know that her companion sisters did not notice anything extraordinary about her. Yet a year after her death, when her autobiography, composed of three manuscripts, was published, an unprecedented flow of letters poured into Lisieux testifying that she was a 'prodigy of miracles'. The Holy See waived its usual fifty-year waiting period, and she was canonized in 1925 with more than a half a million pilgrims present in St. Peter's Square. In recent years, there has been a consistent and extraordinary interest in her life and spirituality. This culminated in the decision of John Paul II in 1997 to proclaim her a doctor of the Church, implying that her teaching has significance for the universal Church.

Unlike other doctors of the Church, whose writings sometime comprise many volumes, Thérèse's contribution consists of her autobiography, plus some letters, poetry, prayers and other minor texts. The autobiography consists of three parts, *manuscript A, manuscript B,* and *manuscript C*. The first, *manuscript A* was addressed to Mother Agnes,

Thérèse's older sister Pauline who was the prioress of the Lisieux Carmel from 1893–96. At the request of Mother Agnes, Thérèse began recounting childhood memories in a simple copybook. These memories are divided into three parts: the first leading up to her mother's death in 1877, the second, 'the most painful of these three periods', when she withdrew into herself and became excessively sensitive. The last, beginning with her fourteenth year, focuses particularly on her Christmas night 'conversion' in 1886, and recounts her trip to Rome and her subsequent entrance into Carmel.

*Manuscript B* was addressed to Sister Marie of the Sacred Heart, who had asked Thérèse to write down her 'little doctrine' during her retreat (September 1896). Having had her first *haemoptysis* (coughing up of blood due to a lung hemorrhage) on Good Friday 3 April 1896, she knew that her death was imminent. This manuscript, consisting of three sheets of folded paper, written in very small handwriting, eloquently expresses a summary of her spirituality. It culminates with the joyful exclamation: 'O Jesus, my Love ... my vocation, at last I have found it ... MY VOCATION IS LOVE! Yes, I have found my place in the Church, and it is YOU, O my God, who have given me this place; in the heart of the Church, my Mother, I shall be Love. Thus I shall be everything, and thus my dream will be realized.'[76] Though not explicitly mentioned here, one sees the kernel of her doctrine of the little way which was her practical response to the problem of reconciling the great desire she had to love God and her experience of imperfection and powerlessness. Her little way to holiness is a 'daring surrender' and abandonment to his mercy.

*Manuscript C*, addressed to Mother Marie de Gonzague, consists of two chapters and recounts some insights she received from sacred Scripture, how she dealt with the other sisters in the community and her great trial of faith. This great trial of faith consisted of the spiritual darkness that gripped her from Easter 1896 until her death. It was not the sort of moral, affective or psychological crisis that Christians sometimes experience; rather it was 'truly a trial of a theological order, imposed by God to purify her faith'.[77] Read carefully, these chapters strip away any notion of sweet sentimentality that is sometimes associated with Thérèse. Written under difficult circumstances and with many interruptions, *Manuscript C* includes her discovery of a 'little way, a way, that is very short, and totally new'.[78] Knowing that she would never measure up to the stature of the saints, she searched Scriptures for a solution. Her insights, especially into Proverbs 9:4 ('Whoever is like a little one, let him come to Me') and Isaiah 66:12-13 ('As one whom a mother caresses, so will I comfort you; you shall be carried at the breasts, and upon the knees they shall caress you'), helped her understand that the heights of holiness would be reached only by abandoning herself figuratively into the arms of Jesus.

St. Thérèse truly lived her 'little way' and proposes to us a spirituality fixed on a confident abandonment of oneself to the merciful love of God. It is a path to holiness for those who feel that they are 'imperfect', 'little', and/or 'weak'. It is a spiritual path for those who have a great desire to know and love God while recognizing that they cannot satisfy these desires by their own effort. Her way is a spiritual path that relies on the purifying love of a God who evokes in us the desire to return love for love. One way to approach Thérèse's understanding of holiness is to concentrate on the theme of purifying love in her writings. In *Manuscript B*, Thérèse asks herself

> O my Jesus! I love You! I love the Church, my Mother! I recall that *'the smallest act of PURE LOVE is of more value to her than all other works together'*. But is PURE LOVE in my heart?[79]

In this passage, Thérèse cites the *Spiritual Canticle* of John of the Cross. Both Thérèse and John refer to a costly love. This love, however, should not appear to be beyond the aim of any truly committed lover of God. So Thérèse's question is as valid for following generations as it was for her: 'But is pure love in my heart?' Two interrelated points emerge in this passage: the centrality of love and the quality of love. In reading *The Story of a Soul* along with her other writings, one discovers that she did nothing but love. She understood both that love is the measure by which we will be judged and that at the end of our lives we come before the Lord with empty hands.

Thérèse shows how the circumstances of life bring their own purification, with the potential of leading to a greater depth of love for God. When on Good Friday 1896 she had her first haemorrhage, she describes the paradoxical awareness that though a painful death was waiting her, she was filled with joy even though she knew the symptoms of tuberculosis. The euphoria of faith was followed by intense suffering. On Easter Sunday, when the liturgy communicates a sense of light and resurrection, Thérèse was trapped in darkness. She says that the thought of heaven, which had previously brought such joy to her, now brought only torment. Feeling that everything was useless, she feared that she would die for nothing. In *Manuscript C*, she describes the depth of her torment:

> It seems to me that the darkness, taking the voice of sinners, says mockingly to me: 'You are dreaming about the light, about a father- land embalmed in the sweetest perfumes; you are dreaming about the eternal possession of the Creator of all these marvels; you believe that one day you will walk out of this fog which surrounds you! Advance, advance; rejoice in death which will give you not what you hope for but a night still more profound, the night of nothingness.'[80]

She says that she does not even want to write more about this because she is afraid of what she might say. This trial of faith continued until she died, and grew worse as it approached. In *Manuscript C,* she confesses openly:

> I may perhaps appear to you to be exaggerating my trial. In fact, if you are judging according to the sentiments I expressed in my little poems composed this year, I must appear to you as a soul filled with consolations and one for whom the veil of faith is almost torn aside, and yet it is no longer a veil for me, it is a wall ... When I sing of the joy of heaven ... I feel no joy in this, for I sing simply what I WANT TO BELIEVE![81]

Immersed in such darkness, Thérèse begins to understand what it is like for people without faith and she enters into solidarity with them. Though assailed by doubt, she continued to exercise an obstinate aban- donment into God's hands and a joy and love that remained despite the intense suffering. Through the crucible of suffering, God purified her love and enabled her to completely abandon herself into his hands.

The *Story of a Soul* demonstrates how Thérèse had experienced the presence and the absence of love, the paradox of profound joy and intense suffering, the light as well as the darkness. These experiences allowed her to understand the depths of Jesus's love and to make a choice to follow him with a total gift of herself. As a doctor of the Church, Thérèse offers Christians an insight into 'the science of divine love' – a love that in her has been generously received and poured out as gift to others – even today.

This insight has practical implications for her understanding of holiness. In the *Last Conversations*, it is recorded that Thérèse said, 'Sanctity does not consist in this or that practice, it consists in a disposition of the heart which makes us humble and little in the arms of God, conscious of our weakness, and confident to the point of audacity in the goodness of our Father.'[82] This means that one lives like a child, recognizing one's nothingness: 'to expect everything from God as a child expects everything from its father; it is to be disquiet about nothing and not to be set on gaining a living.'[83]

Thérèse's path to holiness reminds us that God in his mercy and love is at work in our weakness. God asks from us not dazzling and extraordinary works, but simplicity, humility, and a generous abandonment into his hands. Of course, the surrender to God does not absolve us from taking responsibility for how we live. On the contrary, it calls forth in us the highest level of generosity. And yet, it is not something that we must accomplish alone, for just as a father lifts his child in his arms, so does God lift us up and lead us into the depths of his love so that we too can become love, not only in the heart of the Church, but also in the heart of the world. *The Story of a Soul* ends in the middle of a sentence, for at that point Thérèse was physically too weak to write anymore. The final words are highly significant: 'with confidence and love'.[84] This is her invitation to us as we seek holiness: to go to God with 'confidence and love'.

### Serving the urban poor

Of all the Carmelite saints, Thérèse of Lisieux has probably had the greatest influence on popular piety. The 'Little Flower', as she was called in the early part of the twentieth century, with her 'little way' offered a way of holiness that was particularly accessible to those who tried to live the gospel in the midst of the world.[85] One such woman was Dorothy Day (1897–1980), a social activist from the United States, who was born the year Thérèse died, and who wrote in 1949:

> Either the Little Flower is looked upon (perhaps because of her nickname) with sentimentality, or, as one gets to know her better, with dread ... To her God was a consuming flame. 'It is a terrible thing to fall into the hands of the living God', St. Peter said with exultation. We have to pay a great and terrible price but 'underneath are the everlasting arms'. Thank God for the saints whose feast days come around and remind us that we too are called to be saints.[86]

At first glance, St. Thérèse and Dorothy Day are a study in contrasts. As we have seen, Thérèse grew up in a pious Catholic family with the cultural accoutrement of nineteenth-century bourgeois France. She is best known for her simplicity and purity, her abandonment to God's love and trust that God works in the ordinary circumstances of everyday life to bring us to holiness.

Dorothy Day's somewhat checkered history is in many ways an antithesis of Thérèse's story. Religious practice and belief were not part of her upbringing. At the same time, she admits that throughout her life she felt 'haunted by God'.[87] For example, Dorothy's occasional contact with Christians in her early years had a deep effect upon her. Nevertheless, during her somewhat rebellious period as a young college student, she rejected Christianity as an opiate of the people.[88]

Her decision to become a Roman Catholic in 1928 changed her life in a radical way. Severing ties with Forster Batterham, a man whom she deeply loved, she embarked on a journey of faith – aptly described in her autobiography as *The Long Loneliness*. This journey is characterized by a desire for 'a synthesis', for an authenticity. She wanted 'life', indeed, she wanted 'abundant life', not only for her herself, but 'for others too'. Early on, she recognized her ideal: 'I wanted every home to be open to the lame, the halt, the blind. In such love was the abundant life and I did not have the slightest idea how to find it.'[89] Her subsequent collaboration with Peter Maurin confirmed her deep social concern for the poor and with him she established the Catholic Worker Movement, which included a newspaper, *The Catholic Worker,* written for the working class, as well as Hospitality Houses for the poor, and farming communes.

Lawrence Cunningham notes that, 'Dorothy Day ... was a luminously holy person, but her life included an abortion, a common-law marriage, a period of left-wing politics, and a deep involvement in feminist concerns (her first arrest, before her conversion, was for suffragette activities)'.[90] Even after her conversion to Catholicism, she often stubbornly took positions that were considered unfashionable and that placed her on the fringes of society. For example, she refused to pay income tax, considered herself a pacifist in spite of the atrocities of the Second World War, and picketed and was arrested more than once for her fight against labour injustices. She was a vehement opponent to nuclear arms. Why would this twentieth-century woman from the United States be attracted to the spirituality of the French cloistered Carmelite nun, Thérèse of Lisieux?

Dorothy Day's first encounter with Thérèse came soon after her daughter was born at Bellevue Hospital in New York. At that time, Dorothy was a radical and had no particular religious affiliation. A patient next to her asked what she would call her newborn child: Dorothy replied, 'Tamar Teresa'. The woman asked if Teresa was in honour of the Little Flower, to which Dorothy replied by saying she had never heard of the Little Flower. She was naming the child after St. Teresa of Avila, about whom she had read. The woman handed Dorothy a medal of the Little Flower for the baby, which she reluctantly accepted. Dorothy later commented:

> After hearing of St. Therese as the young novice mistress in her far off convent of Lisieux in Normandy, who had died the year I was born, and whose sisters were still alive, I decided that although I would name my child after the older saint, the new one would be my own Teresa's novice mistress, to train her in the spiritual life. I knew that I wanted to have the child baptized a Catholic and I wanted both saints to be taking care of her. One was not enough.[91]

The baptism of Tamar Teresa, 'cost what it may', was a consuming concern for Dorothy Day. She was determined that she 'was not going to have her floundering through so many years' as she had done, 'doubting and hesitating, undisciplined and amoral'.[92] For herself, she prayed 'for the gift of faith'.[93] Eventually her child was baptized and about a year later, Dorothy took the 'irrevocable step' and became a Catholic.[94] Her decision was surrounded by anguish and suffering, especially in breaking off a relationship with Forster Batterham, the father of her child. She describes how she experienced no consolation upon entering the Church:

> I had no particular joy in partaking of these three sacraments, Baptism, Penance and Holy Eucharist. I proceeded about my own active participation in them grimly, coldly, making acts of faith, and certainly with no consolation whatever. One part of my mind stood at one side and kept saying, 'What are you doing? Are you sure of yourself? What kind of an affectation is this? ... Are you trying to induce emotion, induce faith, partake of an opiate, an opiate of the people?' I felt like a hypocrite if I got down on my knees, and shuddered at the thought of anyone seeing me.[95]

Thérèse of Lisieux remained a silent companion on the journey for the next year, until her confessor, Father Zachary, suggested that she read, *The Little White Flower: The Story of a Soul,* a book with 'a not too attractive picture with a sweet insipid face, holding a crucifix and a huge bouquet of roses'. Feeling 'slightly aggrieved' at Father Zachary, and at men and priests in general who were 'very insulting to women ... handing out what they felt suited their intelligence; in other words, pious pap', Dorothy dutifully read the book, which she found 'colorless, monotonous, too small in fact for my notice'.[96] The problem with Thérèse was that she was too ordinary, too pedestrian for the high idealism which had gripped Dorothy Day:

> What kind of saint was this who felt that she had to practice hero-
> ic charity in eating what was put in front of her, in taking medi-
> cine, enduring cold and heat, restraint, enduring the society of
> mediocre souls, in following the strict regime of the convent of
> Carmelite nuns which she had joined at the age of fifteen? A splash
> of dirty water from the careless washing of a nun next to her in the
> laundry was mentioned as a 'mortification' when the very root of
> the word meant death, and I was reading in my Daily Missal of
> saints stretched on the rack, burnt by flames, starving themselves
> in the desert, and so on.
>
> Joan of Arc leading an army fitted more into my concept of a
> saint, familiar as I was with the history of labor with its martyrs
> in the service of their brothers. 'Love of brother is to lay down
> one's life on the barricades, in revolt against the hunger and injus-
> tice in the world', I told Fr Zachary ... Living as we were in time of
> world revolution, when, as I felt, the people of the world were
> rising to make a better world for themselves, I wondered what this
> new saint had to offer.[97]

During these early days as a Catholic, Dorothy Day was working for the Anti-Imperialist League, a Communist Party affiliate. After some months she obtained other work, as she gradually came to understand the 'basic opposition between Catholicism and Marxism'. She comments though that 'it took me longer to realize the unique position of Therese of Lisieux in the Church today'.[98]

Peter Maurin helped Dorothy Day to reconsider Thérèse as a saint for ordinary people. Only five years a Catholic, she was longing to find a way of integrating her desire to serve the poor with her faith as a Catholic. On 8 December 1932, she prayed at the National Shrine of the Immaculate Conception in Washington, 'that some way would open up for me to use what talents I possessed for ... the poor ... And when I returned to New York, I found Peter Maurin – whose spirit and ideas will dominate ... the rest of my life.'[99] Maurin had spent a short time with the Christian brothers in France and had eventually worked as an itinerant labourer in various parts of the United States and Canada. Through his experience and reading, he developed a theory of social change based on the gospel and Catholic social teaching, but couched in the language of personalism. From 1933 Peter and Dorothy were inseparable co-workers and friends, until his death in 1949. Dorothy Day always insisted upon Maurin's influence upon her:

> My background as a journalist and radical and convert to the faith enabled me to see and to popularize Peter's ideas. I have indeed tried to work them out ... I have learned that one must *be* rather than *do*. The doing follows the being.[100]

Among other things, he helped her to understand Thérèse of Lisieux:

> Peter Maurin was always talking of the primacy of the spiritual. It was in the depths of the Depression that Peter came to me as an answer to prayer, and his way was the Little Way of St. Therese (though I did not think much of the Little Flower and her Little Way at that time).[101]

If on first reading Thérèse, Dorothy was put off by the apparent 'insignificance' of the little way, she eventually was able to penetrate beyond the superficial and see that actually 'love is the measure' by which we will be judged. Dorothy always felt more comfortable with love expressed in concrete acts: taking care of the poor and the weak. This was her way. Through reading Thérèse, she discovered that there are different, but equally valid ways of receiving and returning love. In her weakness, Thérèse returned love 'by doing nothing', and yet this had a powerful impact upon the world. Ultimately, through Thérèse, Dorothy learned that it is not so much what we do, but what God's love does in us and through us which counts. Thérèse's vocation both purified and challenged Dorothy Day's own vocation. She saw that one must live by absolute faith, surrendering to God's will in whatever circumstances. This is a sign of authentic holiness.

Dorothy Day's life resonates with many of the paradoxes and challenges of contemporary society. The reality is that many people live in similar family situations, where faith values are not taught and practised. Broken homes, cohabitation, and single parenthood are all experiences to which many can relate. Yet it is in this context that Dorothy heard the call to follow the radically poor Christ. She understood that Christ not only loved the poor, but he actually became poor and comes to us through the poor.[102] She became aware of the poor around her and allowed them to influence her life. This is a step towards a holiness that flows into a daily life of service to others: allowing oneself to be seized by surrounding realities. Are we willing to feel and to care? Perhaps more often than not, perhaps because of embarrassment or a paralyzing sense of being overwhelmed in the face of great need, we fail to respond. If we want to be open to the gift of doing the truth in love, we need to practise a very real, very radical compassion. 'Without this sensitivity, this awareness, breaking out of the protective numbness, nothing will change, whether in ourselves or in the world', writes Rosemary Haughton. She continues, 'We shall continue to be kind, law-abiding, secure and spiritually in a coma.'[103]

It is not enough simply to be aware, we must also figure out how God is calling us to a concrete response. Through prayer, Dorothy Day understood that her way was to serve the urban poor. This is what she did. She not only served them food, but also began to live with them. Her prophetic call meant letting herself be formed by Christ's way of being and acting. Even then, she struggled with letting go of her own self-interest and desires. Ever a realist, she wrote: 'You can strip yourself, be stripped but still you will reach out like an octopus to seek your own comfort, your untroubled time, your ease, your refreshment.'[104] Dorothy Day's remedy for overcoming the grasping attitude was to follow Christ by living simply and in poverty with the urban poor. This experience gave her eyes to seek and to find Christ in those around her.

Dorothy's was not merely an individualistic quest for holiness; she knew that true fruitfulness to gospel values was fostered by being part of a community of disciples, for alone she could accomplish little. In her book, *The Long Loneliness,* one is struck by the fact that in a life filled with activity and service to others, she struggled with feelings of isolation. It is in the postscript that we find her resolution:

We were just sitting there talking when Peter Maurin came in.

We were just sitting there talking when lines of people began to form, saying, 'We need bread.' We could not say, 'Go, be thou filled.' If there were six small loaves and a few fishes, we had to divide them. There was always bread.

We were just sitting there talking and people moved in on us. Let those who can take it, take it. Some moved out and that made room for more. And somehow the walls expanded ...

It was as casual as that, I often think. It just came about. It just happened.

I found myself, a barren woman, the joyful mother of children. It is not always easy to be joyful, to keep in mind the duty of delight. The most significant thing about *The Catholic Worker* is poverty, some say.

The most significant thing is community, others say. We are not alone anymore.

But the final word is love. At times it has been, in the words of Father Zossima, a harsh and dreadful thing, and our very faith in love has been tried through fire.

We cannot love God unless we love each other, and to love we must know each other. We know Him in the breaking of bread and we know each other in the breaking of bread, and we are not alone anymore. Heaven is a banquet and life is a banquet too, even with a crust, where there is companionship.

We have all known the long loneliness and we have learned that the only solution is love and that love comes with community. It all happened while we sat there talking, and it is still going on.[105]

On the one hand, Dorothy Day reminds us that holiness means moving beyond ourselves – our needs, our wants, our desires – and looking to the needs of those around us. We can do this most effectively if we do it together, with companions who join us on this journey of faith. On the other hand, she recognized that holiness was a gift, given to those who wait on God's mercy. Dorothy Day was influenced by numerous Carmelite saints, including Teresa of Avila, John of the Cross, and Brother Lawrence: yet, the only biography she wrote was of Thérèse. She was convinced that Thérèse had a powerful teaching which spoke to the human condition:

Is the atom a small thing? And yet what havoc it has wrought. Is her little way a small contribution to the life of the spirit? It has all the power of the spirit of Christianity behind it. It is an explosive force that can transform our lives and the life of the world, once put into effect.[106]

In considering Dorothy Day's presentation of Thérèse, the social implications of her teaching come to the forefront. The 'little way' does not excuse us from taking responsibility for the plight of a world racked with suffering, poverty and war. On the contrary, it challenges us to trust that even in our littleness, we can and must make some contribution. It encourages us to embrace the opportunities for service which come our way. The 'little way' purifies us of the 'messiah complex' which so often accompanies social action. Only God can overcome the gigantic problems of the world, but he uses us as instruments of his mercy. The key for both Thérèse and Dorothy is to live a life of holiness – which is none other than union with Christ through love. Dorothy Day wrote that 'responding to that one impulse of grace is of infinitely more power than a cobalt bomb. Therese has said, "All is grace"'.[107]

Seeing Dorothy Day's devotion to Thérèse tells us something about the contemplative dimension of her own social action. All her life, Dorothy Day longed for a 'synthesis', an integration of prayer and action. In turning to Thérèse for inspiration, she discovered that 'love is the measure' by which we shall be judged. Thérèse also said, echoing John of the Cross: 'In the evening of my life, I shall appear before You with empty hands, for I do not ask You, Lord, to count my works'.[108] Objectively speaking Dorothy Day *did* much to help the poor, yet she understood, through her encounter with Thérèse, that ultimately we all come before God with empty hands – just like the poor waiting to be fed at one of the Hospitality Houses: for indeed, *all is grace*.

### An untraditional example of holiness

God's grace knows no bounds and can work in ways beyond our expectations and beyond traditional structures. One example is the life of the enigmatic figure Simone Weil (1909–43), who will never be found in the *Bibliotheca sanctorum* because she was not baptized. This well-known 'Library of the Saints' contains more than 30,000 articles on men and women who have already been canonized and beatified, or whose cause has been opened. At first glance, Simone Weil seems an odd choice for this chapter on holiness. Her life is riddled with paradox.[109] She exemplifies many of the practices traditionally associated with Christian holiness: poverty of spirit, solidarity, obedience and self-giving love. She writes about the importance of humble openness to God and of her experience of waiting before God. She was attracted to the Eucharist and spent long hours in prayer before the Blessed Sacrament. She had a longing to receive communion, but her questioning mind never came to the point of resolving some of the profound difficulties she had with Catholicism. To the end of her days she remained on the threshold of the Church. At the same time, her life and writings contain profound insights into Christian themes and have had an influence on many Catholics. For example, Paul VI considered her to be one of the three figures that most influenced his intellectual development (Bernanos and Pascal were the other two). As Monsignor Montini, he said that Weil could have been proclaimed a saint – if only she had been baptized.[110] When Angelo Roncalli (later John XXIII) was apostolic nuncio in Paris, he too was so impressed by Weil's writings that he wrote her parents a letter after her death.[111]

What is striking about Weil's journey of faith is that in the midst of affliction and against all odds she was attracted to the beauty and holiness of God. She grew up in a non-practising Jewish family in Paris, with loving parents. Her father, a successful physician, and her mother, a dedicated housewife and devoted mother, showed great concern and care for their daughter – something that Simone found somewhat suffocating at times. Her childhood was also marked by the experience of living in the shadow of her brother André, a prodigy, who as an adult became a famous mathematician. In her own right, she excelled academically, graduating in 1931 from the prestigious École Normale Supérieure. Afterwards, she accepted various teaching positions at provincial schools in France while promoting worker unions, writing in left-wing publications, educating adults and helping families of the unemployed. She resigned from teaching in 1934 and for a few years worked in factories and on farms.

It was after a particularly gruelling stint in a Renault factory, when appalling work conditions and severe health problems weakened her physically, that she had her first pivotal religious experience. Having left her factory job, she travelled with her parents to a small fishing village in Portugal. She describes her situation as one of *malheur*. Although difficult to translate into English, this refers to an experience of being in pieces, body and soul. She experienced a strong sense of affliction accompanied by doom and inevitability, and she felt that she had the 'mark of a slave, like the branding of the red-hot iron the Romans put on the foreheads of their most despised slaves'.[112] It is in this context that she had a significant religious insight while watching a religious procession:

> ... in a wretched state physically, I entered the Portuguese village, which alas, was very wretched too, on the very day of the festival for its patron saint. I was alone. It was the evening and there was a full moon over the sea. The wives of the fishermen were, in procession, making a tour of all the ships, carrying candles and singing what must certainly be very ancient hymns of heart-rending sadness ... There the conviction suddenly came to me that Christianity is pre-eminently the religion of slaves, that slaves cannot help belonging to it, and I among others.[113]

At the time, she did not mention this experience to anyone. Instead she continued her eccentric lifestyle, which included joining the Republican forces in the Spanish Civil War in 1936. This adventure ended a month later when she tripped and fell into an open pit filled with oil, badly burning her leg. Her parents faithfully nursed her back to health, though the healing process took nearly an academic year.

In the spring of 1937, she had a second pivotal religious experience while on a trip to Italy.

> There, alone in the little twelfth-century Romanesque chapel of Santa Maria degli Angeli, an incomparable marvel of purity where Saint Francis often used to pray, something stronger than I was ... compelled for the first time in my life to go down on my knees.[114]

A year later she and her mother spent Holy Week and Easter at Solesmes, a Benedictine abbey in north-eastern France. Simone attended all of the services, despite the violent headaches that plagued her the whole week. The beauty of the liturgy taught her an important lesson about 'divine love in the midst of affliction', and it was there that she had her most important religious experience:

I was suffering from splitting headaches; each sound hurt me like a blow; by an extreme effort of concentration I was able to rise above this wretched flesh ... and to find a pure and perfect joy in the unimaginable beauty of the chanting and the words. This experience enabled me ... to get a better understanding of the possibility of divine love in the midst of affliction. It goes without saying that in the course of these services the concept of Christ's passion entered into my being once and for all.[115]

At Solesmes, when an Englishman gave her a copy of 'Love,' the seventeenth century poem by George Herbert, she learnt it by heart and recited it repeatedly.

I used to think that I was merely reciting it a beautiful poem, but without my knowing it the recitation had the virtue of a prayer. It was during one of those recitations that ... Christ himself came down and took possession of me.[116]

The poem is about the priority of God's love. In it Herbert describes the unconditional welcome of a loving God: 'Love bade me welcome', despite all the human unworthiness of those who know themselves to be 'Guiltie of dust and sinne'. Attentively and coaxingly, God invites the timid guest to dine. In light of Simone Weil's lifelong aversion to food, which seems to have been a type of anorexia, this poem, with its meal imagery and invitation by the divine lover to dine is particularly significant.[117]

These religious experiences were kept mainly to herself, but upon encountering the Dominican priest, Joseph Marie Perrin, she was able to recount it and to ask probing questions. She met him in Marseille, where her family had moved because of the dangerous anti-Semitic policies of the French Vichy Government in 1941. Their friendship enabled her to share her insights, many of which are published in *Waiting for God*, where she carefully explains her reasons for not being baptized. Basically, she felt unworthy to receive the sacraments and that by remaining an 'outsider' she would be in solidarity with the many people who are alienated from the Church. She felt called to live a life of sacrificial service and love among the people. In a telling passage from one of her letters to Father Perrin, she says, 'I have always remained at this exact point, on the threshold of the Church, without moving, quite still ... only now my heart has been transported, forever, I hope, into the Blessed Sacrament exposed on the altar'.[118]

In 1942, she and her parents moved to New York, because France was no longer safe for Jews. Weil hated everything about the United States and she left as soon as possible for London, where she worked with the Free French, a government organized in exile. Her great desire was to be parachuted into France as a nurse to support the troops on the front line. Of course, this outrageously impossible plan was never accepted by those in charge. She eventually died of pulmonary tuberculosis on 24 August 1943, and was buried in England in Ashford's New Cemetery.[119]

In the Introduction to the 2001 reprint of *Waiting for God,* Leslie A. Fiedler suggests that 'since her death, Simone Weil has come to seem more and more a special exemplar of sanctity for our time – the Outsider as Saint in an age of alienation'.[120] Simone Weil herself suggests that 'We are living in times that have no precedent ... Today it is not nearly enough merely to be a saint but we must have the saintliness demanded by the present moment, a new saintliness, itself also without precedent.'[121] This new saintliness requires 'genius', for it is 'almost a new revelation of the universe and of human destiny'.[122] And the only way to embrace this new saintliness in 'superabundance' is to ask the Father for it in Christ's name.[123] What Weil teaches us is that we are drawn to God by the beauty of holiness.

### Mary, the Mother of God and the beauty of holiness

Beauty attracts. Holy people, holy places and holy things attract us because they draw us out of ourselves into an experience of the Transcendent. This was Simone Weil's experience, and so it is ours. This beauty is most poignantly manifested in Mary, the mother of God. Her holiness has been explored through the ages in art. These interpretations, these clues, from the earliest images of Mary in the catacombs to more recent mosaics in the *Redemptoris Mater* chapel in the apostolic palace of the Vatican, assist us in opening our minds and hearts to discover her beauty. Poetry and song, theological thought and devotional practices call attention to her and encourage us to meditate on her courageous response to God's call.[124] Theological reflection, especially the teaching of the Second Vatican Council, post-conciliar documents, and, more recently, joint ecumenical documents, also invite us to reflect on how she is a model of holiness.

One example of how a particular culture tries to capture the beauty of Mary's response to God's call in the Annunciation is a small oil painting by Jan van Eyck (c. 1390–1441). This small medieval jewel, containing astonishing lush details, and now displayed in Washington D.C.'s National Gallery, is of a scene well known to us all. The Virgin, dressed in beautiful medieval attire, is recollected in prayer. Above her a multi-coloured messenger appears while a dove hovers over her. The angel waits in suspense as Mary gives her response. This portrayal of Mary is a long way from the simple Jewish woman who lived in Nazareth, but it does offer an insight into her beauty. Understood in the context of the *devotio moderna,* this style of painting aimed at establishing a direct and personal identification with holy figures. For Christians of the Low Countries, it was common to re-enact the annunciation during the Christmas season. During the Golden Mass, when it was time for the gospel reading, young boys playing the roles of Gabriel and Mary came forward. The first pointed with a sceptre and recited the angelic greeting, the same words that are inscribed on this painting, *Ave gratia plena.* The boy playing the Virgin held his hands out in the same open gesture of prayer and blessing, following it with Mary's response to a dove lowered from above. Van Eyck's *Annunciation,* also set in a church, so closely matches the instructions for the Golden Mass that, for the general public, the association must have been understood immediately.[125] One detail in the painting is that Mary's reply to Gabriel's greeting, *Ecce ancilla Domini* ('Behold the handmaiden of the Lord'), is written upside down, just at the right angle for God to read. This painting focuses on Mary as a model: her response to God is to echo in the lives of every Christian. Herein lies one insight into her inner beauty.

A more contemporary expression of this scene is Denise Levertov's poem, 'Annunciation,' where she emphasizes Mary's courageous expression of human freedom:

> We know the scene: the room, variously furnished,
> almost always a lectern, a book; always
> the tall lily.
>           Arrived on solemn grandeur of great wings,
> The angelic ambassador, standing or hovering,
> whom she acknowledges, a guest.

But we are told of meek obedience. No one mentions
courage.

The engendering Spirit
did not enter her without consent.

God waited.

Various types of 'annunciations' occur in one way or another in our lives
too, and sometimes these are rejected. Ordinary life goes on: 'God does
not smite', but an opportunity has been missed. Without a doubt Mary's
was a call 'to a destiny more momentous than any in all of Time'; and
one aspect of her beauty lies in her embrace of human freedom, for 'she
did not quail'.

She did not cry, 'I cannot, I am not worthy,'
nor, 'I have not the strength'
She did not submit with gritted teeth,

raging, coerced.
Bravest of all humans,

consent illuminated her.
The room filled with its light,
The lily glowed in it,

and the iridescent wings.
Consent,

courage unparalleled,
opened her utterly.[126]

One could suggest that these artistic and poetic images of the Virgin are
far removed from the 'real' Mary of Nazareth as she is portrayed in the
New Testament. To enter into the beauty of Mary today, we certainly
need to grasp what it was to be a poor Jewish woman in first-century
Palestine. A recent study, Elizabeth Johnson's *Truly Our Sister A
Theology of Mary in the Communion of Saints,* has provided an insight
into Mary's world that enhances our understanding of the radical
nature of her response.[127] Yet, these various artistic images of Mary
through the centuries also have their validity and importance. What
they say is this: she is truly a woman for all seasons, a woman who
speaks to every age. Whether portrayed in African ebony carving, a delicate Japanese print, the bold mosaics of a modern European chapel or
contemporary poetry, her beauty is celebrated. The foundation of this

beauty is a life of holiness: a life lived in courageous surrender to her God. In attempting to portray her as physically beautiful, artists and poets help us to enter into the inner beauty that is hers, a beauty that is most poignantly manifest in her 'yes' to God.

Doctrinal reflection, especially as expressed in the teaching of the Second Vatican Council, also sets the stage for discovering the beauty of Mary's holiness in the twenty-first century. During the council, a major debate concerned where exactly reflection on Mary should occur in the Council writings. There were some who thought teaching on her should be in a separate document. Others felt that it was more appropriate to include this in the document on the Church. In the closest vote of the Council, on 29 October 1963, 1,114 of the Council fathers voted in favour of inserting the Marian doctrine into the schema on the Church and 1074 voted against it. The result is that Chapter 8 of the Constitution on the Church, *Lumen gentium*, went through several redactions and so the final text, the fruit of much debate and reflection, opens with an introduction (52) that places the Blessed Virgin Mary in the context of salvation history. It then moves to a biblical reflection (55–59). The third part (60–66) touches on Mary and the Church. Mary is portrayed as an eschatological image of the Church, according to which she intercedes for the unity of the people of God. She is both a sign and comfort for the pilgrim people of God. As the pre-eminent member of the Church and the faith-filled mother of Jesus, she who was once herself a pilgrim on earth is now with God in glory.

About ten years after the Council in 1974, Paul VI's *Marialis cultus* offered some important guidelines for renewing Marian devotion in the Church. Among these were the importance of steeping Marian devotions in the wider themes of salvation history and in their proper biblical context; the intricate connection between Marian piety, the liturgical seasons and the liturgy itself, culminating in the Eucharist; the invitation to promote a more ecumenical approach to Mary that honours her while focusing on the centrality of Christ; and a respectful sensitivity to and awareness of changing psychological and sociological conditions which can effect contemporary Marian devotion.[128]

In a well-known passage from that apostolic letter, Paul VI said,

First, the Virgin Mary has always been proposed to the faithful by the Church as an example to be imitated not precisely in the type of life she led, and much less for the socio-cultural background in which she lived and which today scarcely exists anywhere. Rather she is held up as an example for the way in which, in her own particular life, she fully and responsibly accepted God's will (see Lk. 1:38), because she heard the word of God and acted on it and because charity and a spirit of service were the driving force of her actions. She is worthy of imitation because she was the first and most perfect of Christ's disciples. All of this has a permanent and universal exemplary value.[129]

This theme finds a strong resonance in Scripture and is particularly apt for a twenty-first century understanding of Mary's holiness and her influence on Christians, as they seek to live out their own call to discipleship.

One way of deepening our appreciation of this call is to focus on the Gospel of Luke and the Acts of the Apostles, where Mary is described as an exemplary disciple. Her radical discipleship brings us to the heart of her beauty and her holiness. The Gospel of Luke gives more attention to Mary than any other gospel, presenting her as the perfect disciple. In a certain sense, the Annunciation is Mary's formal response to God's call. Her 'yes' at the Annunciation must sooner or later be echoed in the life of every Christian: a 'yes' which requires an unwavering faith in God. The visitation shows Mary's discipleship in action as she goes in haste to help her cousin Elizabeth, and the birth narratives focus on her faithfulness to God. Though these passages are important, the foundation of her discipleship is explicitly developed in Luke 11:27–28:

A woman in the crowd raised her voice and said to him, 'Blessed is the womb that bore you and the breasts that nursed you!' But he said, 'Blessed rather are those who hear the word of God and obey it.'

Mary is proclaimed blessed here because of her openness to the word, the word that she heard, believed, obeyed and pondered. In her own way, she too meets the criteria of what it means to follow Jesus.[130] Focusing on the passage in this light, we can draw some insight into Mary's vocation and into our own call to holiness. She welcomed the Word. Long before the 'yes' at the Annunciation, Mary was a woman of faith who welcomed the word of God into her heart. She did this in her own way and in her own cultural circumstances. Like most of the people of her time, she may not have known how to read, but she certainly would have lived a lifestyle that was open to God's word as it came to her. As an example, she no doubt attentively listened in the word proclaimed in Jewish worship in pilgrimages to the temple in Jerusalem. Above all, as part of the poor of *Yahweh*, she lived in expectation and hope. When the moment came for her 'yes', she proclaimed it with courage. Present at the birth of Jesus and the birth of the Church, from Bethlehem, to Nazareth, to Jerusalem, her 'yes' has remained firm.[131]

Mary as a model of our pilgrimage of faith, as a woman 'upon whom the glory of God's ineffable holiness shines', was also a theme in the pontificate of John Paul II.[132] Recent ecumenical dialogues also have presented Mary as a model of holiness. For example, The Anglican-Roman Catholic's International Commission's (ARCIC) joint statement, *The Gift of Authority II*, said, 'We agree in recognizing in Mary a model of holiness, obedience and faith for all Christians.'[133] This was reiterated in the most recent ARCIC joint statement, *Mary, Grace and Hope in Christ*.[134] In presenting her as a model *par excellence* of holiness, this does not underestimate the uniqueness of her call, for 'in view of her vocation to be the mother of the Holy One, Christ's redeeming work reached "back" in Mary to the depths of her being and to her earliest beginnings'.[135]

In this chapter, we have explored *some* of the various ways to live the call to holiness. Whether as martyrs or monks, as desert or city dwellers, as mendicants or married couples, and even in the life of someone on the threshold of the Church, these 'models' have mirrored to some degree Christ's way of being and acting; they offer us a holiness that convinces. In reviewing the various models of holiness portrayed here, one might object that they are 'Wonderful, but not to be imitated!' A response to this critique is to admit that these 'models' *are* indeed extraordinary. The dwellings they have become by God's grace are particularly splendid. They remind us though that we are all called to holiness and that the communion of saints is real.[136] The same Spirit who was at work in building these extraordinary mansions is at work in our humble dwellings as well. The twentieth-century Catholic lay woman, Madeleine Delbrêl (1904–64), who lived in communist-dominated Paris suburbs, teaches us something about living the call to holiness in all of its ordinariness:

There are some people whom God takes and sets apart.
    There are others he leaves among the crowds ...
These are the people who have an ordinary job, an ordinary household, or an ordinary celibacy. People with ordinary sicknesses, and

ordinary times of grieving. People with an ordinary house, and ordinary clothes. These are the people of ordinary life. The people we might meet on the street.

They love the door that opens onto the street, just as their brothers [and sisters] who are hidden from the world love the door that shuts behind them forever.

We, the ordinary people of the street, believe with all our might that this street, this world, where God has placed us, is our place of holiness.

We believe that we lack nothing here that we need. If we need something else, God would already have given it to us.[137]

Our dwelling may seem rather 'ordinary' when gazing at some of the 'extraordinary dwellings' visited in these pages, yet ours remains a 'place of holiness' because God, the master architect, chooses *how* and *where* to build. Freestanding buildings are not in the blueprint though, because we are all implicated in one another's call to holiness. These few 'mansions' visited along the way, offering only a glimpse of the different calls, remind us that our 'ordinary' dwelling is being built into a spiritual edifice that is bigger and more beautiful than we can imagine. We are linked together with those who have gone before us and those around us in a way that binds us together forever. The holy men and women we have encountered and who make up these mansions challenge us to a new depth of commitment to Christ as we let the full implications of this call penetrate our daily life. In referring to some of these exemplars as 'saints', we must not see them as far removed from us. To Dorothy Day's quip, 'Don't call me a saint – I don't want to be dismissed that easily!',[138] we can respond with the conviction that we need saintly models to challenge and encourage us to become more and more what we are, God's holy dwelling. As we collaborate in the construction of this edifice, extraordinary in its extraordinariness, one sure companion is this process is Mary, both mother and model of holiness *par excellence*, who intercedes for us on the way.

## Notes

1. Though a cult of martyrs and saints has existed since the earliest days of Christianity, the formalization of the canonization process gradually developed over time. A highpoint in this development was Benedict XIV's 1734 treatise, *De Servorum Dei Beatificatione et Beatorum*

*Canonizatione* (*On the Beatification of Servants of God and Their Canonization*), which has influenced the saint-making process up until recent years. The most notable twentieth-century contribution was John Paul II's 1983 Apostolic Constitution, *Divinus Perfectionis Magister* (*The Divine Teacher of Perfection*), which proposed a more collegial approach to the introduction and investigation of the saints' cause by the local ordinary. It also offered new guidelines to the Sacred Congregation for the Causes of Saints, the Vatican dicastery responsible for process. For insight into the present process of canonization, see José Saraiva Martins, *Come si fa un santo*, (ed. Saviero Gaeta, Casale Monferrato: Piemme, 2005).

2. See the following resource on the internet: *www.ca_catholics.net/saints /notes.htm*, which notes that 'the principal source of the information on the saints and blesseds is *Index ac status causarum* (Vatican City, 1999), by the Congregation of the Causes of Saints. Information on saints and blessed proclaimed after the year 1999 are compiled from *Notitiae* and *Vatican Information Service*. Additional information is compiled from various sources. The lists of saints and blesseds have been ensured to be complete. The counts should be accurate'.

3. See John Paul II, Apostolic Letter, *Tertio millennio adveniente* (Vatican: Libreria Editrice Vaticana, 1994), 37: 'It will be the task of the Apostolic See, in preparation for the Year 2000, *to update the martyrologies* for the universal Church, paying careful attention to the holiness of those who *in our own time* lived fully by the truth of Christ. In particular, there is a need to foster the recognition of the heroic virtues of men and women who have lived their Christian vocation *in marriage*. Precisely because we are convinced of the abundant fruits of holiness in the married state, we need to find the most appropriate means for discerning them and proposing them to the whole Church as a model and encouragement for other Christian spouses.'

4. Kenneth Woodward, 'Slow up on saint-making', *Tablet* 253 p.1540 (13 November 1999). Taken from the web page *www.thetablet.co.uk/cgi-bin/register.cgi/tablet-00361*.

5. C. S. Lewis, 'The Weight of Glory', in *The Weight of Glory and Other Addresses* (rev. and exp. ed New York: McMillian Publishing Company, 1980), p.19.

6. See the influential work of Hans Urs Von Balthasar, *The Glory of the Lord. A Theological Aesthetics* (San Francisco: Ignatius, 1991), vol. 5. Also see William M. Thompson, *Fire and Light: The Saints and Theology on*

*consulting the saints, mystics and martyrs in theology* (New York: Paulist Press, 1987). For an overview on recent contemporary considerations on the saints and martyrs, see Lawrence S. Cunningham, 'Saints and Martyrs: Some Contemporary Considerations', *Theological Studies* 60 (1999), pp.529–37, and 'On Contemporary Martyrs: Some Recent Literature', *Theological Studies* 63 (2002), pp.374–81. For a feminist theological perspective on saints, see Elizabeth A. Johnson, *Friends of God and Prophets: A Feminist Theological Reading of the Communion of Saints* (New York: Continuum, 1998). See also the collection of essays which was the result of a seminar organized by the Congregation for Divine Worship and Discipline of the Sacraments, *Il martirologio Romano, teologia, liturgia, santità* (Vatican City: Libreria Editrice Vaticana, 2005).

7. In this short chapter, only a few models could be presented. For a more in-depth study on saints as paradigmatic figures, see Lawrence Cunningham, *The Catholic Heritage* (New York: Crossroad, 1983). See also his most recent book, *A Brief History of Saints* (Malden, MA: Blackwell Publishing, 2005).

8. Robert P. Maloney, 'Models of Being Holy', *America* 176 (15 February 1997), p.17. In focusing on the saints as models of holiness, it is not my intention to underestimate their role as intercessors. For a contemporary reflection on the intercessory role of the saints see Patricia A. Sullivan, 'A Reinterpretation of the Invocation and Intercession of the Saints', *Theological Studies* 66 (June 2005), pp.381–400. I agree with her comment that 'there is a theological inconsistency in recognizing the saints as models but not as intercessors' (p.399).

9. Maloney, 'Models of being Holy', p.22.

10. John Paul II, Apostolic Letter, *Tertio Millennio Adveniente*, 43.

11. Paul Molinari and Peter Gumpel, *Chapter VI of the Dogmatic Constitution 'Lumen Gentium' on Religious Life. The doctrinal contents in the light of the official documents* (Rome: PUG, 1987), pp.35–40. See also Paul Molinari and Peter Gumpel, 'Martyrdom', in *The Way Supplement*, 39 (Winter 1980), pp.14–25, and 'Martire' *Nuovo dizionario di spiritualità* (ed Stefano De fiores and Tullo Goffi, Cinisello Balsamo: Edizioni S. Paolo, 1985), pp.903–13.

12. Adalbert Hamman, *Le prime comunità cristiana* (Milano: Rizzoli, 2001), pp239.

13. William Frend, 'Blandina and Perpetua: Two Early Christian Heroines', in *Les Martyrs de Lyon (177)* (ed M. J. Rouge and M. R. Turcan, Paris:

Éditions du centre national de la richerche scientifique, 1977), pp.167–74.

14. 'The Martyrdom of Saints Perpetua and Felicity', in *The Acts of the Christian Martyrs* (trans. and ed. H. Musurillo, Oxford: Clarendon Press, 1972), pp.108–9. See also the introductory notes in *Atti e passioni dei martiri*, a critical edition and commentary by A. A. R. Bastiaensen, A. Hilhorst, G. A. A. Kortekaas, A. P. Orbán and M. M. Van Assendelft (Milan: Arnoldo Mondadori, 2001).

15. 'The Martyrdom of Saints Perpetua and Felicity', in *The Acts of the Christian Martyrs*, pp.113–17.

16. Two general books on this theme are particularly noteworthy: Andrea Riccardi, *Il secolo del martirio, i cristiani nel novecento* (Milano: Mondadori, 2000), and Robert Royal, *The Catholic Martyrs of the Twentieth Century* (New York: Crossroad, 2000).

17. See the Pontifical Council for Promoting Christian Unity, *Information Service* 104(2000/III), pp.112–32.

18. John Paul, II, *Tertio millennio adveniente*, 37.

19. John Paul II, Encyclical Letter, *Ut unum sint* (Vatican City: Casa Editrice Vaticana, 1995), 84.

20. Edith Stein, *The Mystery of Christmas* (trans. Josephine Rucker, Darlington: Darlington Carmel, 1985), pp.14–15.

21. See Waltraud Herbstrith, *Edith Stein. A Biography* (San Francisco: Harper and Row, 1983), esp. pp.100–08.

22. 'Testament of Father Christian', in *How Far to Follow? The Martyrs of Atlas* by Bernardo Olivera (Kalamazoo: Cistercian Publications, 1997), p.127.

23. *Ibid.*, p.128.

24. *Ibid.*, p.12; Riccardi, *Il secolo dil martirio*, p.317.

25. Olivera, *How Far to Follow?* p.129. For an interpretation of *en-visagé de toi* in light of the thought of Emanuel Lévinas, see Étienne Baudry, 'Envisagé de toi', *Liturgie* (2000), pp.61–73.

26. Kallistos Ware, 'The Seed of the Church: Martyrdom as a Universal Vocation', in *The Inner Kingdom: The Collected Works, 1,* (Crestwood: St. Vladimir's Seminary Press, 2000), p.122. The reference to Cyprian is *On Works and Almsgiving*, 26. Ware also notes that 'The Irish elaborated the idea still further by speaking of a threefold martyrdom, red, white and green: red martyrdom is to shed one's blood for Christ; white martyrdom is "to abandon everything one loves for God's sake," that is, to accept the vocation of wandering, pilgrimage, voluntary

exile for Christ; green martyrdom is "to free oneself from evil desires by means of fasting and labour," pursuing the ascetic way in one's homeland'. See J. Ryan, *Irish Monasticism* (Dublin: Talbot, 1931), pp.197–8, who is citing the so-called Cambray Homily (late seventh or early eighth century) in W. Stokes and J. Strachan, *Thesarus Palaeohibernicus*, (3 vols., Cambridge: Cambridge University Press, 1901/1903), 2: 246–7. See Ware, p.122, n.28.

27. Athanasius, *Life of Antony*, 14 (ed. and trans. Robert Gregg, with a preface by William Clebsch, (New York: Paulist Press, 1980), p.42.

28. William Clebsch, Preface to Athanasius, *Life of Antony*, p.16. See also Samuel Rubenson, *The Letters of St. Antony: Monasticism and the Making of a Saint* (Studies in Antiquity and Christianity, Minneapolis: Fortress Press, 1995). Important sources for understanding desert spirituality in general are *The Sayings of the Desert Fathers: The Alphabetical Collection* (trans. Benedicta Ward, Kalamazoo, MI: Cistercian Publications; Oxford: Mowbray, 1987, this is a revised edition of the 1975 publication); *The Wisdom of the Desert Fathers. The Apophthegmata Patrum, The Anonymous Series* (Fairacres: Oxford, 1986), vol. 48. For some of the women of the desert see Laura Swan, *Forgotten Desert Mothers: Sayings, Lives and Stories of Early Christian Women* (New York: Paulist Press, 2001); Benedicta Ward, *Harlots of the Desert: A Study of Repentance in Early Monastic Studies* (London: Mowbray, 1987). For more general writings on desert spirituality, Belden Lane, *The Solace of Fierce Landscapes: Exploring Desert and Mountain Spirituality* (New York and Oxford: Oxford University Press, 1998); Henri Nouwen, *The Way of the Heart: Desert Spirituality and Contemporary Ministry* (New York: Seabury Press, 1981); John Chryssavgis, *In the Heart of the Desert: The Spirituality of the Desert Fathers and Mothers* (Bloomington, Indiana: World Wisdom, 2003); Roberta Biondi, *To Pray and To Love: Conversations on Prayer with the Early Church* (Minneapolis: Augsburg, 1991); Douglas Burton-Christie, *The Word in the Desert. Scripture and the Quest for Holiness in Early Christian Monasticism* (New York and Oxford: Oxford University Press, 1993); Graham Gould, *The Desert Fathers on Monastic Community* (Oxford Early Christian Studies, New York: Oxford University Press; Oxford: Clarendon Press, 1993).

29. Athanasius, 16, in *Life of Antony*, p.42.

30. *Ibid.* 5, p.34.

31. Abba Moses, 6 in *Sayings of the Desert Fathers*, p.118 (1975 edition)

32. 'It was said of Abba Agathon that for three years he lived with a stone in his mouth, until he had learnt to keep silence.' Abba Agathon, 15 in *Sayings of the Desert Fathers*, p.19.

33. St. Antony, 9 in *Sayings of the Desert Fathers*, p.2 (1975 edition), p.3 (revised edition).

34. Abba Matoes, 13, as quoted by Burton-Christie, *The Word in the Desert*, p.56.

35. Abba Poemen, 183 in *Sayings of the Desert Fathers*, p.102 (1975 edition), pp.192–3 (revised edition).

36. Marcarius the Great, 18, as quoted in Burton-Christie, *The Word in the Desert*, p.234.

37. Burton-Christie, *The Word in the Desert*, p.228.

38. Some would argue that the Dialogues are 'one of the most success-ful forgeries in the history of literature', written by a curial officer in the middle of the seventh century instead of by Gregory. See Francis Clark, *The Gregorian Dialogues and the Origins of Benedictine Monasticism* (Studies in the History of Christian Thought, 108, Leiden and Boston: Brill, 2003). See the review article by Stephen C. Kessler, 'The Gregorian *Dialogues*: A Feature Review' trans. Terrence Kardong *American Benedictine Review* 55 (September 2004), pp.323–8. Though this argument has convincing elements, I still think that with some caution, one can still extract some basic insights into how holiness was perceived in Benedict's life.

39. See Timothy Fry, *RB 1980, The Rule of St. Benedict in Latin and English with Notes* (Collegeville: The Liturgical Press, 1981), p.75 (introduction). All quotations are taken from this edition of the *Rule*, paragraph followed by verse number.

40. André Louf, 'Prayer in the Rule of Saint Benedict', *Word and Spirit* 2 (1981), pp.118–35.

41. *RB 1980*, Prologue 1.

42. Esther de Waal, *A Life Giving Way. A Commentary on the Rule of St. Benedict,* (Collegeville: The Liturgical Press, 1995), p.v. See also *Living with Contradiction, Further Reflections on the Rule of St. Benedict* (London: Fount, Collins, 1988; San Francisco: Harper and Row, 1989).

43. See Simon Tugwell, 'The Spirituality of the Dominicans', in *Christian Spirituality, High Middle Ages and Reformation* (ed. Jill Raitt, New York: Crossroad, 1989), pp.16–31.

44. Keith Egan, 'The Spirituality of the Carmelites', in *Christian Spirituality, High Middle Ages and Reformation*, pp.50–61.

45. Adolar Zumkeller, 'The Spirituality of the Augustinians', in *Christian Spirituality, High Middle Ages and Reformation*, pp.63–74.

46. J. A. Wayne Hellman, 'The Spirituality of the Franciscans', in *Christian Spirituality, High Middle Ages and Reformation*, p.31.

47. This was pointed out in Lawrence S. Cunningham's excellent biography, *Francis of Assisi: Performing the Gospel Life* (Grand Rapids: William Eerdmans Publishing Company, 2004), p.vi. The 1992 special issue of *Time* magazine included Mozart (musician), Gutenberg (inventor), Michaelangelo (artist), Jefferson (statesman), Columbus (explorer), Shakespeare (writer), Galileo and Einstein (scientists) and St. Francis and Martin Luther (religious leaders).

48. For documentation on the 1986 meeting see *Interreligious Dialogue, The Official Teaching of the Catholic Church (1963-1995)* (ed. Francesco Gioia, Boston: Paoline Books and Media, 1997), section 67. For documentation on the 2002 Meeting in Assisi, see *Pro Dialogo* 109 (2002), pp.45–8.

49. Cunningham, *Francis*, pp.6-7.

50. Francis of Assisi, *The Testament* in *Francis of Assisi: Early Documents* (ed. Regis J. Armstrong, J. A. Wayne Hellmann and William J. Short, New York: New City Press, 1999), p.124. This edition is now considered the standard text in English. This first volume *The Saint* is followed by two others: *The Founder* (volume II) and *The Prophet* (volume III). For a commentary on the Rule and Testament see Cajetan Esser, *Rule and Testament of St. Francis. Conferences to Modern Followers of Francis* (Chicago: Franciscan Herald Press, 1977).

51. Cunningham, *Francis,* p.12 cites passages from the *Rule of 1221* where Francis assumes the friars would work with lepers, the *Fioretti* where an entire chapter is dedicated to Francis' love of lepers and the *Mirror of Perfection* where Francis insists that 'whether noble or not' those who enter the order must 'serve lepers and live in their houses'.

52. Bonaventure of Bagnoregio, *Major Legend of St. Francis* (2:4) in *Francis of Assisi, The Founder* (Hyde Park: New City Press, 2000), p.538.

53. See Cunningham, *Francis*, p.20.

54. *Francis of Assisi, The Saint*, p.40.

55. Esser, *Rule and Testament of St Francis*, p.99.

56. See *The Life of Francis by Thomas of Celano* in *Francis of Assisi, The Saint*, pp.201–2. See Cunningham, *Francis*, pp.24–5.

57. Cunningham, *Francis*, pp.73–91, especially p.86 where he notes that

'Greccio and LaVerna were ... two parentheses ... summed up the evangelical vision of Francis.'

58. *The Life of St Francis by Thomas of Celano*, p.224.

59. Cunningham, *Francis*, p.86.

60. 'A Letter to the Entire Order', in *Francis of Assisi, the Saint*, p.118. See Eloi Leclerq, *The Canticle of Creatures Symbols of Union. An Analysis of St. Francis of Assisi* (Chicago: Franciscan Herald Press, 1977), p.180. In his book, *La sapienza di un povero*, Eloi Leclerq imagines a conversation between Francis and Brother Leo on the theme of purity of heart, which captures an important dimension of holiness. Francis explains that 'a heart is pure when it doesn't cease to adore the living and true Lord. It shares deeply in God's life and is so strong that even in all its misery it can be touched by the eternal innocence and joy of God. Such a heart is at one and the same time empty and full to overflowing – that God is God is all sufficient for it. From this certainty, it derives its peace and all its joy. *And holiness of heart – that too then, is nothing else than God.'* Brother Leo pointed out that God calls us to remain faithful to him. Francis replied: 'Certainly, but holiness does not consist in self-realization nor in the fulfilment which one achieves oneself. Holiness is first of all the emptiness which one finds in oneself, which one accepts, and which God fills in an equal measure to which one opens oneself to his fullness.'* See Eloi Leclerc, *La Sapienza di un povero* (Milano: Biblioteca Francescana 2004), pp.111–13 (emphasis mine). I am grateful to Lawrence Cunningham for his comments on this text and on holiness in Francis' writings in general. This quotation of Leclerc is also mentioned in Franz Jalics, *Contemplative Retreat. An Introduction to the Contemplative Way of Life and to the Jesus Prayer* (Munich: Xulon Press, 2003), pp.210–11.

61. This quote is taken from John Paul I's papal audience of 13 September 1978. The context is his greeting to the newlyweds presented at the audience: 'Nel secolo scorso c'era in Francia Federico Ozanam, grande professore; insegnava alla Sorbona, ma eloquente, ma bravissimo! Suo amico era Lacordaire, il quale diceva: « E' così bravo, è così buono, si farà prete, diventerà un vescovone, questo qui! ». No! Ha incontrato una brava signorina, si sono sposati. Lacordaire c'è rimasto male, e ha detto: « Povero Ozanam! E'cascato anche lui nella trappola! ». Ma due anni dopo, Lacordaire venne a Roma, e fu ricevuto da Pio IX. « Venga, Padre, – dice – venga. Io ho sempre sentito dire che Gesù ha istituito sette sacramenti: adesso viene Lei, mi cambia le carte in tavola; mi

dice che ha istituito sei sacramenti, e una trappola! No, Padre, il matrimonio non è una trappola, è un grande sacramento! ».'

62. Robert P. Maloney, 'Models of Being Holy', pp.17–22.

63. The following four books focus on the various exemplars: first, in 1935, Seldon Delany wrote a book entitled *Married Saints* (New York: Longmans, Green, 1935). It was reprinted in 1969 and its purpose was to show that not only those who are celibate but also married couples are called to holiness, which is understood as conformity of one's will with the will of God. The second book, in Italian, is the fruit of the community of Caresto and it is entitled *I santi sposati. Esigenza di una rinnovata agiografia per la spiritualità matrimoniale* (Milan: Edizione O.R., 1989, reprinted 1992). This book suggests that there is a shortage of couples who have been proposed as models of sanctity in the Church and that marital spirituality has been somewhat marginalized. After reflecting on holy virgins, holy politicians, holy mothers, saints with big families and others, the authors plead for a further reflection and development on the theology and spirituality of the laity. The third book is fundamentally a collection of stories about married saints by Ferdinand Holböck, *Heilige Eheleute: Verheiratete Selige und Heilige aus allen Jahrhunderten* (Salzburg: Christiana-Verlag, 2001), which describes more than two hundred married saints. For the English translation see *Married Saints and Blesseds Through the Centuries* (trans. Michael J. Miller, San Franscisco: Ignatius Press, 2002). Finally, in *Marriage as a Path of Holiness, Lives of Married Saints* (South Canaan: St. Tikhon's Seminary Press, 1999), David and Mary Ford present various holy married saints in the orthodox tradition.

64. *Levens der gehouder persoonen die heylighlyck geleeft hebben, al-hoe-wel sy noch niet al in't ghetal der heylighen gestelt en zyn,* (Antwerpen: Johan Cnobbaert, 1631). I am grateful to the Librarian of LIBISMA, Hans Storme, for this reference.

65. See Dionigi Tettamanzi, 'Gesù è stato per lei il punto di riferimento unico', who quotes his predecessor Cardinal Martini, in *Osservatore Romano* 113 (16 May 2004), p.19.

66. As quoted in Fernando daRiese Pio X, *Per amore della vita: Gianna Berettta Mola, medico e madre* (third edition; Roma: Città Nuova, 1994), p.123.

67. Ibid., p.238.

68. Congregatio de Causis Sanctorum, *Canonizationis Servae Dei*

*Ioanae Beretta nuptae Molla matris familias (1922–1962)* (Rome: Tipografia Guerra, 1991), p.11

69. 'Gianna Beretta offered her life for her child', *Osservatore Romano* 17 (27 April 1994), p.2.

70. Frances Kennedy, 'Gianna's Choice', *Tablet* 22 (May 2004). Taken from the webpage *www.thethablet.co.uk/cgi-bin/arcive_db.cgi?tablet-00895.*

71. *Questi Borghesi ... I Beati Luigi e Maria Beltrame Quattrocchi* (Siena: Cantagalli, 2001), pp.6–7.

72. John Paul II, *Tertio millennio adveniente*, 37.

73. Basil Hume, 'Spirituality for the Year 2000', B.R.E.S. Termly Lecture (6 November 1997), pp.10–11.

74. Thérèse of Lisieux, 'My Vocation is Love,' in *Story of a Soul. The Autobiography of St. Thérèse of Lisieux* (Washington, DC: ICS Publications, 1996), pp.187–88.

75. Godfried Cardinal Danneels, Preface, *Saint Thérèse of Lisieux: Her Life, Times and Teaching* (Washington, DC: ICS Publications, 1997), p.5.

76. 'My Vocation is Love', *Story,* p.194.

77. Emmanuel Renault, 'Thérèse in the Night of Faith', in *Saint Thérèse of Lisieux: Her Life, Times and Teaching*, p.223.

78. Thérèse of Lisieux, 'The Trial of Faith', *Story* p.237.

79. Thérèse of Lisieux, 'My Vocation is Love', *Story* p.197.

80. Thérèse of Lisieux, 'The Trial of Faith', *Story* p.213.

81. Ibid. p.214.

82. Thérèse of Lisieux, *Last Conversations* (trans. John Clarke, Washington DC: ICS, 1977), p.129. There is a question regarding the authenticity of this passage. See note on p.129.

83. Ibid. p.138.

84. Thérèse of Lisieux, *Story* p.259.

85. For some recent articles on the relationship between Dorothy Day and Thérèse, see J. Leon Hooper, 'Dorothy Day's Transposition of Thérèse's "Little Way"', *Theological Studies* 63 (2002): pp.68–88 and Peter Casarella, 'Sisters in Doing the Truth: Dorothy Day and St. Thérèse of Lisieux', *Communio* 24 (Fall 1997), pp.468–98. My comments here are a re-working of a short study I did for the Carmelites (O. Carm.) in 1997 that has not yet been published..

86. Dorothy Day, 'On Pilgrimage', *The Catholic Worker* (October 1949), p.1.

87. '"All my life I have been haunted by God," a character in one of Dostoyefsy's [sic] books says. And that is the way it was with me.' *From Union Square to Rome* (second edition, London: Geo. E. J. Coldwell, 1939), p.18.

88. See Dorothy Day, *The Long Loneliness, An Autobiography* (San Francisco: Harper and Row, 1952, reprinted 1981), pp.26–49 for an account of her university years.

89. Ibid. p.39.

90. Lawrence Cunningham, *Catholic Prayer* (New York: Crossroad, 1989), p.147.

91. Dorothy Day, *Therese* (Springfield: Templegate Publishers, 1991), pp.vi–vii (preface). Day uses an American spelling of the name Thérèse. Consequently when quoting her directly or when mentioning her book, we shall do the same. At all other times, the accents will be inserted.

92. Day, *The Long Loneliness* p.136.

93. Ibid., p.136.

94. Ibid., pp.145, 148.

95. Ibid., p.148–9.

96. Day, *Therese* pp.vii–viii (preface).

97. Ibid., p.viii.

98. Ibid., p.xiii.

99. Day, *The Long Loneliness* p.166.

100. Dorothy Day, 'The Catholic Worker', *Integrity* 1 (November 1946): pp.17–19 as quoted by Brigid O'Shea Merriman, *Searching for Christ: The Spirituality of Dorothy Day* (Notre Dame and London: University of Notre Dame, 1994), p.205.

101. Dorothy Day, 'On Pilgrimage', *The Catholic Worker* (February 1977): 1.

102. Dorothy Day, 'Room for Christ,' *Catholic Worker* 12 (December 1945), p.2. Reprinted in *The Catholic Worke*r 46 (1980), p.7.

103. Rosemary Haughton, 'Prophetic Spirituality', in *Spiritual Life* (Spring 1989), p.11.

104. Dorothy Day, *Loaves and Fishes* (New York: Maryknoll, 1963), p.84.

105. Day, *The Long Loneliness* pp.285–86.

106. Day, *Therese* p.175

107. Ibid. p.175.

108 Thérèse of Lisieux, 'Act of Oblation to Merciful Love', *Story*, p.277.

109. The bibliography is quite extensive. See *Ouevres Complétes* (eds. André A. Devaux and Florence de Lussy, Paris: Gallimard, 1991–2000). The English translation of *Attente de Dieu* was first published as *Waiting for God*, (trans. Emma Craufurd, New York: G.P. Putnam's Sons, 1951). This edition, recently reprinted by Harper-Collins Perennial Classics

(2001), is the one used here. Other works in English include, *First and Last Notebook*, trans. Richard Rees, New York and Toronto: Oxford University Press, 1970); *Formative Writings, 1929-1941* (ed. and trans. Dorothy Tuck McFarland and Wilhelmina Van Ness; London, Routledge and Kegan Paul, 1987) and *Gravity and Grace*, trans. Emma Craufurd, New York/London: Rouledge Press, 1963). Some significant secondary sources are the following: André A. Devaux, 'Weil, Simone', *Dictionnaire de spiritualité* (Paris: Beauchesne, 1994) vol. XVI, cols. 1346–55; Francine du Plessix Gray, *Simone Weil* (London: Weidenfeld & Nicolson, 2001); Joseph-Marie Perrin and Gustave Thibon, *Simone Weil as We Knew Her* (London: Routledge & Kegan Paul, 1953); Simone Pétrement, *La vie de Simone Weil* (Paris: Librairie Arthéme Fayard, 1973). The English translation by Raymond Rosenthal is *Simone Weil: A Life* (New York: Pantheon Books, 1973); Diogenes Allen, *Three Outsiders: Pascal, Kierkegaard, Simone Weil* (New York: Cowley Publications, 1983); Giulia P. DiNicola and Attilio Danese, *Simone Weil. Abitare la contraddizione* (Roma: Edizioni Dehoniane, 1991); Gabriela Fiori, *Simone Weil. Biografia di un pensiero* (Milan: Garzanti, 1981); Thomas Nevin, *Simone Weil: Portrait of a Self-Hating Jew* (Chapel Hill: University of North Carolina Press, 1991).

110. Gray, *Simone Weil*, p.223, DiNicola and Danese, *Simone Weil*, p.57.

111. DiNicola and Danese, *Simone Weil*, p.57.

112. Weil, *Waiting for God*, p.25.

113. Ibid. p.27, See also Gray, *Simone Weil*, p.120

114. Weil, *Waiting for God*, p.26.

115. Ibid. p.26.

116. Ibid. p.27.

117. Gray's discussion of this is particularly helpful.

118. Weil, *Waiting for God*, pp.32–3.

119. Pétremend, *Simon Weil, A Life*, p.538.

120. Weil, *Waiting for God*, p.vii.

121. Ibid. p.51.

122. Ibid. p.51.

123. Ibid. p.51.

124. Timothy Verdon, *Maria nell'arte europea* (Milan: Mondadori, 2004), pp.9ff. See also John Saward, *The Beauty of Holiness, Art Sanctity and the Truth of Catholicism* (San Francisco: Ignatius Press, 1996), especially pp.113–59, the Chapter entitled '*Tota Pulcra*, The Beauty of Our Lady and the Renewal of Christian Culture'.

125. Barbara Moore and Carla Brenner, *Map and Guide, National Gallery of Art, Washington DC*. (London: Scala Publishers, 2001), pp.16–17.

126. Denise Levertov, *A Door in the Hive* (second edition New York: New Directions Book, 1989), pp.86–88.

127. Elizabeth Johnson, *Truly Our Sister. A Theology of Mary in the Communion of Saints* (New York and London: Continuum, 2003). See especially the fourth part of this book, pp.137–208. See also her synthesis of this book, *Dangerous Memories: A Mosaic of Mary in Scripture* (New York: Continuum, 2004). Other bibliography of particular interest for this topic are the following: Beverly Gaventa, *Mary: Glimpses of the Mother of Jesus* (Columbia, SC: University of South Carolina Press, 1995); Beverly Gaventa and Cynthia L. Rigby (eds), *Blessed One: Protestant Perspectives on Mary* (Louisville: John Knox Press, 2002); Francis J. Moloney, *Woman First Among the Faithful* (Notre Dame: Ave Maria Pres, 1986); Donald Senior, 'Gospel Portraits of Mary: Images and Symbols from the Synoptic Tradition', in Doris Donnelly (ed.), *Mary Woman of Nazareth. Biblical and Theological Perspectives* (New York: Paulist Press, 1989), pp.92–108; See also his 'New Testament Images of Mary', *The Bible Today* 24 (1986), pp.143–52. I am grateful to Donald Senior, CP, for drawing my attention to some of this bibliography.

128. Johnson, *Truly Our Sister*, pp.132–33.

129. Paul VI, Apostolic Exhortation, *Marialis Cultus* (Devotion to the Blessed Virgin Mary), (Vatican City: The Vatican Polyglot Press, 1974), p.35.

130. Raymond Brown, K. Donfried, J. Fitzmyer and J. Reumann, *Mary in the New Testament: A Collaborative Assessment by Protestant and Roman Catholic Scholars* (Philadelphia: Fortress Press, 1978), p.172.

131. Brown. *et. al. Mary in the New Testament*, p.177.

132. See for example, the Encyclical Letter, *Redemptoris Mater*, (Vatican City: casa Editrice Vaticana 1987),36.

133. ARCIC, *The Gift of Authority in the Church II* (1990) n.30 at www.prounione.urbe.it/dia-int/arcic/doc/e_arcic_authority 2.html.

134. ARCIC, *Mary, Grace and Hope in Christ* (2005). See also the article, Jared Wicks, 'The Virgin Mary in Recent Ecumenical Dialogues', *Gregorianum* 81 (2000), pp.25–75 and *A Commentary on Mary, Grace and Hope in Christ of the Anglican-Roman Catholic International Commission (ARCIC)*. Two other dialogues are of particular interest: Lutheran-Catholic Dialogue in the United States, Dialogue VIII, *The*

*One Mediator, the Saints, and Mary* (Minneapolis: Augsburg Press 1992); *Mary in the Plan of God and the Communion of Saints* (New York: Paulist Press, 2002) trans. Matthew J. O'Connell, from *Marie dans le dessein de Dieu and la communion des saints*, by the Alain Blancy, Maurice Jourjon and the Dombes Group (Paris: Bayard /Centurion 1999), which states, 'Mary, who was so close to the human Jesus as his mother, had to experience the passion and death of her Son in order to become a disciple in the church. She thereby warns Christians that they cannot bypass the cross and resurrection in entering the community of their Lord' (par.189, p.69).

135. ARCIC, *Mary, Grace and Hope in Christ*, 78.

136. Woodward, 'Slow up on Saint-Making' *The Tablet* 253 (13 November 19990 p.1539.

137. Madeleine Delbrêl, *We, the Ordinary People of the Streets* (trans. David Louis Schindler, Jr. and Charles F. Mann, Grand Rapids: William Eerdmans Publishing Co., 2000), p.54. In 1993 Carlo Maria Cardinal Martini wrote, 'Personally, I esteem her as one of the great mystics of our century'. *A Prophetic Voice in the City. Meditations on the Prophet Jeremiah* (Collegeville: Liturgical Press, 1999), p.101. The Italian edition of this was published in 1993.

138. A comment by Dorothy Day made to a journalist as quoted in Jim Forest, 'The trouble with Saint Day', *U.S. Catholic* 62 (November 1997), p.18.

'If we linger before the mosaic, we notice that this Cross is in reality a tree, from beneath which four sources of water originate, at which deer slake their thirst. The thought of the four rivers of paradise arises, and the phrase in the psalm comes to mind: "As a deer longs for flowing streams, so longs my soul for you, O God" (ps 42:1–2).'
Joseph Cardinal Ratzinger (Pope Benedict XVI) *Images of Hope* (San Francisco: Igantius, 2006), pp.75–6.

# 3
# Ordinary Maintenance for an
# Extraordinary Dwelling

*Since Baptism is a true entry into the holiness of God through incorpo-*
*ration into Christ and the indwelling of his Spirit, it would be a contra-*
*diction to settle for a life of mediocrity, marked by a minimalist ethic and*
*a shallow religiosity. To ask catechumens: 'Do you wish to receive*
*Baptism?' means at the same time to ask them: 'Do you wish to become*
*holy?' It means to set before them the radical nature of the Sermon on the*
*Mount: 'Be perfect as your heavenly Father is perfect' (Mt. 5:48).*
John Paul II, Apostolic Letter *Novo millennio ineunte*
(Vatican City: Libreria editrice Vaticana, 2000), 31

*Lax suddenly turned around and asked me the question:*
    *'What do you want to be, anyway?' ...*
*'I don't know; I guess what I want is to be a good Catholic.'*
*'What do you mean, you want to be a good Catholic?' ...*
    *'What you should say – he told me – what you should say is that*
*you want to be a saint.'*
    *A saint! The thought struck me as a little weird. I said: 'How do*
*you expect me to become a saint?'*
    *'By wanting to,' said Lax, simply ... 'Don't you believe that God*
*will make you what he created you to be, if you will consent to him to do*
*it? All you have to do is desire it.'*
Thomas Merton, *The Seven Storey Mountain*
Orlando: A Harvest (HBJ Book, 1948, reprint 1976), p.237

Basic care and general upkeep are required for every house – be it
cottage or castle. Regular house-cleaning, routine maintenance tasks
and, at times, even major renovations are necessary to keep a building
functional. These essential tasks, along with cultivating a sense of liveable style, lend themselves to transform a simple shelter into a home.
There is an intimate relationship between physical structure and the

life it shelters, between design and function. Housekeeping and maintenance require a certain sort of attention and, if one 'does it right', an element of anticipation. Interior design, which is a non-negotiable in the matter of soulful 'live-ability', also requires concerted attention, tidiness, and knowledge of the occupants. Attention and care are important. The ordinary maintenance for the extraordinary dwelling, which we are in Christ Jesus, requires just as much mindful attentiveness as do our homes and apartment units, convents and monasteries, dorm rooms and cells. Throughout the ages, Christians have been encouraged to care for their interior lives and their lives together as a community through the basic means of prayer and fasting, almsgiving, works of compassion, Scripture and spiritual reading, the sacraments and sacramentals, and physical/psychological stewardship of our bodies and minds. Practising these various essentials of 'good housekeeping' are the means for establishing and maintaining a home – a castle even, according to Teresa of Avila, where God delights to dwell.[1]

This chapter explores the amazing renovation project and maintenance program to which God invites us to collaborate. Some sacraments like baptism, confirmation, matrimony and holy orders are similar to a major renovation to the dwelling that we are, whereas Eucharist, Penance, and anointing of the sick are paradoxically akin to 'ordinary', yet 'extraordinary' means of preserving the building. Prayer and daily contact with the word of God, almsgiving and fasting, sacramentals and popular piety are all practical ways of fostering holiness and making the dwelling strong and graceful. These 'routine' yet paradoxically special moments of grace transform us. The responsible use of our freedom also leads us to virtuous living and an openness to the gifts of the Spirit granted to us in baptism and confirmation. Care for the physical structure of this temple of the Holy Spirit which we have become includes also stewardship of our bodies and minds.

## Sacraments

The most important gifts that God has given for the total renovation of this structure are the sacraments. Included among the purposes of the sacraments is that as we celebrate them in a full, conscious and active way, they make us holy.[2] Sacraments effect what they signify, thereby serving as vehicles of God's transforming presence and power in human lives. In our celebration of the sacraments, we open ourselves, often incrementally, to the wide and varied scope of God's reality. We discover new horizons by finding the extraordinary in the ordinary. Ordinary things like water, oil, bread and wine, and gestures such as the touch of an anointing hand become extraordinary ways, tangible ways, of communicating God's love and presence to us. The sacraments are '"powers that come forth" from the Body of Christ, which is ever-living and ever-giving. They are actions of the Holy Spirit at work in ... the Church'.[3] They are dynamic activities, living realities. Through the sacraments, the Holy Spirit gradually heals and transforms us, conforming us to Christ and making us into a holy people for God and for others.[4]

Contemporary theological reflection sees the sacrament as an encounter between God and the human person through a symbol. A symbol has meaning pointing beyond itself to the grace which God wishes to confer. An earlier sacramental theology used to ask: what sort of causality was exercised by the sacraments (for example, how would water and the word confer grace)? Now the question is re-presented, and we look much more to God using the sacraments to confer grace. Sacraments are an encounter between the person in need, Christ, and the Church, with the Holy Spirit effecting the transforming grace.

In early Christian art, the sacraments are often represented as streams of water flowing from the foot of the Cross. Gathered at the base of the cross are deer or lambs who slake their thirst in the life-giving waters. This image reminds us that the sacraments flow from Christ crucified and become through his death and resurrection the source of life for all who draw near.[5] Our human and spiritual hungers and thirsts are fed and slaked by the sacraments. The *Office of Readings* for Good Friday, in a text attributed to St. John Chrysostom, makes the connection between the cross and the sacraments explicit:

> The gospel related that when Christ had died and was still hanging on the cross, the soldier approached him and pierced his side with the spear, and at once there came out water and blood. The one was a symbol of Baptism, the other of the mysteries [the Eucharist]. That soldier, then, pierced his side: he breached the wall of the holy temple, and I found the treasure and acquired the wealth ... There came out from his side water and blood.' Dearly beloved, do not pass the secret of this great mystery without reflection.[6]

Here the focus is on baptism and the Eucharist, but all seven sacraments find their source in Christ crucified and risen. While Christians differ on the precise number of sacraments and some communions do not believe in 'sacraments' at all, but will allow for 'ordinances', all agree that God's extraordinary grace comes to us in the ordinary. The common conviction is something that we all share. As we explore the various sacraments, we will discover that each sacrament, in its own way, touches on our basic longing for holiness.

### Sacraments of initiation

In the early Church, the three sacraments of initiation – baptism, confirmation and Eucharist – were celebrated together at the Easter vigil after a long period of spiritual preparation known as the catechumenate. Today in the West, while infant baptism is common, confirmation and Eucharist usually occur at the age of 'discretion' – often, with Eucharist preceding confirmation. However, since the *Rite for the Christian Initiation of Adults* (*RCIA*) was published in 1972, the sacraments of initiation are celebrated, in the case of adult conversion, in their ancient order. This approach reflects the Roman Catholic view that these three sacraments are 'foundational' for Christian life and holiness.[7] They are the underlying base or support of the Christian life.

### *Baptism*

Baptism is both a personal experience of union with God and the means whereby we become a people gathered into the Church, into the family of God, into communion with one another. Through baptism, we have become 'living stones' and we are built into a spiritual house.[8] Through baptism we are bound together with others in the Church as we grow in holiness. A text written by Sixtus III c.432–40 and placed above the baptismal font of St. John Lateran in Rome expresses this point well: 'the brood born here to live in heaven has life from water and the fructifying Spirit ... No barrier can divide where life unites: one faith, one fount, one Spirit makes one people ... The stream that flows below sprang from the wounded Christ to wash the whole world clean and give it life. Children of the water: ... birth in this stream is birth to holiness.'[9]

Baptism is, for all believers, their 'birth into holiness.' A few years ago, I attended the Easter vigil at a Roman Catholic church in the United States. There were several baptisms that evening. Adults and babies and, to my surprise, an entire family – parents and their children – were baptized by immersion into a full-sized baptismal pool shaped like a tomb. As I watched the catechumens about to be completely drenched, many of them seemed to instinctively brace themselves against the physical placement of their bodies under water. Their physical reaction symbolized in many ways what we believe happens in this wonderful sacrament. In the early Church many baptismal fonts were designed in such a way as to remind the liturgical participants of death. They often had three steps leading in and out of the tomb-like pool to symbolize the three days Jesus spent in the sepulchre prior to his resurrection. Entering into the baptismal pool was seen as death to sin and rebirth in the water of life. Baptisms, during the days of early Christianity, were by full immersion, not unlike the baptisms I witnessed during the Easter vigil. Old ways and old lives die hard – even with the supportive encouragement of a believing community and a sensitive presider. Sin resists being extinguished and birth is hard, both in the small act of a religious rite and in real life. No wonder the catechumens braced themselves!

Many of us, having been baptized as infants, are not blessed with vivid memories of our baptisms. We find it challenging to even begin to grasp the radical nature and meaning of the rite. However, even a rudimentary understanding of the far-reaching relationship between baptism and holiness is necessary in the mind and life of a Christian. One of the central New Testament images for baptism that helps us do this is found in Paul's Letter to the Romans:

> Do you not know that inasmuch as we have been baptized into Christ Jesus we have been baptized into his death? We were buried therefore with him through baptism into death, so that as Christ was raised from the dead by the glory of the Father, we too might walk in newness of life. (Rom. 6:3–5)

In the waters of baptism we are enveloped in Christ's resurrected life by entering into his death. This new life brought about by baptism is the foundation of Christian holiness because it marks a new relationship with God who is Father, Son and Spirit.

In Greek, the word 'to baptize' literally means 'to plunge' or 'to immerse', and 'to be baptized' can mean 'to be drowned'. Baptism is a 'drowning', a dying to sin in order to surrender to a new way of life. One way of grasping what it means is to think about baptism as learning to drown, or perhaps more aptly, of learning to live under water, immersed in God. As Catherine of Siena understood it, we are in God just as, in the

sea, a fish is in the water and the water is in the fish. Our Christian existence is in God. It is a mutual indwelling.[10] As baptized Christians, we
need to become like fish that live under water. Comprehending the
significance of baptism in every day life involves trusting ourselves to
live in life long surrender to the holy waters of our own baptism. We are
invited to never completely 'dry off' after our baptismal immersion so
that this sacrament becomes a living reality in our daily lives.[11] It initi-
ates us into the God's life, into life itself and puts to death all that is not
holy in us. 'To breathe under water means to breathe death', says
Richard Fragomeni. 'It means to live an alternative way of life. It is a
new mode of surviving, breathing water instead of air. Now death is the
mode of survival. Drown! This is the Baptismal imperative.'[12] To be
baptized is also to live in surrender to God and to nurture in ourselves
a certain attentive responsiveness to all that is holy, to all that is of God.
Baptism restores in us a spiritual vitality and squelches the creeping
cancer of sin and eventual death.

The implications of living 'underwater' are several. To remember our
baptism into Christ, to reflect on the original sacrament of initiation, is to
deliberately focus on God's love for us and dwell in this love just as a fish
lives in the sea. Remembering our baptism is to recall the identity and
dignity we have in and through Christ. The identity and dignity of our
baptism carry with them the responsibilities of our new life, our Christ
life. 'Let us rejoice and give thanks,' wrote St. Augustine, 'we have not
only become Christians, but Christ himself ... Stand in awe and rejoice:
We have become Christ.'[13] This point of view, of the Christians becoming
'Christ', illustrates the relationship between baptism and holiness. A
scriptural passage that brings together the two basic images associated
with baptism, namely death and resurrection, along with washing and
sanctification is Titus 3: 4–7. 'But when the goodness and kindness of God
our Saviour appeared, he saved us, not because of any works of righteousness that we had done, but according to his mercy, through the water
of rebirth and renewal by the Holy Spirit. This Spirit he poured out on us
richly through Jesus Christ our Saviour so that, having been justified by
his faith, we might become heirs according to the hope of eternal life.'

This 'birth to holiness' offered to the 'children of the water' goes
beyond immersing the newly baptized in the sea of God. It also unites
all Christians before any distinctions are made. Baptism is the foundation for the universal call to holiness as described in the Second Vatican
Council's Dogmatic Constitution on the Church, *Lumen gentium*. After

portraying the mystery of the Church with a rich medley of images in Chapter 1, *Lumen gentium* devotes an entire chapter to the Church as primordially the People of God.[14] This scripturally-based description of the Church accentuates the basic equality and unity of all the baptized, who have become in Christ 'a chosen race, a royal priesthood, a holy nation ... once no people, but now God's people.'[15] Indeed, the Church must be a holy building formed by the Spirit.

Baptism is also the foundation for our unity with all Christians. The 1982 Lima, Faith and Order Ecumenical Document, *Baptism Eucharist and Ministry*, emphasized that 'Baptism is a sign and seal of our common discipleship. Through baptism, Christians are brought into union with Christ, with each other and with the Church of every time and place. Our common Baptism, which unites us to Christ in faith, is thus a basic bond of unity ... Our one Baptism into Christ constitutes a call to the Churches to overcome their divisions and visibly manifest their fellowship.'[16] Christianity firmly negates the idea of second-class citizens in the Church.[17] Holiness is a free gift given in baptism and it is also a call given to all the baptized without distinction. The baptismal invitation to die and to rise in Christ is not limited to individuals but is offered to the community of the Church as a whole. There too, we find ourselves as a community flinching or bracing ourselves in light of the demands of our baptismal commitment. Opening ourselves to the grace and spirit of baptism, individually and as a community, we are transformed more into Christ: living stones, a dwelling for God.

## Confirmation

Confirmation, closely linked with baptism, is best understood as the sacrament that strengthens us with the Holy Spirit. Though already incorporated into the Church through baptism, confirmation binds us even more perfectly to the Church. Through this sacrament, we are also empowered to embrace more fully our responsibilities as Christians.[18] Above all, confirmation is the sacrament that keeps the gifts of the Holy Spirit alive and active in our hearts.[19] Without the Holy Spirit, it is impossible to respond to God's call to holiness. As St. Catherine of Siena wrote regarding the role of the Holy Spirit in our lives, 'without this guide we cannot go on'.[20] The gift of the Spirit was at work in our baptism, and we are specifically given the gift of the Spirit in confirmation; hence we are challenged not only to live by the Spirit, but also to be guided by the Spirit (Gal. 5:25).

When focusing on confirmation in the *RCIA*, the Greek word *paraklete* (*paraclitus* in Latin) has been brilliantly translated by two words, 'helper' and 'guide'. We can add to these rich personal phrases, the teaching of St Thomas Aquinas on the Holy Spirit as 'friend'.[21] With these three words, we are reminded of the possibility of a deep personal relationship with the Holy Spirit as guiding friend. As in any healthy friendship, we can expect to be enriched by our life in the Spirit and be drawn out of ourselves to be more fully all that God has destined us to be. In the context of confirmation, the emphasis is on the Gift who is the Spirit. The Spirit gives the seven messianic gifts, the fruit of the Spirit (Gal. 5:22-23), and the Spirit draws us into God's light and holiness (cf. Romans 8).

Confirmation, like baptism, is celebrated only once. How do we keep the transforming power of this sacrament effective throughout our lives? One simple way to recall the gift of the Spirit given in these sacraments is to pray daily for the coming of the Holy Spirit, using, perhaps, the prayer *Veni Creator Spiritus* (Come Holy Spirit). This prayer, attributed to Rabanus Maurus (776–856), is traditionally recited on special occasions such as Pentecost or the dedication of a church when the Holy Spirit is solemnly invoked. Yet if we, as a people, are God's dwelling, it seems appropriate if not necessary to ask *daily* for the renewal of the Spirit's gift given in Baptism and Confirmation, to 'fan into a flame' this gift of God (2 Tim. 1:6). In the first stanza of this ancient hymn, we invoke the Creator Spirit to fill our hearts and dwell within us anew, recognizing that the Spirit is the 'font of life' and 'fire of love'. With Maurus's remaining stanzas, we welcome the seven-fold gifts of the Spirit and we recognize the power of the Spirit at work in our lives – in our walk and talk, in our ways of behaving and speaking, in our practical acts of compassion and care, in our practice of virtue as well as in our inner posture of peace and good will, speech and acts, at work in overflowing love, patience, virtue and peace.

The gifts of the Spirit (cf. Isa. 11:2) are those permanent fixtures that bring lightness to the daily task of being attentive and open to the Holy Spirit.[22] These seven gifts – wisdom, understanding, counsel, fortitude, knowledge, piety and fear of the Lord – attune us to divine inspirations. Above all they remind us to whom the dwelling belongs: 'For all who are led by the Spirit of God are sons and daughters of God ... if children, then heirs, heirs of God and fellow heirs with Christ.'[23] Like the gifts, the fruit of the Spirit (Gal. 5:22–23) bring vitality to the dwelling because they are signs of God's love at work in our lives, moulding us into the image and likeness of Jesus. They include charity, joy, peace, patience, kindness, goodness, generosity, gentleness, faithfulness, modesty, self-control and chastity.[24] Whether praying the ancient prayer 'Come Holy Spirit' or another, consistently remembering our confirmation and asking that the Holy Spirit be vibrantly alive in us fosters growth in holiness.

*Eucharist*

The Eucharist, the font and summit of the Christian life, in the words of Francis Moloney, 'is not a prayer wheel that we spin every morning and a little more solemnly on Sunday. It is the grammar and syntax of Christian life.'[25] The sacramental re-presentation of the paschal mystery is the source of holiness where we express our creatureliness before God in adoration and praise, where God teaches us in the word, and where we pray for the world and receive healing for it and for our own lives.[26] At the same time, the Eucharist is where we bring our desires, our successes and our failures, that like loaves and fishes are transformed (cf. Mt. 15: 34–7) and where we are given the gift to 'offer to the Father a solemn pledge of undivided love' and 'to our brothers and sisters a life poured out in loving service of (the) kingdom'.[27]

In the Eucharist we celebrate the power of the transforming love of God in our lives, in the Church and in the world. Through Christ's sacrifice, through the living sacrifice of the Eucharist, we are reconciled to God the Father in the Holy Spirit. The same Holy Spirit, given in baptism and cconfirmation, transforms ordinary bread and wine into the body and blood of Christ, and makes those who participate in the Eucharist one body and one spirit.[28] To the newly baptized who were to receive communion for the first time, St. Augustine said:

> If you are the members of the body of Christ, your sacrament is placed on the table of the Lord. It is your sacrament that you receive. To that which you respond, 'Amen' ('yes, it is true!') and by responding to it you assent to it. For you hear the words, 'the Body of Christ' and respond 'Amen'. Be then a member of the Body of Christ that your Amen may be true.[29]

St. Augustine insists on the communal dimension of the Eucharist. Christ is always 'we'. The Eucharist is not only Christ's mystery. *It is also our mystery*. The Eucharist tells us most clearly about who we are, as God's holy people, and how we are to live. It is the celebration of Jesus's total gift of himself to us, even unto death, something which moves us to praise God for his goodness and imitate Jesus in our lives. When Jesus says, 'Do this in memory of me', he is not just suggesting that we perform a ritual. He is reminding us that just as his body was broken and his blood was spilled, so we, like the fragile disciples who followed him, are invited to be broken and given to others in love.[30] We celebrate the Eucharist as a community and this is an invitation to live in ecclesial communion. It does not make sense to receive the Eucharist exclusively focused on the Lord without recognizing the bond between Christ and his body the Church.

Christ's transforming of bread into his body and wine into his blood is the beginning of a series of transformations leading up to that point when 'God will be all in all' (cf. 1 Cor. 15:28) in our lives and in the world.[31] An analogy between food for our bodies and spiritual food helps us to understand the personal transformation that takes place. Like food for the body, the Eucharist sustains us, and builds us up. There is, however, one big difference:

> When we eat a meal ... the food we consume is digested and assimilated into our bodies to nourish and strengthen us. It is not we who are changed according to the food, but the food that is changed according to us. Spiritual food is different. When we eat the body and drink the blood of Christ, it is not Christ who is changed according to us, but we are changed according to Christ.[32]

This is the nature of spiritual food. St. Thomas echoes St. Augustine who once heard the Lord say to him: 'You will not change me into yourself as you would do with food of your flesh, but you will be changed into me.'[33]

This earthy comparison brings out an important aspect of the Eucharistic celebration; the sacrament of the Eucharist transforms us. We are challenged to take on Christ's way of being and acting.[34] This eucharistic transformation gathers momentum and flows into our everyday lives to bring life and healing and reconciliation to the world around us. This transformation is, according to Benedict XVI, like inducing nuclear fission in the very heart of being – the victory of love over hatred, the victory of life over death:

'Only this intimate explosion of good conquering evil can then trigger off the series of transformations that little by little will change the world ... This first fundamental transformation of violence into love, of death into life, brings other changes in its wake. Bread and wine become his body and blood. But it must not stop there; on the contrary, the process of transformation must now gather momentum. The body and blood of Christ are given to us so that we ourselves will be transformed in our turn. We are to become the body of Christ, his own flesh and blood.[35]

## Sacraments of reconciliation and healing

The sacraments of penance and the anointing of the sick also foster transformation and growth in holiness. Through penance or reconciliation, God forgives sin, which by its nature, breaks off our communion with God, with one another, and with ourselves. The consequences of sin, both personal and social, shatter relationships and bring about personal confusion and blindness. When we bring this woundedness to God through sacramental reconciliation, we open ourselves up to forgiveness and the healing of relationships. The sacrament is a way of acknowledging the holiness of God in the sense that we acknowledge honestly who God is and who we are. It is a celebration of God's merciful love.[36] 'Mercy works, protecting, enduring, vivifying, and healing, and it is all of the tenderness of love, and grace works with mercy', writes the fourteenth-century English mystic Julian of Norwich. 'And this is from the abundance of love, for grace transforms our dreadful failing into plentiful and endless solace: and grace transforms our shameful falling into high and honourable rising; and grace transforms our sorrowful dying into holy, blessed life.'[37]

In recent years, many Catholics have questioned the importance of this sacrament, and in some parts of the world, its celebration is infrequent. A superficial and formalistic approach to the sacrament in the past led some people to be disillusioned with it. In some parts of the world, a shortage of ministers of the sacrament has led to the decline in its celebration.

Some would suggest that Catholics have, in the past, focused too much on sin and guilt, while others are all too aware of their imperfections, weaknesses and sin, and sometimes lack the courage to face them head-on. Perhaps we are afraid of the human element involved in sacramental reconciliation. And yet, for each of us, when we take time to reflect upon our lives, we discover that there are things that weigh on us – relationships gone wrong, injustices to others, areas where we experience fragmentation and need reconciliation and healing. The communal dimension of reconciliation through individual confession to a minister of the Church is a liberating way to grow in holiness. Sin and reconciliation have a social dimension. The act of seeking reconciliation in this way helps us to realize how our personal and social sin wound others.

Many of the saints known for their close union with God tell of their growing awareness of the gap between God's holiness and their very real human shortcomings. It seems that the more God's love and holiness penetrates our lives, the more we are aware of our sin and imperfection. This awareness, not to be confused with an oppressive heaviness or psychological pathology, comes as an invitation to authentic freedom and unconditional abandonment into the hands of God. John of the Cross uses the image of the sun shining on a smudgy window to explain the result of divine light on those who are seeking God.[38] When a window is exposed to direct sunlight, every speck of dust is visible. So it is for us as the love of God scrutinizes our lives. Those who experience this divine light want the window cleaned to reflect the splendour of God. Using another image, John of the Cross says that at times our lack of freedom makes us seem like a bird that cannot fly because its leg is tied by a thread. 'It makes little difference whether a bird is tied by a thin thread or by a cord. For even if it is tied by thread, the bird will be prevented from taking off just as surely as if it were tied by cord – that is, it will be impeded from flight as long as it does not break the thread.'[39] Here the cord symbolizes deliberate sin and the thin thread is some distorted attachment.

The sacrament of reconciliation is a means of being set free from what holds us back from God and from loving relationships with others. The *New Rite of Penance* offers creative ways of celebrating the sacrament. For example, both the rite for reconciliation of individual penitents and the rite of reconciliation for several penitents aim to place individual confession and absolution in the context of the celebration of the word of God.[40] Focusing on the word of God reminds us of God's personal love and mercy while setting before us the challenges of Christian discipleship. The *New Rite* also stresses the communal dimension of the sacrament. Sin affects other members of the community and through the sacrament, we acknowledge that as members of the Church we need ongoing healing from sin. We who are members of the Church are in need of cleansing from our moral flaws and imperfect practice of holiness in order to become who we are, a holy dwelling for our God.

During the period before the Second Vatican Council, sin was regarded very much as a personal matter between God and oneself, except in situations where the social dimension was obvious, as with stealing or calumny. In the 1920s, the Spanish Carmelite B. M. Xiberta emphasized that the sacrament involved both reconciliation with God and with the Church. This theologically mature idea was widely accepted by Karl Rahner and other theologians. This theologically mature idea eventually entered into the teaching of the Second Vatican Council and subsequent liturgical documents.[41]

One helpful approach to the sacrament as a path for growth in holiness is suggested by Carlo Maria Cardinal Martini in *Ministers of the Gospel*.[42] Acknowledging that some people are disappointed with a quick celebration of the sacrament, he suggests that we consider taking more time to celebrate it with greater depth and meaning. The first step is to begin with a 'confession of praise' (*confessio laudis*). Quite simply, this focuses on the most profound meaning of 'confession', namely the praise of God for his holiness and mercy: one could ask, 'Since my last celebration of the sacrament, what do I want to thank God for?' The second step, a 'confession of life' (*confessio vitae*), is an invitation to query: 'What weighs on me since my last confession? Where do I experience the burden of sin and fragmentation in my life?' Here one simply confesses one's sin to a priest, expressing sorrow and accepting absolution and penance. The last step, a confession of faith (*confessio fidei*), is a final act of faith, of trust in the merciful and forgiving God. Seeing this sacrament in the context of holiness as God's building project is a reminder of the regular maintenance needed to maintain a beautiful dwelling. The joyful celebration of this sacrament is one of the ways that God transforms the 'feeblest ... of us into ... a dazzling, radiant, immortal creature, pulsating all through with such energy and joy and wisdom and love as we cannot now imagine, a bright stainless mirror which reflects back to God perfectly (though, of course, on a smaller scale) His own boundless power and delight and goodness'.[43]

Anointing of the sick, the second sacrament of healing, comes to our aid when our dwelling is damaged and in need of repair. Throughout the centuries this sacrament has swung between being understood as an anointing of the sick, and extreme unction, the anointing of the dying. The Scriptural foundations for praying for the sick and anointing them with oil are Jesus's ministry of healing, exemplified in Mark 6:13 and Mark 16:17-18, and also, the practice of the early Church, specifically explicated in James 5:14–15: 'Are any among you sick? They should call for the elders of the Church and have them pray over them, anointing them in the name of the Lord. The prayer of faith will save the sick, will raise them up; and anyone who has committed sins will be forgiven.'

From the fifth to the eighth centuries, the bishop (or in some cases the priest) blessed the oil, but the actual anointing was done by a priest, or a family member. At times, even the sick person did the anointing. In the eighth century, a decisive shift took place, where the administration of the sacrament was reserved for priests alone and where it was understood as complementary to the sacrament of penance. As the centuries passed, the sacrament was given mainly to those who were dying. By the twelfth and thirteenth centuries, when its sacramental nature was explicitly developed, the name was changed officially to extreme unction. It is noteworthy that some of the bishops and theologians at the Council of Trent (1545–63) tried to ban the term because it seemed to be new and without support in the tradition. In the final document, both terms – *extrema unctio* and *sacra infirmorum unctio* – were used at Trent.[44] The sacrament was seen primarily as a means for healing the spiritual wounds of sin in preparation for death. The practice, until the Second Vatican Council, was to celebrate the sacrament, if possible, immediately before death.

In the Constitution on the Liturgy, *Sacrosanctum concilium*, the Second Vatican Council devotes three paragraphs to the sacrament (*SC* 73–75), where it states that the more fitting name is 'Anointing of the Sick', and that the sacrament is not only for those for whom death is imminent, but for all who suffer from infirmity, old age or disease. This conciliar teaching was put into practice with the *Pastoral Care of the Sick; Rites of Anointing and Viaticum*. Whether celebrated with the sick or the dying, the sacrament strengthens one with a particular grace of the Holy Spirit to overcome the difficulties associated with old age and/or illness. In the *New Rite*, there is an acknowledgement that the prayer may lead to a cure, but as Christopher O'Donnell notes, 'in a person properly disposed it always leads to healing, that is the sick, whatever their state are brought into the fullness of life (cf. Jn 10:10) which will be spiritual and almost always also psychological (cf. GI [General Instruction] 6).'[45] This spiritual healing also includes the forgiveness of sins. Since holiness is, as we have seen, about union with Christ, it is significant that the *Catechism of the Catholic Church* notes that the second effect of the sacrament is that the sick are consecrated to bear fruit by letting themselves be configured to the suffering of Christ and by associating their sufferings with his redemptive passion.[46] The sick person is encouraged through the grace of the sacrament to contribute 'to the sanctification of the Church and to the good of all'.[47] Sickness can lead either to a preoccupation with self or to a mature assessment of what is really important and a search for or a return to God.[48] Anointing of the sick can help those who are sick to be united more closely with Christ, as they experience the realities of paschal living. Sickness can become, through the grace of the sacrament, a path of holiness.

This sacrament also changes the relationship between the sick person and the Church. Recognizing the healing power of the sacrament in no way negates the redemptive value of suffering. 'The vision of the opening pages of the *Ordo* stands in prophetic judgement on the human impulse to negate the social value of the weak and suffering.' Mary Collins continues, 'People with seriously impaired physical or mental health, the elderly, and sick children are seen here to hold a key to the mystery of life.'[49] Sickness is not to be seen as merely a physical evil. According to John Paul II, 'it is at once also a time of moral and spiritual testing. The sick person has a great need for interior strength to come victorious from this trial. Through the sacramental anointing Christ shows the sick his love and gives them the necessary interior strength.'[50]

The sacrament is also a way for the Church to show care for the sick and to help them witness to God's grace in suffering. Finally, the sacrament may also prepare those on the point of death for their transition into eternal life, with *viaticum* (the final Eucharist for the dying person) as the proper sacrament for the dying. The sacraments of initiation mark the beginning of our pilgrimage of faith while the anointing of the sick and the Eucharist as *viaticum* are the sacraments that accompany the believer at 'the end of Christian life'. For the dying, they are 'the sacraments that prepare for the heavenly homeland' or the sacraments that complete the earthly pilgrimage.[51]

## Vocational sacraments

Two particular vocations in the Church are marked by sacraments: holy orders and the sacrament of matrimony. This does not deny that other vocations are paths to holiness, but in this section, these two will be discussed because they are included among the seven sacraments. It is significant that the *Catechism of the Catholic Church* lists matrimony along with holy orders as sacraments at the service of communion. They are directed towards the salvation of others.[52]

Holy orders includes not one, but three separate ordinations: to the diaconate, to the presbyterate and to the episcopate. This is why *orders* is in the plural. It is *holy* orders about which we speak. This is one of three sacraments (baptism and confirmation are the others) with an indelible character, meaning not only that the sacrament cannot be repeated or be conferred temporarily, but also that in this case there is 'a permanent configuration of the recipient to Christ by a special grace of the Holy Spirit'.[53] Christ himself, present and at work in the one ordained, guarantees an objective sacramental holiness that is independent of one's personal holiness. This dimension of the sacramentality of orders is a reminder that the work of sanctifying begins with God, the Father through Jesus Christ in the Holy Spirit. This is an important message for today, especially in view of scandals in the Church. Centuries ago, St. Augustine said that, at the end of the day, it does not matter whether you have been baptized by John or Judas, as long as you have been baptized in Christ: 'That you have been baptized by a drunk or an assassin or an adulterer, if you are focused on Baptism in Christ it is always Christ who has baptized. I am not afraid of the adulterer, drunk or assassin because I look at the dove (the Catholic Church) who says to me: It is he who baptizes.'[54]

The ordained's personal vocation to holiness can be understood in the context of the sacrament itself, which involves a new consecration to God in ordination.[55] Seeking holiness of life is an even greater responsibility for him because of his call to lead others on this path.[56] The primary way that the ordained grow in holiness is through celebrating the sacraments and exercising their ministry of service to others. By frequently using the liturgical books as a source of personal prayer, they can reflect more deeply on the eucharistic prayers or the General Instructions so that the liturgy comes alive for them personally, and later for others. In every dimension of ministry and life, the ordained are invited, as the Rite of Ordination reminds them when they receive the offertory gifts from the faithful, 'to live the mystery that has been placed in your hands'.[57]

Like holy orders, matrimony is a vocational sacrament. In acknowledging that matrimony is a sacrament, the Church recognizes that this ordinary human institution, shared by most cultures, becomes sacred and holy, through the consecration that takes place. The marital relationship, in all of its dimensions, is blessed by God. Married Christians share in the fruitful love which exists between Christ and the Church. Through their lives together, the spouses help one another grow in holiness.

The sacraments are best understood in a dynamic way. As we stretch our understanding of them to include the idea of sacred activity or progress, we see that the grace of the sacrament of matrimony is at work not only during the celebration of the sacrament, when the two spouses, as ministers of the sacrament, before God and in the presence of a minister of the Church, confer this sacrament on each other, but also in daily life where the matrimonial partners become 'sacraments' (i.e. visible signs of God's grace), to one another.[58] During the rite, the couple pledge their life-long commitment to love and fidelity 'for better, for worse, for richer, for poorer, in sickness and in health, until death'. The gift of God's fidelity and love to the couple made present through the sacrament will help the spouses become instruments of holiness and salvation to one another as their life together unfolds. In *A Daring Promise: A Spirit-uality of Christian Matrimony*, Richard R. Gaillardetz describes the dynamics of the sacrament at work in ordinary life in terms of salvation:

> Put simply, while salvation is always God's work in us and there-fore a free gift, it often *feels* like our work as we struggle to remain open to God's saving action. In any event, I have become con-vinced that my 'salvation,' the spiritual transformation that God wishes to effect in me, transpires within the crucible of my rela-tionship with my wife and children.[59]

Each of the seven sacraments is a means for growth in holiness. Through the ordinary means of word, touch, anointing, and feeding, we are being transformed and sustained in an edifice. All the sacraments involve some sort of consecration or renewal of consecration. To consecrate lit-erally means to set aside or displace something from ordinary use.[60] Through baptism and the other sacraments, we are set aside for God. We have become God's dwelling, and our lives are not our own anymore. Whenever a sacrament is celebrated it is a reminder that we, as mem-bers of the Church, belong to God and to one another.

## Prayer and the word of God

Another essential way of growing in holiness and maintaining the extraordinary dwelling that we are in Christ is by a life of prayer and reflection on the word of God. One of the best descriptions of prayer and its practical implications for holiness comes from St Teresa of Avila. Whether prayer is vocal, meditative or contemplative, it places us before the Holy One. Insisting that prayer is about communication, Teresa explains that 'contemplative prayer (*oración mental*) is ... nothing else than a close sharing between friends; it means taking time frequently to be alone with him who we know loves us'.[61] As Teresa searches for words to describe the intimacy between the person praying and God, she settles on the image of a close friendship. As this close friendship unfolds through frequent, mutual communication and shared silence, we become aware that we are in the presence of the one who loves us.

For Teresa, the point of prayer goes beyond personal consolation to bring us more fully into conformity with the nature of God and his purposes. Furthermore, it is meant to bear fruit in loving relationships in our everyday life. She explains this by using the metaphor of watering a garden. The person praying is like a helper in the garden that God owns is God. Our role is simply to take care of the plants and flowers in the garden by watering them so that they will thrive. She explains the four ways to water a garden, moving from the laborious first stage of watering the garden by manually, drawing water with a bucket from a well, to the final stage when God's abundant rain waters the garden for us.[62] It is important for us to note that the garden belongs to the Lord who chooses the plot and invites us to join him in this enterprise. 'You did not choose me, it was I who chose you to go forth and bear fruit,' Jesus said in the Gospel of John (Jn 15:16). This being stated, we must acknowledge that the initiative in prayer belongs to God.

Secondly, the water is for the plants. The water is prayer, often experienced as consolation, and the good plants are the virtues.[63] Prayer helps us to grow in virtue. Prayer transforms our lives and the garden begins to produce vibrant and thriving plants and flowers (the virtues) that give glory to God. Some of the virtues that Teresa stresses are faith, hope, love, humility, self-forgetfulness, sensitivity to the needs of others and zeal for God.[64] Prayer moves us beyond ourselves into service of others.

Personal prayer is nurtured by communal prayer and vice versa. Communal prayer can take many forms, including the Liturgy of the

Hours, rosary, Taizé prayer around a cross, and centering-prayer groups. Whether a monastic community chanting the full liturgy of the hours, lay people gathered together (like the *Sant'Egidio* community in Rome) for vespers and for serving the poor, or families praying around the dinner table, some sort of communal prayer is important. With the challenges of family life, it is important that married couples and their children make an intentional effort to find creative ways of sharing prayer. One option is to mark the different seasons of the liturgical year by establishing family traditions of communal prayer.[65]

All of us are invited to a life of surrender to God in prayer, for prayer is communion with and recognition of God's presence and activity in all of life. The Orthodox Theologian, Paul Evdokimov once wrote, 'It is not enough to *say* prayers, one must become, *be* prayer, prayer incarnate'.[66] Prayer is to become an expression of who we are and how we relate to others. To merely 'say prayers' is inadequate, just as we do not simply 'say words' to friends. Prayer is a way of joining our hearts and lives to our self-revealing, personal, Triune God. Prayer makes us increasingly aware of the Lord's presence in our lives and among the stuff of our living. Prayer keeps us sensitive to his presence in church, in nature, in friendship, and even, as St Teresa of Avila recognized, 'among the pots and pans'.[67]

In prayer God is calling us to respond to his pervasive presence. Meister Eckhart, a fourteenth-century German mystic, was very much aware of this responsibility of responding to God moment by moment, and wrote that such attentive responsiveness in all of life was wise. 'Wisdom', he wrote, 'consists in doing the next thing.'[68] The practical dimension of this dictum emerges especially when faced with sickness. In an interview given just before he died of cancer, the Jesuit Joseph Whelan wrote:

> There's a new inability with sickness, an inability to think. I can't think anymore ... I have been very much helped by something from Meister Eckhart ... It's where Eckhart says, 'Do the next thing.' When you think about your life and look at the next week coming up or the next month, you say, 'I just don't see how I can get through all that.' But can you do the 'next thing'? If the next thing were to listen to me for 20 minutes, could you do that? Ordinarily you'd be able to say, 'Yeah, I can do that.' So I find that the prayer I most frequently say is: 'With your help, dear Lord,

Jesus, I can do the next thing.' Then I try to see what the next thing is, and I try to do it, because I often can just get no further than that.[69]

Familiarity with the word of God complements prayer as a means for growth in holiness. One way of helping individuals and parish communities to become more attuned to the word of God and to apply it to their lives is a method of praying with scripture called *lectio divina*. Briefly, *lectio divina*, a continual reading of the Bible, involves four steps. The four steps, reading (*lectio*), meditation (*meditatio*), prayer (*oratio*) and contemplation (*contemplatio*), are a simple way of allowing the word of God to take effect in one's life. *Reading* the text carefully in its historical, geographical, and cultural setting and in the context of the Church's living tradition is the first step. This also involves reading the text several times while paying attention to verb forms, key words, and the feelings expressed. The next step, *meditation,* poses the question, 'what is this text saying to me today?' The word falls on rocky ground (Mt. 13: 20) unless it is allowed to take root by penetrating a person existentially. *Prayer* is a response to the text which may include a petition, praise, thanksgiving, or reconciliation. Above all, it is prayer that emerges out of the prayerful meditation on Scripture. *Contemplation* involves silently allowing the word to be formed in one's heart. Contemplation in the strict sense is a gift, but in the context of *lectio divina*, it means surrendering to God by waiting in silence and adoration. Some add another step to the traditional monastic teaching, namely *actio*. The challenge here is to take clear steps to make the word come alive in one's daily life, be it in the workplace, at home, at school, or on public transport.[70]

John Chrysostom (344–407 CE) and Gregory the Great (540–604 CE) were insistent that familiarity with the word of God was particularly important for Christians in the midst of their daily activities. Chrysostom's reply to a sceptical lay person is telling: 'You say, "I am not a monk" ... But in this you have made a mistake, because you believe that Scripture concerns only monks, while it is even more necessary for you faithful who are in the midst of the world.'[71] Gregory makes a similar point in a letter (c. 595) to the physician of the emperor who was too busy to read sacred Scripture everyday. Adding an interesting twist, Gregory says:

What is Sacred Scripture if not a letter from Almighty God to his creatures? If ... [you] lived somewhere else and received mail from an earthly monarch ... [you] would have no peace ... [you] would have no rest ... [you] would not shut your eyes until ... [you] had learned the contents of that letter. The king of heaven, the Lord of men and angels has written that you might live, and yet, illustrious son, you neglect to read it with ardent love. Strive therefore, I beg you, to meditate each day on the words of your Creator. Learn to know the heart of God in the words of God ... May the Spirit fill your soul with his presence, and in filling it make it ... free.[72]

## Almsgiving and fasting

Maintaining God's holy dwelling also involves a genuine concern and care for the poor. It is not enough to pray and listen to the word of God; this needs to be accompanied by actions consistent with the message heard. The early Christians considered almsgiving, along with prayer and fasting, an essential element of the call to holiness. Perhaps today, almsgiving is best understood in terms of stewardship and charitable giving, justice and a preferential option for alleviating poverty. It is significant that in the Hebrew Scriptures, the same word is used for both 'alms' and 'justice', inferring that they are intimately intertwined, for almsgiving restores God's just order to society. The Israelites gave a tenth of their produce away (Deut. 14:28–29) when they harvested their fields, they also allowed the poor to collect the gleanings (Lev.19:9–10, 23:22).[73] The Hebrew prophets insisted that holiness relates to justice. The care of the most vulnerable of society – orphans, widows and strangers – indicated how Israel was responding to God's covenant love. This call for justice carries over into Jesus's teaching with even more insistence. 'In the Christian scriptures', writes Ronald Rolheiser, 'one out of every ten lines deals directly with the physically poor and the call from God for us to respond to them. In the Gospel of Luke, that becomes every sixth line, and in the epistle of James, that commission is there, in one form or another, every fifth line.'[74]

Closely related to almsgiving is fasting. Fasting is really fasting *only* when alms are given to the poor, according to St. John Christostom.[75] The *Shepherd of Hermas*, an even earlier writer, is more specific: 'In the day on which you fast you will taste nothing but bread and water; and having reckoned up the price of the dishes of that day, which you intended to have eaten, you will give it to a widow, or to an orphan, or to a person in want, so that the one who has received benefit from your humility may fill his own soul.'[76] Fasting is more than showing solidarity with the poor, it is a way of recognizing that our lives and resources belong to Another.

Prayer (rooted in the word of God), fasting and almsgiving are meant to be held together, in a delicate balance. These are some of the ordinary ways that God invites us to maintain the extraordinary dwelling that we are in Christ. Recognizing that the 'tasks' themselves are gifts from God evokes in us a sense of gratitude. Without gratitude, our prayer, fasting and almsgiving are hollow.

## Sacramentals and popular piety

God's building project is also maintained by sacramentals and popular piety.[77] They remind us that growth in holiness is in no way limited to the seven sacraments; there are other prayers, actions and objects that put us in touch with God's grace in Jesus Christ. A sacramental usually includes a prayer, sometimes accompanied by sprinkling with holy water, making the sign of the cross, or the laying on of hands.[78] They include blessings (of persons, meals, objects and places), consecrations of persons or places to God, such as blessings of an abbot or abbess, the consecration of virgins and widows, the rites of religious profession and the blessing of certain ministries in a church. Other forms of piety and devotion also surround the lives of the saints. More popular ones today include pilgrimages, the stations of the cross, and the rosary. Underlying these sacramentals and devotions is the notion that Christ is the primary sacrament of our encounter with God and there are a variety of ways through which we can come into contact with God.[79] The sheer variety of popular devotions rooted in diverse cultural realities is a reminder that almost any material thing that is properly used can be directed to our sanctification and the praise of God.[80]

## Embracing the virtues

Just as a house does not become a home without effort, so also holiness does not just happen. Saints are incremental people – consciously attentive to little things and in the process becoming more open to God's transforming power in their lives. We have a great capacity for either virtue or vice. A 'marvellous mixture of well being and woe' is how Julian of Norwich puts it.[81] Responding to God's call to holy living is a daily choice. Consistently choosing virtue through repeated actions gradually leads to a transformation and allows us to become who we are meant to be, God's holy people, cleaving to and enjoying God.[82]

The theological virtues of faith, hope and love serve as a point-  counterpoint in the on-going relationship between the believer and God. These qualities are gifts given in baptism and our responsibility. We graciously receive them from a generous Lord to facilitate our growth in holiness and effective Christian living. God entrusts these virtues to us with the expectation that we use them creatively and wisely. They are tools, the metaphorical hammers and brooms that allow us to build and maintain the dwelling that we are. These gifts of faith, hope and love are given to us with the wish that we cultivate them as growing dispositions, making them our primary attitudes, and allow them to become our fundamental responses to life. From time to time the dust must be brushed off common religious rhetoric to reveal its simple, uncomplicated beauty. Faith, hope and love are rich, strong words that shine with meaning. Faith, referring to our belief in God and what has been revealed by God, enables us to see and do God's will. With hope, firmly rooted in the paschal mystery (Rom. 5:6–11), we yearn for the kingdom of God, and rely on the Holy Spirit to reach our goal. Charity, God's love poured into our hearts through the Holy Spirit, leads us to love God and our neighbour as ourselves.

The cardinal virtues (or 'hinges', from the Latin *cardo*) are prudence, justice, fortitude and temperance. They are about self-mastery or self-possession. They orient us towards God and others in a life of self giving love. As we are conformed to Christ, to his dying and rising, the cardinal virtues translate the implications of that paschal living into our daily experience. Prudence enables us to judge rightly what to do in specific circumstances. Justice evokes in us not only a profound respect for the rights of other people, society and individuals, but also insures that we act appropriately. Especially today, the implications of social justice for Christian spirituality needs to be emphasized. A story that is well-known in social-justice circles illustrates this point:

Once upon a time there was a town that was built just beyond the bend of a large river. One day some of the children from the town were playing beside the river when they noticed three bodies floating in the water. They ran for help and the townsfolk quickly pulled the bodies out of the water.

One body was dead so they buried it. One was alive, but quite ill, so they put that person into a hospital. The third turned out to be a healthy child, whom they then placed with a family who cared for it and who took it to school.

From that day on, every day a number of bodies came floating down the river, and every day, the good people of the town would pull them out and tend to them – taking the sick to hospitals, placing the children with families, and burying those who were dead.

This went on for years; each day brought its quota of bodies, and the townsfolk not only came to expect a number of bodies each day but also worked at developing elaborate systems for picking them out of the river and tending to them. Some of the townsfolk became quite generous in tending to these bodies and a few extraordinary ones even gave up their jobs so that they could tend to this concern full-time. And the town itself felt a certain pride in its generosity.

However, during all these years and despite all that generosity and effort, nobody thought to go up the river, beyond the bend that hid from their sight what was above them, and find out why, daily, those bodies came flowing down the river.[83]

When we exercise the virtue of justice, we are led up the river to figure out why there are homeless, wounded and dead bodies. Holiness without the exercise of justice is incomplete; holiness coupled with the virtue of justice can change the world. We may not be Mother Teresa, Oscar Romero or Dorothy Day, but in our own way, we can make a difference: for example, by advocating healthy markets in impoverished neighbourhoods and decaying urban areas, being involved in local politics, participating in literacy initiatives, coordinating visitors to check shut-ins, 'adopting' a highway and cleaning up the litter while pushing for environmental causes, or writing politicians thoughtful letters. Exercising justice also means being alert to buying goods from developing countries, noting carefully the ethical standards of multi-national companies and investing in stocks only in those companies that support justice and equality.

Reflecting on the relationship between holiness and justice may lead us also to choose a simpler lifestyle. The point is that holiness manifests itself in deeds and not only in prayer and piety. Our response to God's call to holiness influences our approach to work, the way we respond to our political responsibilities, our economic ideology, and our care for the environment.

Two more virtues, fortitude and temperance, also foster holy living. Fortitude, also a confirmation gift (like the other cardinal virtues), is according to St. Thomas Aquinas given in two forms. First of all, it empowers us to exercise courage in the face of difficulties, to face adversity without despondency, and to be resolute in confronting immediate danger. Above all, fortitude protects us from fear, especially the fear of danger and death. Fear paralyzes us, while fortitude enables us to act with firmness and strength in times of adversity.[84] The other understanding of fortitude, which St. Thomas considers higher, is the strength and courage needed for long-term problems, continuing illness, and difficult life situations, for example caring for elderly relatives. These never ending challenges require courage of a very high order. Linked with fortitude is temperance which encourages us to use creative goods moderately. It also assists us in channelling our emotions to virtuous living and in making good decisions when faced with the attraction of pleasure. Our call to holiness means a commitment to 'live sober, upright and godly lives in this world'.[85] The metaphorical hammers and brooms that the virtues are have the capacity of making a mediocre house into an extraordinary dwelling where Christ is pleased to dwell.

## Physical and psychological stewardship of bodies and minds

A dwelling, be it cottage or castle, requires constant attention. If neglected or abandoned, slowly, yet perceptibly, it begins to fall apart. Just as this is the case for our physical homes, so it is with the dwelling which we are in God. Those of us who live in the developed world sometimes spend much energy, time and money chasing after improved physical health and psychological well-being. These efforts lead to a level of increased physical wellness and indeed an enhanced psychological vitality.[86] Such improvements occurring on the basic human plane do have positive ramifications in our pursuit of holiness, since we believe that grace builds on nature. The psychosomatic unity of the person, the body–spirit connection, effects how we perceive ourselves, God, others and the world. One might even go as far as saying that to be holy, one must first 'be' – that is, a perquisite to self-transcendence requires a self and that self-transcendence goes beyond the narrow confines of self-actualization or self-fulfillment.[87]

We are better aware today of what makes us function psychologically.[88] We know something about complexes, defence mechanisms, and repression of emotions and the effect they can have on various dimensions of our health – physical, psychological and spiritual. This knowledge can be incorporated into our discernment as we seek to open ourselves up to

God's gift of grace, in commitment to truth, justice and holiness of life. In recent years, many practitioners of Ignatian spirituality have introduced a revealing change in translating the Spanish *esamen de consciencia* as 'consciousness examen' instead of 'examenation of conscience'.[89] Discernment begins with consciousness, awareness of who we are and of our concrete reality. Not only do we need to be able to identify and assume responsibility for the ways in which we fail to act in accordance with our conscience, *we also benefit much by developing our consciousness – by coming to an awareness of what is really going on within us*. A greater self-awareness can be of much help in our attempt to correct faults, thanks to our becoming more skilled at identifying emotional factors and hidden motives. Psychological growth and a balanced awareness of self can work with grace and assist us to grow in holiness. In the end though, it is not in itself holiness.

This has gone along, sometimes in a somewhat subjective, in a 'me-first' society with a growing concern for self – *self*-improvement, *self*-fulfillment, *self*-recognition. Concomitant with the positive value of greater self-awareness has been the tendency, at times, to become self-absorbed. This tendency seems to clash with a Christian understanding of holiness, especially when considering the Gospel call to *deny* self. For this reason, we are at times reluctant to focus today on the cross, self-denial, and sacrifice. In this context, it is important to realize that true self-fulfilment is, paradoxically, the fruit of genuine self-denial, but this self-denial is always in view of some higher good, principally love. Self-denial, which is motivated by anything less than love for a good of some kind – for truth, for love of God or of others – is not a Christian value. It is not possible to grow in holiness or to achieve Christian virtue without self-denial. Nor indeed is it really possible to achieve true human happiness without it. One way of putting it is to see it as a matter of going beyond self, or self-transcendence, which means leaving behind immature stages to open oneself to higher levels of growth in an ever-expanding commitment to truth and justice.

While recognizing the legitimate connection between health and holiness,[90] we must be careful not to exclude God's gift of holiness at work in those who are physically or psychologically weak. 'We know that we hold a treasure in earthen vessels', writes St. Paul, 'so that we know that the extraordinary potential comes from God and not from us' (2 Cor. 4:7). Many of the saints have had psychological pathologies, and still God's gift of holiness was evident in their lives.[91] This reality is particularly important today, when we may at times place a tremendous burden on ourselves and others, when for one reason or another we experience limits, woundedness and vulnerability, by implying that one has only succeeded if one has overcome illness, whether physical or psychological. 'The tradition', says the philosopher Gillian Rose who died in 1995, 'is far kinder in its understanding of the human predicament that to live, to love, is to be failed, to forgive, to have failed, to be forgiven for ever and ever.' She further points out that 'A crisis of illness, bereavement, separation, natural disaster, could be the opportunity to make contact with deeper levels of the terrors of the soul ... To grow in     love-ability is to accept the boundaries of oneself and others, while remaining vulnerable [and] woundable.'[92] The view of holiness I am proposing allows us to realize and accept our vulnerability and so helps us to grow 'in love -ability'. This really is *love's work*, and in the Christian tradition, we would say that it is *love's redeeming work*, in us.

## Conclusion

Attentiveness to sacramental living, prayer, the Word of God, the virtues and gifts of the Spirit are the tools God has given us to foster holy living. A wise person once said that it is quite easy to drift away from God simply by not paying attention. To grow in holiness calls for constant, continual attentiveness, allowing the yearning that we have for God to permeate all that we are and all that we do. At times, we may share Thomas Merton's question, 'How do you expect me to become a saint?' And we need to hear his friend, Lax's response, "By wanting to ... All that is necessary to be a saint is to want to be one. Don't you believe God will make you what He created you to be, if you will consent to let Him do it? All you have to do is desire it".[93] We show signs of our desire and consent by the way we wisely use the gifts God has given, the ordinary means God provides to maintain an extraordinary dwelling.

## Notes

1. Thomas Merton, *The Seven Storey Mountain* (Orlando, Florida: Harvest/ HBJ, 1948, reprinted in 1976), pp.237–38. I am grateful to Mary Popio for drawing my attention to this quotation, which I cite in full here:

   Lax was much wiser than I, and had clearer vision, and was in fact, corresponding much more truly to the grace of God than I, and he had seen what was the only important thing. I think he has told what he had to say to many people besides myself: but

certainly his was one of the voices through which the insistent
Spirit of God was determined to teach me the way I had to travel.

Therefore, another one of those ties that turned out to be historical, as far as my own soul is concerned, was when Lax and I were
walking down Sixth Avenue, one night in the spring. The street was
all torn up and trenched and banked high with dirt and marked
out with red lanterns where they were digging the subway, and we
picked our way along the fronts of the dark little stores, going down-
town to Greenwich Village. I forgot what we were arguing
about, but in the end Lax suddenly turned around and asked me the
question:

'What do you want to be, anyway?'

I could not say, 'I want to be Thomas Merton the well-known
writer of those book reviews in the back pages of the *Times Book
Review*' or 'Thomas Merton the assistant instructor of Freshman
English at the New Life Social Institute for Progress and Culture,'
so I put the thing on the spiritual plane, where I knew it belonged
and said:

'I don't know; I guess what I want is to be a good Catholic.'

'What do you mean, you want to be a good Catholic?'

The explanation I gave was lame enough, and expressed my confusion, and betrayed how little I had really thought about it at all.

Lax did not accept it.

'What you should say' – he told me – 'what you should say is that
you want to be a saint.'

A saint! The thought struck me as a little weird. I said: 'How do
you expect me to become a saint?'

'By wanting to,' said Lax, simply.

'I can't be a saint,' I said, 'I can't be a saint.' And my mind dark-
ened with a confusion of realities and unrealities: the knowledge of
my own sins, and the false humility which makes men say that they
cannot do the things that they *must* do, cannot reach the level that
they *must* reach: the cowardice that says: I am satisfied to save my
soul, to keep out of mortal sin, but which means, by those words: I
do not want to give up my sins and my attachments.

But Lax said: 'No. All that is necessary to be a saint is to want to
be one. Don't you believe that God will make you what he created
you to be, if you will consent to him to do it? All you have to do is
desire it.'

A long time ago, St. Thomas Aquinas had said the same thing and it is something that is obvious to everybody who ever understood the Gospels. After Lax was gone, I thought about it, and it became obvious to me.

The next day I told Mark Van Doren:

'Lax is going around saying that all a man needs to be a saint is to want to be one.'

'Of course,' said Mark.

All those people were much better Christians than I. They understood God better than I. What was I doing? Why was I so slow, so mixed up, still, so uncertain of my directions and so insecure?

2. Teresa of Avila, *The Interior Castle (The Collected Works of Teresa of Avila)*, vol. II (Washington: ICS Publications, 1980), Ch.1, 1, p.283.

3. See *The Constitution on the Sacred Liturgy, Sacrosanctum Concilium*, 59: 'The purpose of the sacraments is to make people holy, to build up the body of Christ and finally, to express a relationship of worship to God.' All references to the Second Vatican Council, unless otherwise indicated, are taken from Norman P. Tanner, *Decrees of the Ecumenical Councils* (London: Sheed and Ward Limited; Washington DC: Georgetown University Press, 1990), vol. II.

4. *Catechism of the Catholic Church* (Vatican City: Libreria Editrice Vaticana; Washington, DC: United States Catholic Conference, 2000, 2nd ed 1116. Further references are to this edition and are indicated by the abbreviation *CCC*.

5. *CCC*, 1129. Excellent insights into the significance of baptism and confirmation for ordinary Christians are offered by Richard N. Fragomeni, *Come to the Light* (New York: Continuum, 1999), see pp.23–25.

6. Carlo Rocchetta, 'I sacramenti, sorgenti di santità', in Emanno Ancilli, *Santità Cristiana: Dono di Dio e Impegno dell'Uomo* (Rome: Pontificio Istituto di Spiritualità Teresianum, 1980), p.270. Flowing from the paschal mystery, the sacraments are vehicles of holiness (*SC* 61).

7. *The Divine Office, The Liturgy of the Hours According to the Roman Rite* (London: Collins, 1974), vol. II, pp.297–98.

8. *CCC*, 1212.

9. See 1 Pet 2:5 and *CCC*, 1268.

10. The translation is taken from Aurelie Hagstrom and Irena Vaisvilaité, *A Pilgrim's Guide to Rome and the Holy Land for the Third Millennium* (Allen, Texas: Thomas More, 2000), p.238.

11. Catherine of Siena, *Dialogue of Divine Providence* (trans. Suzanne Noffke New York: Paulist Press, 1980), p.27. 'The soul is in God and God is in the soul, just as the fish is in the sea and the sea is in the fish.' In *The Life of Catherine of Siena*, her spiritual director Raymond of Capua describes how on 18 August 1370, after receiving communion, 'she felt herself drawn into God, and God into her soul, in the same way as a fish in the sea is in the water, and the water is in the fish.' The edition used here is translated by Conleth Kearns (Dublin: Dominican Publications, 1980), II, VI, p.192.

12. See Paul J. Philibert, *The Priesthood of the Faithful. Key to a Living Church* (Collegeville: Liturgical Press, 2005), p.22. He writes, '[If] you are a serious Christian, then you never completely "dry off" from your baptism, to use a wonderful phrase of Gerard Baumbach. The sacrament is a living reality, not merely an unrepeatable event in the past.'

13. Fragomeni, *Come to the Light*, p.29.

14. St. Augustine, *Tractus on the Gospel of John*, 21,8 as quoted in John Paul II, *Christifideles laici. The Vocation and Mission of the Laity in the Church and in the World* (Vatican City: Libreria editrice Vaticana, 1989), 17.

15. The significance of this chapter in its historical context is particularly interesting, though beyond the scope of this chapter. See, for example, Yves Congar, 'The People of God', in *Vatican II: An Interfaith Appraisal* (ed. John H. Miller: Notre Dame: University of Notre Dame Press, 1966), pp.197–249.

16. *LG*, 9 (quoting from 1 Pet. 2:9–10).

17. *Faith and Order Paper* 111 (Geneva: WCC, 1982), n.6. See Christopher O'Donnell, 'Baptism', in *Ecclesia, A Theological Encyclopedia of the Church* (Collegeville: The Liturgical Press, 1996), p.41.

18. See Yvers Congar, *Lay People in the Church* (London: Geoffrey Chapman, 1985), p.11. This ecclesial perspective also negates the notion sometimes expressed in the Middle Ages that there are two classes of Christians: those called to perfection and those who simply obey the commandments. The lay state is not simply a concession to human weakness: rather the laity with all others in the Church form part of 'a people made one by the unity of the Father, the Son, and the Holy Spirit' (*LG*, 4, quoting Cyprian, *The Lord's Prayer*, 23), and through baptism they are called to holiness.

19. See *LG*, 11.

20. See the final prayer for the rite of confirmation, in *The Rites of the Catholic Church*, (Study edition New York: Pueblo Publishing Company, 1983), p.333.

21. St. Catherine of Siena, *Epistolario*, Le Letter di Santa Caterina da Siena, edited by Piero Misciattelli, (Florence: Giunti, 1970), Lettera 335.

22. St. Thomas Aquinas, *Summa contra gentiles* 4:19–22. See Mary Ann Fatula, *The Holy Spirit. Unbounded Gift of Joy* (Collegeville: Liturgical Press, 1998).

23. According to John of St. Thomas, 'Although the forward progress of the ship may be the same, there is a vast difference in it being moved by the laborious rowing of the oarsmen and its being moved by sails filled with a strong breeze' as quoted by George Evans, 'Gifts of the Holy Spirit', *New Dictionary of Catholic Spirituality*, p.438. See also pp.193–231; Paul Wadell, *The Primacy of Love* (New York: Paulist Press, 1992), especially Chapter 8.

24. *CCC*, 1831.

25. *CCC*, 1830–2. See also Michel Ledrus, *I frutti dello Spirito. Saggi di 'Etica Evangelica'* (ed. Angelo Tulumello, Cinisello Balsamo: Edizioni S. Paolo, 1998).

26. Cf. the interview of John Allen with Francis Moloney, 'The Word from Rome', 21 October 2005 in www.nationalcatholicreporter.org/word/word/102105.htm, where this theme is mentioned in the context of a lecture Maloney gave at the Lay Centre at Foyer Unitas on the 'Eucharist as Memory and Sacrifice'.

27. On the theme of adoration of Christ in the Blessed Sacrament as deriving from the actual celebration of the Eucharist, see Jeremy Driscoll, *Theology at the Eucharistic Table* (Herefordshire: Gracewing, 2005), pp.237–44.

28. This is part of the alternative opening prayer for the Feast of the Body and Blood of Christ.

29 *CCC*, 1353.

30. St. Augustine, *Sermo* 272 (PL 38, 1247), as quoted in *CCC*, 1396.

31. Cf. the interview of John Allen with Francis Moloney, 'The Word from Rome'.

32. See 'Il dono dell'amore', in Benedict XVI, *La rivoluzione di Dio* (Cinisello Balsamo: Edizioni San Paolo, 2005), p.70. This is from the World Youth Day Homily at Marienfield, 21 August 21 2005.

33. Paul Wadell, 'The Role of Charity in the Moral Theology of Thomas

Aquinas', in *Aquinas and Empowerment: Classical Ethics for Ordinary Lives,* ed. G. Simon Harak; Washington: Georgetown University Press, 1997), p.162. See also St. Thomas Aquinas, *Summa Theologica,* III, 73, 3.

34. Aquinas, *ST* III, 73, 3, See Wadell, 'The Role of Charity', p.169.

35. Waddell, 'The Role of Charity', p.162.

36. See Benedict XVI, 'Il dono dell'amore', pp.70–1. This can also be found on the Vatican webpage (www.vatican.va) in different languages. 'This transformation is', according to Benedict XVI,

> 'like inducing nuclear fission in the very heart of being – the victory of love over hatred, the victory of love over death. Only this intimate explosion of good conquering evil can then trigger off the series of transformations that little by little will change the world ... This first fundamental transformation of violence into love, of death into life, brings other changes in its wake. Bread and wine become his Body and Blood. But it must not stop there; on the contrary, the process of transformation must now gather momentum. The Body and Blood of Christ are given to us so that we ourselves will be transformed in our turn. We are to become the Body of Christ, his own flesh and Blood.
>
> We all eat the one bread, and this means that we ourselves become one. In this way, adoration, as we said earlier, becomes union. God no longer simply stands before us as the One who is totally Other. He is within us, and we are in him. His dynamic enters into us and then seeks to spread outwards to others until it fills the world, so that his love can truly become the dominant measure of the world.'

37. *CCC*, 1456.

38. Julian of Norwich, *Showings* (trans. and ed. Edmund Colledge and James Walsh: New York: Paulist Press, 1978), *Long Text*, 48, p.262.

39. John of the Cross, *The Ascent of Mount Carmel* (*The Collected Works of John of the Cross*) (trans. Kieran Kavanaugh and Otilio Rodriguez: Bangalore: AVP Publications, 1981) II, 5, 6.

40. John of the Cross, *Ascent of Mount Carmel.* I, 11, 4.

41. The third rite, to be used only for emergency situations, involves general absolution.

42. See *Lumen gentium*, 11 and the *General Instruction on the Rite of Penance*, n.5, 'Reconciliation with God and with the Church'.

43. Carlo M. Martini, *Ministers of the Gospel. Meditations on St. Luke's*

*Gospel* (Middlegreen: St. Paul's Publications, 1983) pp.48–52. This book is based on a recording of a retreat and was not revised by the author.

44. Clive Staples Lewis, *Mere Christianity* (revised. and amplified edition San Francisco: HarperSanFrancisco, 2001), p.205–6. This was first published in 1952.

45. H. Denzinger, 907–8, as quoted in Philippe Rouillard, 'The Anointing of the Sick in the West', in Anscar Chupungco, *Handbook for Liturgical Studies, Sacraments and Sacramentals* (Collegeville: Liturgical Press, 2000), vol. IV, p.176. This section follows closely the historical analysis in this article.

46. O'Donnell, 'Anointing of the Sick', in *Ecclesia*, p.14.

47. *CCC*, 1521.

48. *CCC*, 1522.

49. *CCC*, 1500–1501. See Michael Joncas, *The Catechism of the Catholic Church on Liturgy and Sacraments* (San Jose: Resource Publications, 1995), p.38.

50. Mary Collins, 'The Roman Ritual: Pastoral Care and Anointing of the Sick', *Concilium* (1991/92), pp. 3–18, see especially p.3.

51. *Osservatore Romano* (Eng. edn), 30 April 1992.

52. *CCC*, 1525. See Joncas, *The Catechism of the Catholic Church*, pp. 37–40.

53. *CCC*, 1534.

54. *CCC*, 1581.

55. St Augustine, *Tractatus on the Gospel of John*, 18 (cc. 36, 51) as quoted in Gisbert Greshake, *Essere preti Teologia e spiritualità del ministero sacerdotale* (Italian edn ed. Enzo Valentino Ottolini: Brescia: Queriniana, 1995), p.170.

56. PO, 12. See also John Paul II, *Pastores Dabo Vobis. Post-synodal Apostolic Exhortation on the Formation of Priests in the Circumstances of the Present Day* (Vatican City: Libreria Editrice Vaticana 1992), 19–20 (*PDV* hereafter).

57. PO, 12: 'Already in the consecration of Baptism, along with all Christ's faithful, they have received the sign and gift of so great a grace and call that, even in the weakness of the human condition; they both can and should aspire to perfection, as our Lord said: "You, therefore, must be perfect, as your heavenly Father is perfect" (Mt. 5, 48). But priests are specially bound to attain perfection because they are consecrated to God in a new way by receiving the sacrament of

order and are made living instruments of Christ the eternal priest; to carry out through time his wondrous work with which heavenly power restored the whole human family.'

58. *PDV*, 24. See PO, 13, 16–17; O'Donnell, 'Priests, Ministerial', in *Ecclesia*, pp.383–85.

59. This was developed in more detail in: Donna Orsuto, 'Discovering the Extraordinary in the Ordinary: Towards a Christian Marital Spirituality', *INTAMS* 7 (Spring 2001), pp.3–12.

60. Richard Gaillardetz, *A Daring Promise: A Spirituality of Christian Matrimony* (New York: Crossroad, 2002).

61. Rolheiser, *The Holy Longing: Search for a Christian Spiritiuality* (New York: Doubleday, 1999), p.124.

62. Teresa of Avila, *The Book of Her Life* (*The Collected Works of St. Teresa of Avila*, vol. I (trans. Kierian Kavanaugh and Otilio Rodriguez: Washington DC: ICS, 1976), ch. 8, 5, p.67. The fourth part of the *Catechism of the Catholic Church* cites this passage (*CCC* 2709).

63. St Teresa of Avila, *The Book of Her Life*, See Chapters 11–23.

64. Thomas Green, *When the Well Runs Dry. Prayer Beyond the Beginning* (Notre Dame: Ave Maria Press, 1979), p.34.

65. Green, *When the Well Runs Dry,* p.34.

66. Aldegonde and Hubert Brenninkmeijer, 'The Year of the Lord in Married Life. I: Time of Preparation', *INTAMS Review* 5 (1999), pp.199–204; 'The Year of the Lord. Part II: Marital Sharing in the Domestic Church', *INTAMS Review* 6 (2000), pp.112–19.

67. Paul Evdokimov, *The Sacrament of Love* (Crestwood, NY: St Vladamir's Seminary Press, 1985), p.62.

68. Teresa of Avila, *The Book of Her Foundations* (*The Collected Works of St Teresa of Avila* vol. III, trans. Kieran Kavanaugh and Otilio Rodriguez: Washington DC: *ICS* 1985), ch. 5, 8, pp.119–20.

69. As quoted in Donald Nicholl, *Holiness* (London: Darton, Longman and Todd, 1996), p.106.

70. 'How I Pray Now. A Conversation: Joseph P. Whelan, S. J.', *America* 169 (20 November 1993) p.17.

71. See Carlo Maria Martini, 'Il ruolo centrale della parola di Dio nella vita della Chiesa. L'animazione biblica dell'esercizio pastorale', *Civiltà Cattolica* 3727.4 (2005), pp.24–35. See also Simon Tugwell, *Ways of Imperfection* (Springfield IL.: Templegate Publishers, 1985), where he gives, in Chapters 9–11, a summary of the *Ladder of*

*Monks* by the Carthusian, Guigo II (d. 1188). His 'spiritual exercise' is similar to what today would be referred to as *lectio divina*. It consists of four stages: reading, meditation, prayer and contemplation. A comprehensive and classical study on *lectio divina* can be found in Mariano Magrassi, *Bibbia e preghiera: La lectio divina* (Milano: Ancora, 1990). The English translation by Edward Hagman is *Praying the Bible: An Introduction to Lectio Divina* (Collegeville: Liturgical Press, 1998).

72. John Chrysostom, *Homilies on Matthew*, 5.5.

73. Gregory the Great, *Epist.* IV, 31 (PL 77, 706ab), as quoted by Magrassi, *Praying the Bible*, p.126.

74. William Short, 'Almsgiving,' *NDCS*, p.33.

75. Ronald Rolheiser, *The Holy Longing: The Search for a Christian Spirituality* (New York: Doubleday, 1999), pp.64–5.

76. John Chrysostom, *Homilies on Matthew*, 77.6, as quoted in Shawn Madigan, 'Fasting', *NDCS*, p.391.

77. *Shepherd of Hermas*, 3.5.3, as quoted in Madigan, 'Fasting', p.391.

78. See the latest document from the Congregation for Divine Worship and the Discipline of the Sacraments, *Directory on Popular Piety and the Liturgy* (Vatican City: Editrice Vaticana, 2001).

79. *CCC*, 1667.

80. Cf. Keith F. Pecklers, *Worship: A Primer in Christian Ritual* (Collegeville: The Liturgical Press, 2003), pp.138–60 on worship and popular religion.

81. *SC*, 61. See also Patrick Bishop, 'Sacramentals', in *The New Dictionary of Sacramental Worship* (ed. Peter Fink: Collegeville: The Liturgical Press, 1990). Thomas Marsh, 'The Sacramentals Revisited', *Furrow* 33 (1982), pp.272–81.

82. Julian of Norwich, *Showings, Long Text*, 52, p.279.

83. According to St. Thomas Aquinas, living a virtuous life to the full means 'cleaving to God and enjoying him' (*ST* II,II, q.24, a.9).

84. As quoted in Ronald Rolheiser, *The Holy Longing*, pp.168–9. See also Jim Wallis, *The Call to Conversion, Recovering the Gospel for Our Times* (San Francisco: Harper and Row, 1981).

85. St. Thomas Aquinas, quoting St.. Augustine, speaks of fortitude as 'Love readily enduring all for the sake of what is loved'. See *ST*, II–II, 123.4. The *Catechism of the Catholic Church* focuses on this virtue in section 1808.

86. *CCC*, 1809.

87. See Benedict Ashley and Kevin O'Rourke, *Ethics of Health Care* (Washington DC: Georgetown University Press, 2002), p.25. They describe a holistic concept of health as 'an optimal functioning of the human organism to meet biological, psychological, social and spiritual needs'.

88. See Walter E. Conn, *The Desiring Self. Rooting Pastoral Counseling and Spiritual Direction in Self-Transcendence* (New York: Paulist Press, 1998).

89. For a brief history of the relationship between psychology and spirituality, see Kees Waaijman, *Spirituality: Forms, Foundations, Methods* (Leuven: Peeters, 2002), pp.414–18.

90. See Herbert Alphonso, *The Personal Vocation* (Rome: LitoPomel, 1996), pp.72–82.

91. One of the early books that came out on this topic was Josef Godbrunner's *Holiness is Wholeness* (New York: Pantheon, 1955). His purpose was to demonstrate the significance of modern psychology for spirituality. He discusses conditions for a healthy spiritual life and the three theological virtues and their influence on health. Now the intersection between psychology and spirituality is a given, as evidenced by the various articles on that topic in dictionaries of spirituality. For a more recent book on the relationship among the physical, spiritual, psychological dimensions of the call to holiness, see Wilkie Au, *By Way of the Heart. Toward a Holistic Christian Spirituality* (Mahwah: Paulist Press, 1989).

92. See Michály Szentmártoni, 'Psychopatologia e santità', *La santità* (Napoli: Cirico, 2001), pp.165–77.

93. Cf. Gillian Rose, See *Love's Work* (New York: Schocken Books, 1995), p.105.

94. Thomas Merton, *The Seven Storey Mountain*, pp.237–8.

'*The Cross as vine points us from the mosaic below to the altar, on which the fruit of the earth again and again is changed into the wine of the love of Jesus christ. In the Eucharist the vine of Christ grows into the whole breadth of the earth. In its worldwide celebration, God's vine extends its circles over the earth and carries its life in fellowship with Christ. In such a way the image itself shows us the way to reality: Let yourself be drawn into the vine of God, it tells us. Give your life over to the holy tree that grows ever new from the Cross. Become a branch of it yourself. Keep your life in the reconciliation that comes from Christ, and let yourself be drawn upward by him.*'
Joseph Cardinal Ratzinger (Pope Benedict XVI) *Images of Hope*,
(San Francisco: Ignatius Press, 2006), p.77.
Basilica of Saint Clement, Rome
Apse Mosaic, 12th Century
The Acanthus (The Tree of Life)
Reproduced by Courtesy of the Irish Dominican Fathers.

# 4
# Beyond Basic Floor Plans:
# Towards a contemporary
# understanding of holiness

*It is necessary therefore to rediscover the full practical significance of Chapter 5 of the Dogmatic Constitution on the Church* Lumen gentium, *dedicated to the 'universal call to holiness'. The Council Fathers laid such stress on this point, not just to embellish ecclesiology with a kind of spiritual veneer, but to make the call to holiness an intrinsic and essential aspect of their teaching on the Church.*

John Paul II, Apostolic Letter, *Novo millennio ineunte*
(Vatican City, Libreria editrice Vaticana, 2001), 30

*One expects the central shrine of Christendom [The Holy Sepulchre] to stand out in majestic isolation, but anonymous buildings cling to it like barnacles. One looks for numinous light, but it is dark and cramped. One hopes for peace, but the ear is assailed by a cacophony of warring chants. One desires holiness, only to encounter a jealous possessiveness: the six groups of occupants – Latin Catholics, Greek Orthodox, Armenians, Syrians, Copts, Ethiopians – watch one another suspiciously for any infringement of rights. The frailty of humanity is nowhere more apparent than here: it epitomizes the human condition. The empty who come to be filled will leave desolate; those who permit the church to question them may begin to understand why hundreds of thousands thought it worthwhile to risk death or slavery in order to pray here.*

Jerome Murphy O'Connor, *The Holy Land*
(Oxford Archaeological Guides: Oxford:
Oxford University Press, 1998), p.45.

*I admire them all [different religious orders]. I belong to one of them by observance, but to all of them by charity. We all need one another; the spiritual good which I do not own and possess, I receive from others. In this exile, the Church is still on pilgrimage and is, in a certain sense, plural: she is single plurality and a plural unity. All our diversities, which make manifest the richness of God's gifts, will continue to exist in the one house of the Father, which has many rooms. Now there is a division of grace: then there will be distinctions there of glory. Unity, both here and now, consists in one and the same charity.*

St. Bernard of Clairvaux, *Apologia to William of Saint Thierry*, 4, 8
as cited by John Paul II, Apostolic Exhortation *Vita Consecrata*
(Vatican City, Libreria editrice Vaticana, 1996), 52, 118.

House renovations require an intimate awareness of the original design. Studying the blue prints and recalling the basic floor plans help to determine how to make the best use of the space available and to decide how rooms are arranged, where furniture is placed, and what parts of the abode are appropriate for certain activities. The strategic placing of the home's hearth, for example, is a fundamental decision because this is where the family gathers, where guests are welcomed, and where the bonds of love are strengthened. Less important, but still necessary, are closets and storerooms, attics and basements.

Aged buildings require even more care when refurbished. Older Roman *palazzi*, for example, have a special charm, but they require greater attention than newer buildings, especially when changes are on the horizon. The beauty of the past can easily be obscured or even destroyed by lack of concern for detail or hasty changes made in favour of modern conveniences. A linoleum floor may be more efficient to clean than antique tiles, but would totally clash, with the décor of an Italian *palazzo*. Eyes need to be trained to see the value of the tiles and how they fit into the environment. Some changes may be necessary over time, but these need to be in harmony with and respectful of the original design. Other alternations may not be possible, because they could destroy the building's integrity.

With regard to holiness, God's building project which we are in Christ, there are certain features that determine our identity; these are non-negotiable. Without them, the building would not be what it is. There are other elements where changes that respect the integrity of the dwelling actually may bring out a new depth of beauty that was not visible before. This chapter explores the radical holiness of the Church by reviewing the basic floor plans as they appear today. It begins with a re-reading of Acts 2:42–47 which sets forth a vision of how we are meant to live out our holiness together. Then we move to a consideration of key themes for reflecting on holiness at present: holiness as described by the Second Vatican Council, holiness of the Church despite its need of reform, the universal call to holiness, and finally, holiness lived in the ordinary circumstances of everyday life.

## Living holiness together

In Acts 2:42–47 we have an early expression of what holiness lived out together looks like for the Christian community:

> They devoted themselves to the apostles' teaching and fellowship, to the breaking of bread and the prayers ... Wonders and signs were being done by the apostles ... [they] were praising God and having the goodwill of all the people.

This ideal picture of the first Christian community still has its drawing power; it continues to be a model for Christians. First of all, the early Christian community devoted themselves to the apostles' preaching. The Christian community is not a chance gathering: it is summoned and unified by teaching. The central teaching is about the death, resurrection and glorification of Jesus, that he is the Messiah and his life and teaching are the sure way that God has planned to lead us to holiness. The Christian community still gathers to be taught. In Chapter 1 we saw the importance of scripture for a life of holiness. The way many Christians hear the word of God is in Church, as it is unfolded throughout the liturgical year. The Church year not only enables us to hear substantial teaching from sacred Scriptures, but it also draws us into the mystery of Christ: his birth, his ministry of teaching and healing, the paschal mystery and the gift of the Spirit given at Pentecost. The liturgical year also presents outstanding saints who are models, friends and intercessors for us. As Karl Rahner notes:

> The nature of Christian holiness appears from the life of Christ and of his Saints; and what appears there cannot be translated absolutely into a general theory but must be experienced in the encounter with the historical which takes place from one individual case to another. The history of Christian holiness (of what, in other words, is the business of every Christian, since everyone is sanctified and called to holiness) is in its totality a unique history and not eternal return of the same. Hence this history has its always new, unique phases;

hence it must always be discovered anew (even though always in the imitation of Christ who remains the inexhaustible model), and this by all Christians. Herein lies the special task which the canonized Saints have to fulfil for the Church. They are the initiators and the creative models of the holiness which happens to be right for, and is the task of, their particular age. They create a new style; they prove that a certain form of life and activity is a really genuine possibility; they show experimentally that one can be a Christian even in 'this' way; they make such a type of person believable as a Christian type.[1]

The Christian community gathered to hear the apostolic teaching is a school for holiness. Furthermore, as we allow the liturgical year shape our spirituality, and as we focus on the exemplars of holiness that have gone before us, we are being built into a dwelling where God abides.

Secondly, the apostles' teaching invites people to come together. The Greek word *koinonia* implies what is common or shared, a joint partaking, and, most of all, fellowship. Sharing life with others, and love of neighbour and of those in need are indispensable for genuine holiness. We are called to live a practical, down-to-earth holiness, and this is done together. While, in the early Church, the community shared its gifts and sought to live in harmony, we also know from the first books of the New Testament that sin and disunity emerged. The community was soon to know the sin of Ananias and Saphira. Within a relatively short time after the events recorded in of Acts 2:24–27, Paul would be warning his communities about the dangers of sins that they must avoid. He even writes to the Corinthians about sins which he says not even the pagans would commit (see 1 Cor. 6:1). So from the beginning, sin and failure mar the holy Church. This need not surprise us, as Jesus had warned his disciples through parables that holiness and sin would coexist in the Church until the end of time (see the parables of the good and bad seed, and the good and bad fish, Mt. 13:24-30, 47-50).

The third mark of the apostolic community was its breaking of bread. We have already seen the importance of the Eucharist, the sacrament towards which all others tend,[2] the source and summit of the whole Christian life. The breaking of bread as public worship is a priestly task for the whole community (*Sacrosanctum Concilium*, 7). One of the important teachings of the Second Vatican Council was about the common priesthood of all believers and the ways in which all Christians through baptism share in the triple office of Christ as priest, prophet and king. The meaning of the council on this teaching grew from the initial exposition in the second chapter of *Lumen gentium*, 'The People of God'. There we find clearly the priestly dimension (*LG* 10–11) and the prophetic (*LG* 12), but the sharing of all the faithful in Christ's triple office as priest, prophet and king is most clearly developed in the chapter on the laity (*LG* 34–36). All the members of the Church share in Christ's priesthood by offering the sacrifice of Christ, by prayer and works in the Spirit. They are to be prophetic, speaking for God in word and deed. They are to share in the lordship of Jesus by working for the kingdom and by being dedicated to truth and life, holiness and grace, justice, love and peace.[3]

The fourth mark of the community is its prayer. In the previous chapter we considered the place of prayer in the lives of those who want to grow in holiness. The point to be made here is that prayer has to be taught and sustained. As children we are taught our prayers; if we were fortunate we may have learned to listen and speak to God out of our daily lives. On the spiritual journey, though, we need many skills; we also need to be alert to dangers along the way. For the spiritual journey and especially for prayer, we do not start off with a *tabula rasa* or clean slate. There is acquired wisdom to be found in schools of spirituality, which offer us 'historical syntheses' of a variety of ways to live out this holiness in daily life.[4] The *Catechism of the Catholic Church* reminds us that 'the different schools of Christian spirituality share in the living tradition of prayer and are essential guides for the faithful. In their rich diversity they are refractions of the one pure light of the Holy Spirit.' It goes on to quote St. Basil on the Holy Spirit: 'The Spirit is truly the dwelling of the saints and the saints are for the Spirit a place where he dwells as in his own house, since they offer themselves as a dwelling place for God and are called his temple.'[5]

Today, various paths of praying and living the call to holiness are offered by diverse ecclesial movements, associations and groups in the Church,[6] like the Neocatechumate Way, the Charismatic movement, and Communion and Liberation. Chiara Lubich's Focolari movement (Work of Mary), begun in 1943, also seeks to overcome the modern sense of isolation by providing a communal experience of unity with God and others. Another effort to combat isolation, particularly intense for hand-icapped women and men, is Jean Vanier's L'Arche, which began in 1964 and offers a community of love and healing. In all of their diversity, these various initiatives, of which only a few have been mentioned here, desire to promote a spirituality that acknowledges the universal call to holiness and encourages women and men to live an evangelical life in the midst of the world. Opus Dei (literally the Work of God), founded by St Josemaría Escrivá de Balauguer, proposes still another path. Not a movement, but a personal prelature established by the pope, Opus Dei aims to help laity and clergy live the universal call to holiness in the midst of the secular world.[7] For most Christians, ordinary parish life provides the context for living out the call to holiness. The 'parish is the "place" in the world for the community of believers to gather together as a "sign" and "instrument" of the vocation of all to communion. It is to be a house of welcome to all and a place of service. Pope John XXIII called the parish the "village fountain" to which all would have recourse in their thirst.'[8]

All of these different paths witness to the beauty of the diverse ways that God leads people to holiness of life. They are not in competition with one another; rather they manifest diverse ways of living the one call to holiness. Today we are accustomed to speak of pluralism in the Church: there are many theologies but one truth. The same sacred mysteries are celebrated in different ways according to places and cultures. There is only one focus though: a sharing in the life of the Trinity and being moulded according to the paschal mystery of Jesus Christ. The gospel call to holiness is summarized by Jesus as love of God and of neighbour (see Mt. 22:37–40), but there are many ways in which people in different times and places can fulfil this command. Different cultures, various social circumstances, changed times and ways of thinking all give diverse possibilities of expressing holiness.

Pluriformity, not uniformity, characterizes life in the church and ways of living out holiness. This pluriformity is meant to promote and guarantee communion and unity. What Bernard of Clairvaux wrote regarding religious orders, as cited in the epitaph to this chapter, can easily be applied to the various ways of living out holiness today: movements, associations, groups, secular institutes, and forms of consecrated life.

I admire them all [different religious orders]. I belong to one of them by observance, but to all of them by charity. We all need one another; the spiritual good which I do not own and possess, I receive from others. ... In this exile, the Church is still on pilgrimage and is, in a certain sense, plural: she is single plurality and a plural unity.

All our diversities, which make manifest the richness of God's gifts, will continue to exist in the one house of the Father, which has many rooms. Now there is a division of grace: then there will be a distinctions of glory. Unity, both here and there, consists in one and the same charity.[9]

To summarize: Acts 2:24–27 has had enormous fecundity in the history of spirituality, particularly for those called to consecrated life. Founders of various religious orders returned to this text time and again and presented it as an ideal for their followers. Devotion to the apostolic teaching, communion or fellowship, the breaking of bread, and prayer are non-negotiable elements that still inspire us as we respond to the invitation to live out the call to holiness in our time.

### Holiness today

For Catholics, the Second Vatican Council is a benchmark for developing a systematic understanding of Christian holiness, and may help us to discover a do-able, liveable holiness for our times. The Council was, in many ways, a major renovation project (or *aggiornamento*, as the Italians like to say) in the Church. We can grasp the influence that it had on our understanding of holiness only if we consider the wider context in which this teaching developed.

This wider picture is clearly delineated in the final Report of the 1985 Extraordinary Synod that took place in Rome to celebrate the twentieth anniversary of Vatican II. It affirmed that despite inevitable difficulties with the reception of the Council, its teaching was a sure foundation for the future. The four Dogmatic Constitutions – on the Church (*Lumen gentium*), on the Church in the Modern World (*Gaudium et spes*), on the liturgy (*Sacrosanctum concilium*) and on Divine Revelation (*Dei Verbum*) – were strong pillars upon which to continue the building project in process. These four Constitutions, said Basil Hume (1923–97), the former Archbishop of Westminster, 'probe its inner mystery; they outline its agenda for the transformation and the sanctification of the world; they celebrate the source and summit of its life; they point to the Word of God revealed in scripture and tradition as the sure guide for its ongoing pilgrimage.'[10] The Council is both a point of arrival and a point of departure: while it needs to be interpreted in continuity with earlier councils and the great tradition of the Church, it also offers new insights that help the Church be an effective witness in today's world.[11]

The Second Vatican Council presents holiness in a positive way. Though it does not offer an 'official' definition of holiness, it does suggest a solid doctrine on its nature, a doctrine that is in harmony with the tradition that came before.[12] In the context of the mystery of Christ and the Church, holiness is understood as a sharing in the fullness of divine life, given through the gift of the Spirit, to unite us with Christ in charity. There is but one holiness – that is 'cultivated by all who are led by the Spirit of God, and who, in obedience to the voice of the Father and worshipping God, the Father in spirit and truth, follow Christ, poor and humble in carrying his cross so that they may deserve to be sharers of his glory' (*LG* 41). According to the teaching of the Council, Christian holiness assumes our participation in the paschal mystery it is specifically a sharing in the death and resurrection of Christ.

### The Church: Holy, yet in need of renewal and reform

The Church, holy and beautiful in its teaching, its liturgy and the lives of saintliness, manifests holiness in its members here and in glory.[13] The Council presents the Church as marked with a holiness that, while genuine, is imperfect (*LG* 48). This paradoxical statement can only be understood if we accept that the Church is a 'mystery', consisting of both human and divine elements. As *Lumen gentium* 8 says:

> Christ, the one mediator, set up his holy church here on earth as a visible structure, a community of faith, hope and love; and he sustains it unceasingly and through it he pours out his grace and truth on everyone. This society, however, equipped with hierarchical structures, and the mystical body of Christ, a visible assembly and a spiritual community, an earthly church and a church enriched with heavenly gifts, must not be considered as two things, but as forming one complex reality comprising a human and a divine element.

The Church is the people of God that is made holy by the Holy Spirit and is therefore objectively holy. Yet the Church is made by people who are marked by sin, and so there is an element of imperfection. It is only if we recognize its complex nature that we will avoid the error of imagining *two* Churches: one, the 'mystical body' and 'bride of Christ' and the other, a corrupt and sinful hierarchical society.[14] This one Church is holy because Christ the Lord, the 'fountain of all holiness', sent the

Holy Spirit, who continually sanctifies and 'now dwells in the church and in the hearts of the faithful, as in a temple' (*LG* 4).

Each time we profess the Creed, we proclaim our faith in the 'One, Holy, Catholic and Apostolic Church'. Thus, to say that the Church is holy is a matter of faith. Holiness, as one of the four marks of the Church, has been acknowledged from the earliest creeds.[15] *Lumen gentium* 39 expresses the foundations or grounds for this affirmation:

> The church ... is held to be indefectibly holy as a matter of faith. For Christ, the Son of God, who with the Father and the Spirit, 'alone is holy', loved the church as his bride and delivered himself up for it that he might sanctify it (see Eph. 5:26–26), and he joined it to himself, as his body and bestowed on it the gift of the holy Spirit to the glory of God.

Some translate the council's Latin, *indefectibiliter sancta*, as 'unfailingly holy'. It can also mean: 'holy in a way which can never fail'.[16] As Francis A. Sullivan notes, '*Indefectibiliter* does not mean "without defect", but "without the possibility of being lost".'[17] There are basically three reasons why this is so. The Church is holy, first of all, because of its Trinitarian foundation. As we have seen in previous chapters, a Christian understanding of holiness always begins with the unmerited gift of God's grace. Holiness is always gift before it becomes response and responsibility. Along these lines, *Lumen gentium* reminds us of the specific way that God, who is Father, Son and Holy Spirit, manifests holiness in the Church. The Church is unfailingly holy because it is founded upon Christ's death and resurrection. Secondly, the Church is holy because of the strong bond of love between Christ and his bride. The image of the Church as bride demonstrates the intricate and definitive relationship of Christ and his people. Finally, the Church is holy because of the abiding gift of the Spirit. The Spirit, the gift of the risen Christ, dwells in the Church forever and this implies that 'it is unthinkable that the Holy Spirit could either abandon the church or abide in her without actually causing the church to be a holy people'.[18]

One of the images used for the Church in *Lumen gentium* is that it is the people of God. Baptized, gathered together in worship at the Eucharist, and guided by their pastors, the Church is a structured people. In other words, there are formal structures, instituted by Christ, that are part of the reason for an insistence on objective and effective elements. These include the word of God, the sacraments, and the gifts or charisms that prepare people for the upbuilding of the Church. *Lumen gentium* 12 makes this point explicitly:

> The ... holy Spirit not only sanctifies and guides the people of God by means of the sacraments and ministries and adorns it with virtues, he also apportions his gifts 'to each individually as he wills' (1 Cor.12:11), and among the faithful of every rank he distributes special graces by which he renders them fit and ready to undertake the various tasks and offices which help the renewal and building up of the church, according to the word: 'to each is given the manifestation of the Spirit for the common good' (1 Cor.12:7). These charismatic gifts, whether they be very outstanding or simpler and more widely diffused, are to be accepted with thanksgiving and consolation, since they are primarily suited to and useful for the needs of the church.

The Holy Spirit is at work through the sacraments and ministries and also through the various charisms, gifts given for the upbuilding of the Church. These make the Church objectively holy because the come directly from Christ. They are Christ's gift given in the power of the Spirit to the church and do not depend on the often subjective and sometimes dubious holiness of individuals. This is important because sacraments are holy even if the persons administering or receiving them do so unworthily. Similarly, the holiness of the word of God is not dependent on the holiness of the preacher or hearer. Furthermore, the exercise of charismatic gifts does not necessarily imply the personal holiness of a person.[19]

Holiness is witnessed not only in its formal elements, but also in the priestly people set apart to worship God alone. Consecration by God into the priesthood of all the faithful comes through the sacraments of initiation and is considered a 'participation in the priesthood of Christ' (*LG* 10). Consequently, the 'character' or 'spiritual mark' of this holiness of consecration always remains in the baptized, even if they commit grave sins, and even if they separate themselves from the Church by schism or heresy.

One way of expressing these two dimensions of holiness is to speak of the holiness *of* the Church and holiness *in* the Church. This distinction was made in the International Theological Commission's document, 'Memory and Reconciliation: The Church and Faults of the Past':

> The Church is holy because, sanctified by Christ who has acquired her by giving himself up to death for her, she is maintained in holiness by the Holy Spirit who pervades her unceasingly. We believe that the church ... is indefectibly holy ... One can distinguish the *holiness of the church* from *holiness in the church*. The former – founded on the missions of the Son and Spirit – guarantees the continuity of the mission of the people of God until the end of time and stimulates and aids the believers in pursuing subjective personal holiness ... Personal holiness is always directed toward God and others, and thus has an essentially social character: it is holiness 'in the church' oriented toward the good of all.[20]

We have seen why the Church is considered holy, but the Second Vatican Council also emphasizes that the Church needs to be purified. Two important passages from the Council are pertinent here: *Lumen gentium* 8 and *Unitatis redintegratio* 6, respectively:

> While Christ 'holy, blameless, unstained' (Heb.7:26) knew no sin (see 2 Cor.5:21), and came only to expiate the sins of the people (see Heb. 2:17), the church, containing sinners in its own bosom, is at one and the same time holy and always in need of purification and it pursues unceasingly penance and renewal (*sancta simul et semper purificanda, poenitentiam et renovationem continuo prosequitur*).

> In its pilgrimage on earth Christ summons the church to continual reformation (*perennem reformationem*), of which it is always in need, in so far as it is an institution of human beings here on earth. Thus if, in various times and circumstances, there have been deficiencies in moral conduct or in church discipline, or even in the way church teaching has been formulated – to be carefully distinguished from the deposit of faith itself – these should be set right in the proper way at the opportune moment. (*UR* 6)

Only with the coming of the kingdom, when Christ will be all in all, will the Church be 'without spot and wrinkle'. Meanwhile, the Church will always be in need of purification, renewal and reform. Though the

Church will always have members who are holy and so be considered indefectibly holy, there will also be members who are sinners. It is not as if the church is neatly divided into saints and sinners. The fact is that all of the 'holy ones' are also sinners.[21] In the words of René Latourelle:

> 'The church's holiness is a dialectic of *already* and *not yet*. The Second Vatican Council speaks of a holiness which is real, but imperfect [*vera sanctitate licet imperfecta*] (*LG* 48). Though holy, the church will always needs to be purified (*LG* 8). In baptism ... [it] is consecrated to God, but like Israel, also consecrated to God ... [it] has to live this fundamental holiness which comes to ... [it] as a pure gift from God. There is therefore a tension between what has been given and received and what must be conserved and realized ... The Church is called to live always more fully and more perfectly her fundamental holiness.[22]

During his pontificate (1978–2004), John Paul II, who beatified and canonized more people than any other pope in history, also called for a general confession of sin to mark the Jubilee year, saying:

> The history of the church is a history of holiness ... Yet it must be acknowledged that history also records events which constitute a countertestimony to Christianity. Because of the bond which unites us to one another in the mystical body, all of us, though not person- ally responsible and without encroaching on the judgement of God, who alone knows every heart, bear the burden of the errors and faults of those who have gone before us. Yet we too, sons and daugh- ters of the church, have sinned and have hindered the bride of Christ from shining forth in all her beauty ... As the successor of Peter, I ask that in this year of mercy the church, strong in holiness which she received from her Lord, should kneel before God and implore forgiveness for the past and present sins of her sons and daughters. All have sinned and none can claim righteousness before God.[23]

Pope John Paul II presided at this act of repentance on the first Sunday of Lent during the Jubilee year when, after his homily, seven prelates of the Roman Curia each made a general confession of sins – first of sins in general, and then of particular kinds of sin. After each confession, the Pope prayed for forgiveness. This act was and is an important gesture, especially in light of recent scandals in the Church, for it helps us to recognize that we are bound together in one body and when one sins, it affects all. As we struggle with the tension of recognizing that the Church is holy, yet in need of reform, we can also draw inspiration from St. Catherine of Siena (1347–80), who lived in one of the saddest periods of ecclesial history. Faced with schism and grave moral problems in the Church, Catherine was able to hold in delicate balance her love for holy Church and her recognition of its need for reform. In our days when there are signs of disillusionment with the Church, especially in light of the handling of recent sexual scandals, Catherine has a particularly important message. When we look at this fourteenth-century mystic with all of the problems of the Church of her time, we see that in spite of them all, Catherine lived her life at the heart of the church. In spite of the problems that beset the Church, she loved it as few people have. Pope Paul VI called her the saint who most loved the Church. Her love for the Church was not blind, for she saw only too clearly its defects; rather it was love clothed in a truth which could penetrate beyond appearances to the beauty and holiness of the Church.

Catherine did not live in a dream world. She saw the Church as it was: leprous, infected by greed, pride, division, arrogance, rebellion and schism; these are just a few of the descriptive words that she used in her book, *The Dialogue of Divine Providence*. In one of her letters, she also used the terms 'devils incarnate' and 'evil counsellors' of those cardinals who tried to discourage Gregory XI from leaving Avignon for Rome.[24] Catherine was not afraid to speak the truth, but she always spoke the truth in love. It was her great love for the Church that led her to call for its reform. She insisted that this reform must come from within and that it had to begin with herself by taking personal responsibility through continuous prayer, work and sacrifice.

**The universal call to holiness in the Church**
A direct consequence of this vision of the Church as holy is the universal call to holiness. *Lumen gentium* 40 specifically focuses on the invitation of all the baptized to personal sanctity:

> The lord Jesus, the divine master and model of all perfection, preached holiness of life, which he himself both initiates and perfects,

to each and every one of his disciples, no matter what their condition of life: 'You, therefore, must be perfect, as your heavenly father is perfect' (Mt. 5:4–8). To all of them he sent the holy Spirit to inspire them from within to love God with all their heart, all their soul, all their mind, and with all their strength (see Mk 12:30) and to love one another even as Christ has loved them (see Jn 12:34; 15:12). The followers of Christ, called by God not for their achievements but in accordance with his plan and his grace, and justified in the lord Jesus, by their baptism in faith have been truly made children of God, and sharers in the divine nature, and are therefore really made holy. Their holiness, therefore, which they have received by the gifts of God, they must maintain and perfect by their way of life. They are warned by the apostle to live 'as is fitting among saints' (Eph. 5:3), 'as God's chosen ones, holy and beloved,' to put on 'compassion, kindness, lowliness, meekness and patience' (Col. 3:12); to possess the fruits of the Spirit for sanctifications (see Gal. 5:22; Rom. 6:22). And since all of us commit many faults (see Jas. 3:2), we are in continuous need of the mercy of God and our daily prayer has to be: 'And forgive us our trespasses' (Mt. 6:12).

It is therefore evident to everyone that all the faithful, whatever their condition or rank, are called to the fullness of the Christian life and the perfection of charity.[25]

This passage stresses the fact that holiness, which manifests itself in the love of God and neighbour, is a gift of the Holy Trinity, which is given in baptism along with the responsibility to maintain it and put it into practice. It is God who calls, the Lord Jesus who justifies, and the Holy Spirit who inspires us from within to live this call. Through baptism, believers are made God's children and sharers in God's nature. Again the pattern of gift, response and responsibility emerge.

The bottom line is that there are no second-class citizens in the Church. This holiness is lived out in diverse ways, but all Christians are called to live out this sanctity 'in the measure in which they have received this as Christ's gift' (*LG* 40). This means following in the footsteps of Christ and conforming themselves to Christ's likeness. Holiness is about following God's will, for only then will it produce fruit in abundance.

It is common to speak of different states of life in the Church (as the Council does). Theologically there are two states: clergy and laity. But canonically there is another state, that of consecrated life, whose members comprise both clergy and laity.[26] Perhaps today we really should be thinking also in more sociological categories. There are many diverse 'states' of life: for example, one has only to think of Shakespeare's seven ages of the human. Each has different possibilities and challenges for holiness. There are people who are single – temporarily or permanently – consecrated or not; there are people who are married; and people who are separated and widowed. A person may have been in several states of life. There are consecrated persons, in cloistered monasteries, in active apostolic orders, in secular institutes. There are religious priests and bishops and diocesan ones. The point is that the appropriate way of seeking holiness needs to be adapted to the particular state and capabilities of an individual in his or her cultural context. In the first part of his *Introduction to the Devout Life* (written between 1602 and 1608), St. Francis de Sales already suggested that each individual was called to live out the call to holiness in light of his or her particular life situation and capabilities.[27]

## Lay sanctity: an emphasis of the Council

One of the fruits of the Second Vatican Council was a renewed appreciation of the vocation and mission of the laity in the Church and in the world, and especially of the call of the laity to holiness. Yet many lay women and men still ask: how can we respond to this call to holiness in the midst of our family, work, political, and social responsibilities? In other words, how can one live a 'secular sanctity'? Part of the problem is that there has been a scarcity of lay models, especially when searching among the canonized saints. In her introduction to the collection of essays *Lay Sanctity, Medieval and Modern: A Search for Models*, Ann Astell maps out the multiple and shifting understandings of lay sanctity through the ages.[28] After a careful historical survey, Astell explores lay sanctity in the context of the postmodern challenge. By a clever juxtaposition of quotations, one from John Chrysostom where he exhorted the laity of his time to 'conduct themselves like monks', and another from Paul VI who reminded the participants in a congress on the lay apostolate that 'you are not hermits who have withdrawn from the world in order to devote yourselves to God. It is in the world and in its activities that you must sanctify yourselves', Astell showed that there has been a paradigm shift in the Church's understanding of lay sanctity. The profound ascetical and theological implications of this shift bring one to the question (posed by Astell): 'If the laity are not to "conduct themselves as monks", what models of holiness are appropriate to them? What are the distinctive characteristics of their spirituality?'[29]

*Exploring lay sanctity*

As lay persons seek their own paths to sanctity, we need to take into account the concrete circumstances they find ourselves in. Too often in the past, many lay people have felt guilty because family and work responsibilities have prevented them sometimes from dedicating large amounts of time to 'churchy' activities. Holiness has sometimes been associated almost exclusively with pious practices that take place in church. In reality, however, all time and space have a sacred dimension, for they are shot through with God's presence. The call to holiness for laity is lived precisely in and through relationships at home, at work, and in the marketplace. The challenge, as we have seen through this book, is for us to discover extraordinary grace ever active in our ordinary lives. Called to be leaven, light and salt, lay women and men face the challenge of finding God in the midst of ordinary human relationships and of being a Christian presence in the world.

For people who are trying to live out the call to holiness by integrating faith and everyday life, the social teaching of the Church has a special relevance. Less known than other areas of Church doctrine, some have referred to the social teaching as the best kept secret in the Roman Catholic Church.[30] Its relevance is particularly evident with regard to the connection between work and holiness. Since the vast majority of people spend a major portion of their day in the workplace, it is important to consider the relationship between work and the call to holiness. This can only be understood in the context of the relationship between labour and leisure: or more precisely, the link between work and worship.

In contemporary culture, work is an ambiguous reality. Some tolerate or even disdain it as a necessary evil to achieve something else – to support a family or simply to pay the bills.[31] The real pressure of making ends meet financially in contemporary society often forces people to work harder and longer than they would like. Others, like the 'workaholics' are so consumed with work that nothing else matters. As Barbara Killinger notes in *Workaholics, The Respectable Addiction*, 'The roots of workaholism lie in the old Calvinistic philosophy that work redeems the believer and that indulging in pleasure ... will bring eternal damnation. Even three hundred years later, this joyless dictum that work is virtue and play is sin still pervades our society.'[32] For the workaholic, work takes over to such an extent that family and social relationships suffer or become non-existent. Others are forced by their professions to work longer hours than they would prefer, because this is what is expected. For example, it is quite normal for attorneys to clock eighty to ninety hours per week in the United States. Still others ardently seek work, yet because of economic realities and high unemployment find it impossible to find a job.

Three major social encyclicals of John Paul II – *Laborem exercens* (1981), *Sollicitudo rei socialis* (1987), and *Centesimus annus* (1991) – grapple in one way or another with a Christian understanding of human work, but only *Laborem exercens* specifically suggests some considerations for a spirituality of work. In the fifth section of that encyclical, Pope John Paul II offers elements for this spirituality which portray work as a means of drawing closer to God. Reflecting on it in the context of God's salvation plan for humanity and for the world, he sees work as a way of participating in Christ's priestly, prophetic and kingly mission.[33] Ideally, we work not exclusively for personal and family needs, but also to serve society, to cultivate resources for the common good, and to transcend ourselves.

Underlying this teaching is the affirmation that there is an inherent dignity in human work. Since we are made in God's image and likeness, our work, whether manual or intellectual, reflects in some way God's work. At the same time, our inherent dignity comes from who we are (human beings created in God's image and likeness), and not simply from what we do (our work).[34] A Christian notion of work insists that ultimately work does not define a person. We are always more than our work (*GS* 35; *LE* 26). This is important, especially when considering those who cannot work because of ill health, old age, or high unemployment. However, this notion is counter-cultural, because the common tendency is for people to be identified and recognized for the work they do.

*Co-creators with the Creator: The positive dimension of human work*
A Christian vision of work maintains that through our labour we share in the work of the Creator. Genesis 1 portrays creation as a 'work' of God done over a six-day period. After each day of creation, we read, 'And God saw that it was good.' The author presents the creative process as something good and positive. The culmination of God's creative activity is humanity, created in the image and likeness of God. We become partners in God's creative act through the work that we do. Insofar as we

are faithful stewards of God's creation, our work is an unfolding of the Creator's work. Seven is the number of completeness, so the number six, one less than seven, implies incompleteness. In this context, the Genesis account of creation might not imply a challenge to women and men to complete through their work the creative work of God.[35]

Following the teaching of *Gaudium et spes*, Pope John Paul II, in *Laborem Exercerns* insists that there is an inherent unity between human work and God's creative power. Indeed, 'Christians are convinced that the triumphs of the human race are a sign of God's greatness and the flowing of his own mysterious design' (*GS* 34; *LE* 25). In striving for excellence in a particular field, such as science or technology, we are sharing in the creative activity of God. As a way of advancing human history towards its fulfilment in Christ, work is integral to one's spirituality. What we think about work is directly related to our understanding of the Christian's role in the world. Just as the end result is integral to a football game, so also for the Christian at work in the world intention is not enough: the end is important. It is not enough to act in such a way that the outcome does not matter just as long as we do not fall into sin. The outcome does matter because it is in our small way a participation in the work of Christ, who is directing all history to its final goal. Through our work, we give glory to God. *Gaudium et spes* 43 forcefully suggests that the split between faith and daily life is one of the more serious errors of our age. Those who neglect their responsibilities in society, their duty towards 'their neighbour and even God, jeopardize their eternal salvation' (*GS* 43).

The deepest meaning and value of all creation has its foundation in the Risen Christ. In light of this, all reality is shot through with the presence of God. As Teilhard de Chardin vividly expresses in *Le Milieu Divin*:

> God, in all that is most living and incarnate in Him, is not far away from us, altogether apart from the world we see, touch, hear, smell and taste about us. Rather He awaits us every instant in our action, in the work of the moment ... There is a sense in which He is at the tip of my pen, my spade, my brush, my needle – of my heart and of my thought. By pressing the stroke, the line, or the stitch ... to its ultimate natural finish, I shall lay hold of that last end towards which my innermost will tends.[36]

*Toil: Sharing in the paschal mystery*

If the first chapter of Genesis expressed the positive dimension of human work, Gen. 2:2–25 presents the negative dimension of it (*LE* 27). Here the punishment of Adam and Eve's disobedience in the garden includes 'toil', which will be relieved only through death itself. 'Cursed is the ground because of you; in toil you shall eat of it all the days of your life' (Genesis 3:19). The encyclical letter *Laborem exercens* interprets this negative dimension of work in light of the paschal mystery. Through toil, the Christian shares in a small way in the cross of Christ and collaborates with him in his redemptive mission. At the same time, in light of the resurrection, one finds 'a glimmer of new life ... precisely through the toil that goes with work' (*LE* 27). Toil, difficulty and boredom are at times inevitable in the workplace. The key is to see these real experiences in light of Christ's death and resurrection. In this way, Christ enters the workplace not as a furtive guest, but as the One who permanently abides with and within us. He invites us to see the ups and downs of work as a way through which we can share in the paschal mystery, and thus in his mission.

*Labour and leisure*

Even with all of the pressures of contemporary society with regard to work, especially as families try to make ends meet under often difficult financial circumstances, a Christian vision of work still insists that work is not an end in itself. Labour without leisure robs us of our humanity.[37] The first account of creation, part of the 'gospel of work', hints at this rhythm between labour and leisure. It ends with the pregnant words:

> And on the seventh day, God finished the work that he had done, and he rested on the seventh day from all the work that he had done. So God blessed the seventh day and hallowed it, because on it God rested from all the work that he had done in creation. (Gen. 2:1–3).

Seven symbolizes perfection; and so creation reaches its completion only in this divine repose. The rhythm of God's six days of creative activity and God's rest points to the inherent interconnection between labour and leisure. The underlying theological message is that labour and leisure are complementary. The Sabbath rest exists not simply to renew our creative capacities, but it is a way of entering into the divine repose. If we want to attain our greatest potential as human beings created in the image and likeness of God, we mus include the invitation of the divine rest.

Before entering into the religious dimension of the Sabbath, there is also a human dimension which cannot be underestimated. There is more to life than human work and if this is not recognized, the human spirit eventually will be destroyed. One of the sayings from the desert fathers illustrates this point. A hunter in the desert who saw Anthony the Great enjoying himself with the brethren was scandalized. Abba Anthony asked the hunter to shoot his arrow. After doing so several times, Anthony asked the hunter to continue doing so continuously. When the hunter replied that the bow would break, Abba Anthony pointed out that also the human spirit would snap if it remained taut.[38]

In light of the challenges of our consumer and materialistic society, it is important to explain exactly what we mean by leisure. Leisure is not escapism, laziness, or boredom. For example, it is not spending time watching television or glued to one's computer, activities which can leave one numb and dazed.[39] Instead of leading to consumption and waste, authentic leisure expands into wonder and gratitude. Leisure is a way of wasting time, but it is a wasting of time that is life-giving, and energizing. In his *Leisure. The Basis of Culture*, Josef Pieper describes leisure as

> an attitude of non-activity, of inward calm, of silence; it means not being 'busy', but letting things happen.
>
> Leisure is a form of silence, of that silence which is the prerequisite of the apprehension of reality: only the silent hear and those who do not remain silent do not hear ... Leisure is a receptive attitude of mind, a contemplative attitude, and it is not only the occasion but also the capacity for steeping oneself in the whole of creation.[40]

Specifically, in the Christian tradition, leisure builds up friendship, family and community. It cultivates an appreciation of the arts and the beauties of creation. It leads to an integrated and wholesome lifestyle that harmonizes labor and leisure; it leaves space for God's work of holiness.[41]

### Leisure and worship

The celebration of worship is the centre of leisure. We most affirm the world and our experience of it when we praise the Creator. Thus, 'the most festive feast it is possible to celebrate is divine worship'.[42] The

Sabbath is a day of rest, but it is also a day of worship, because on this day we acknowledge publicly that we belong to another. In his apostolic letter *Dies Domini*, Pope John Paul II observes that:

> This is precisely why it is also *the day of rest.* Speaking vividly as it does of 'renewal' and 'detachment', the interruption of the often oppressive rhythm of work expresses the dependence of man [and woman] and the cosmos upon God. *Everything belongs to God!* The Lord's Day returns again and again to declare this principle within the weekly reckoning of time. The 'Sabbath' has therefore been interpreted evocatively as the determining element in the kind of 'sacred architecture' of time which marks biblical revelation. It recalls that *the universe and history belong to God.*[43]

Because, for the Christian, the Sabbath *is* the person of Jesus Christ who through his death and resurrection has become Lord of the Sabbath, it is a day of joy and celebration. From earliest times, Christians have gathered on the first day of the week because Jesus rose from the dead on that day. The first day is also the eighth day, which together symbolize not only the beginning of time, but also the fullness of time, reminding us of the 'festal gathering' at the end of time.[44] Sunday is not only the day of the Lord, but it is also the day of the Church. It is the day we gather together for the Eucharistic celebration which 'feeds and forms the church'. This is why 'the Sunday celebration of the Lord's Day and his Eucharist is at the heart of church life'.[45] This day of joy and rest is also a day of sharing, of solidarity with others. It is a day to turn towards God and towards others.

*Practical implications*

If we take seriously the understanding of work and leisure as outlined here, several practical implications emerge that may have an effect on our understanding of holiness. Firstly, work, as understood as a share in God's creation, becomes an opportunity for growth in holiness. A Christian vision of work insists that God can be found in the workplace and that this is one place where we can carry on Christ's creative and redemptive mission. Concretely this means that our attitude towards work, our relationship with employers or employees, and our promotion of a just and peaceful workplace are all ways that we live out our Christian vocation and mission in the world.

Secondly, the importance of leisure in the Christian life challenges us to evaluate how we spend our time. The refrain 'I don't have time' characterizes the experience of many women and men who feel themselves fighting against time or running against the clock. When the clock controls our life to such an extent that we lose a sense of balance, it is time to ask some serious questions: 'in this consumer society, how can I develop a healthy detachment from things and avoid the temptation to assess who I am by what I have? How do I strike a balance between labour and leisure that enlarges my capacity for friendships, for family life, for community?'[46]

Thirdly, we must ask ourselves how we celebrate the Lord's Day. 'Is the Sunday liturgy really the 'font and summit' of my life, as it is for all of the Church's activity?[47] Do all of my activities during the week flow into and find their culmination in the Sunday Eucharistic celebration?' In his book, *Giorno del Signore Giorno dell'uomo*, Enzo Bianchi sounds an alarm about the widespread neglect of the Lord's Day. He is convinced that the future of Christianity depends on living Sunday in a profoundly Christian way. Indeed, 'without living Sunday one cannot live the communal reality of the church: in that case the church is destined to become a movement and faith is reduced to a personal relationship of women and men to Jesus Christ'.[48] The Sunday celebration is intricately intertwined with what it means to be church, with our identity as women and men of faith bound together in communion, formed together into the body of Christ. This was certainly important for the early Christians, some of whom were martyred because of their celebration of the Lord's Day. One of the most moving testimonies comes from the *Acta Saturnini:*

> Turning towards Emeritus, the Proconsul asked: 'Were meetings, forbidden by the decrees of the Emperor, held in your house?' Emeritus, full of the Holy Sprit, said: 'In my house we celebrated the Sunday Eucharist.' And the other asked: 'Why did you allow them [other Christians] to enter?' He replied: 'Because they are my brothers and I cannot stop them.' ... the Proconsul replied: 'You had the responsibility to stop them.' And he said: 'I could not because we are Christians and we cannot be without the Sunday Eucharist ... The Proconsul then turned to Felix: 'Do not tell us if you are a Christian. Respond only if you participated in that meeting.' But Felix responded: 'As if the Christian can exist without the Sunday Eucharist or the Sunday Eucharist can be celebrated without the

Christian! Don't you know ... that the Christian finds his foundation in the Sunday Eucharist and the Sunday Eucharist in the Christian such that one cannot exist without the other? When you hear the name Christian, you know that he joins his brother before the Lord and, when you hear one speaking about a gathering, you recognize in that the name Christian. We have celebrated the gathering with great solemnity and we will always gather for the Sunday Eucharist and for reading the Scriptures of the Lord.'[49]

Celebrating Sunday is more than simply keeping the commandment to honour the Lord. It defines our Christian identity and helps us to live out the call to holiness. When Sunday becomes just another day, we lose a sense of celebration which is at the heart of Christian faith. By integrating a theology of festival with a theology of work, we will recover an equilibrium which is essential for holy living.[50]

## Holiness, justice and political action

Holiness, which is union with Christ in charity, has both a vertical and horizontal dimension. In recent years, tensions have emerged regarding the vertical and horizontal experience as a starting point for spirituality. For example, those committed to social justice and political action, often characterized by the horizontal approach, react against a more traditional spirituality which generally emphasizes the vertical. They suggest that the vertical approach promotes an individualistic and escapist attitude to holiness which lacks a social dimension. Those who accentuate the vertical approach suggest that social activists lack depth. Their restless activity, void of prayerful reflection, often masks a smoldering anger which is destructive to themselves and to others.[51] An authentic Christian approach to holiness today holds both the vertical and horizontal in careful balance. The key is integration, promoting both prayer and action in a faith that does justice. As the US Bishops wrote some years ago in *Economic Justice for All*:

The road to holiness for most of us lies in our secular vocations. We need a spirituality that calls forth and supports lay initiative and witness not just in our churches but also in business, in the labor movement, in the professions, in education, and in public life. Our faith is not just a weekend obligation, a mystery celebrated around the altar on Sunday. It is a pervasive reality to be practiced every day in homes, offices, factories, schools, and businesses across our land. We cannot separate what we believe from how we act in the marketplace and in the broader community, for this is where we make our primary contribution to the pursuit of economic justice.[52]

An authentic spirituality transforms hearers into doers of the word. In his apostolic letter, *A Call to Action, Octagesima Adveniens*, Paul VI suggests a methodology which moves towards this integration. The first step consists of analyzing the contemporary situation, of trying to see it objectively. This assumes that Christians are aware of political and economic realities and that they attempt to understand them. The second is to make a judgment based on prayer, discernment and reflection in light of the Gospel and the social teaching of the Church. This presupposes familiarity with Scripture and a formation in the social doctrine of the Church. Finally, the third step moves from theory to practice by taking concrete steps to work for the transformation of society in light of Gospel values.[53] Echoing the 'See, Judge, Act' formula of Joseph Cardijn, this is a practical strategy for integrating faith with social and political action in the here and now.

### Eschatological or final holiness: the communion of saints
In this life, our holiness is always incomplete. We are united to God and God lives in us but we see now 'as in a mirror, in an enigmatic way' (1 Cor. 13:12): it is only in eternity that we will come to the fullness of holiness. We are holy now, because in the Spirit we are united to Christ and our lives do give glory to the Father, but our holiness is fragile and vulnerable. For this reason, *Lumen gentium* 48 reminds us that 'The church, to which we are all called in Christ Jesus, and in which through the grace of God we attain sanctity, will reach its completion only in the glory of heaven, when the time for the restoration of all things will come (see Acts 3:21) and along with the human race the whole universe, which is intimately united to humanity and through it attains its goal, will be established perfectly in Christ (see Eph. 1:10; Col. 1:20; 2 Pet. 3:10–13).'

When we recite the Apostles' Creed, we profess our belief in the communion of saints. The Greek and Latin texts have an ambiguity: it can be a communion, that is, a sharing, of either holy persons or holy things. Here we return again to the liturgy as teacher of holiness. In the Eucharist we have a sharing of the body and blood of the Lord, of the word of God, of grace and love. But it is also a sharing among holy persons. In each eucharistic prayer we remember the Church and people throughout the world. We also commend to God those who may be in need of purification or healing after death, but we also celebrate in union with the Virgin Mary, the angels and saints. The Eucharist is a celebration of the whole family of God. The saints and the Virgin Mary are models and intercessors, spurring us on to holiness. In the liturgy we find a model, a hope and inspiration. We also see the consummation of all our yearnings.

We do not worship alone, but with those who have gone before us, with the whole communion of saints. Holiness is not an individual quest of the here and now, but is a journey or pilgrimage in the company of others – especially the martyrs and saints who have gone before us. As we worship God in communion with them, we have a privileged opportunity to grow in holiness. Their example and intercession invite us to a deeper experience of union with Christ. The presence of the saints and martyrs, along with the Virgin Mary, fills us with eschatological hope, that we will join them in full communion as we sing an unending hymn of praise to God.[54]

## Notes

1. Karl Rahner, 'The Church of the Saints', *Theological Investigations*, (London: Darton, Longman and Todd 1971), vol. III, pp.99–100.
2. St. Thomas Aquinas, *ST*, 3a, q.65, a.3.
3. Paul J. Philibert, *The Priesthood of the Faithful* (Collegeville: Liturgical Press, 2005).
4. For an overview of the different schools of spirituality, see Kees Waaijman, *Spirituality, Forms, Foundations, Methods* (Leuven: Peeters, 2002), pp.116–211).
5. *CCC*, 2684. The quote from St. Basil is *De Spiritu Sancto*, 26, 62 (PG 32, 184).
6. For an overview of these movements and their significance today, see Jesús Castellano Cervera, *Carismi per il terzo millennio, i movimenti ecclesiali e le nuove comunità* (Roma Morena: Edizioni OCD, 2001); Bruno Secondin, *I nuovi protagonisti* (Cinisello Balsamo: Edizioni Paoline, 1991); Fidel González Fernández, *I movimenti. Dalla Chiesa degli apostoli a oggi* (Milan: RCS Libri, 2000). See especially the postscript of the book by the (then) Cardinal Joseph Ratzinger (now Pope Benedict), 'Movimenti ecclesiali e il loro collocazione teologica',

pp.303–36; Christoph Hegge, *Il Vaticano II e i movmenti ecclesiali una recezione carismatica* (Roma: Città Nuova Editrice, 2001); *Movements in the Church, Proceedings of the World Congress of Ecclesial Movements (Rome, 27-29 May 1998)* (The Laity Today: Vatican City: Vatican Press, 1999) the English edition of Cardinal Ratzinger's essay is translated here: 'The Ecclesial Movements: A Theological Reflection on their Place in the Church', pp. 23–51. Also important is *The Ecclesial Movements in the Pastoral Concern of the Bishops* (The Laity Today: Vatican City: Vatican Press, 2000).

7. See John Allen, *Opus Dei* (New York: Doubleday, 2005).

8. *Christifideles laici* (Vatican City: Liberia editrice Vaticana, 1989), 27.

9. St. Bernard of Clairvaux, *Apologia to William of Saint Thierry* 4, 8 as cited by John Paul II, Apostolic Exhortation *Vita Consecrata* (Vatican City: Libereria editrice Vaticana, 1996), 118.

10. Basil Hume, *Towards a Civilization of Love, Being Church in Today's World* (London: Hodder and Stoughton, 1988).

11. Avery Dulles, 'The Reception of Vatican II at the Extraordinary Synod of 1985', in *The Reception of Vatican II* (eds. Giuseppe Alberigo, et al.: Washington DC: Catholic University of America Press, 1987), p.350.

12. Paolo Molinari, 'Santo', in *Nuovo dizionario di spiritualità* (Cinisello Balsamo: Edizioni San Paulo, 1985), p.1370. This whole dictionary article provides a masterful synthesis of the conciliar teaching on holiness (pp.1369–85) and what is developed here has been strongly influenced by it, and by the course I had many years ago with Fr Molinari at the Gregorian University on this topic.

13. Christopher O'Donnell, 'Love of the Church', in *A Church with a Future: Challenges to Irish Catholicism Today* (eds N. Coll and P. Scallon; Dublin: Columba, 2005), pp.72–3.

14. Cf. *Lumen gentium* 39. All references to the Second Vatican Council, unless otherwise indicated, are taken from Norman P. Tanner, *Decrees of the Ecuminical Councils* (London: Sheed and Ward Limited; Washington DC: Georgetown University Press, 1990) vol. II. Cf. Francis A. Sullivan, *The Church We Believe In. One, Holy, Catholic and Apostolic* (New York: Paulist Press, 1988), pp.66–7; Christopher O'Donnell, 'Holy', in *Ecclesia: A Theological Encyclopedia of the Church* (Collegeville: Michael Glazier, Liturgical Press, 1996), pp.198–202; René Latourelle, *Christ and the Church. Signs of Salvation* (Staten Island NY: Alba House, 1972) especially pp.127–33, 211–64.

15. This observation was made by Paul O'Callaghan, 'The Holiness of the Church in Lumen Gentium', *Thomist* 52 (1988), p.673, n.1.

16. See Walter A. Abbott, S. J. (ed.), *The Documents of Vatican II* (New York: America Press, 1966), pp.65–6.

17. Francis A. Sullivan, 'Do the Sins of Her Members Affect the Holiness of the Church?' This article has not yet been published. I am grateful to Fr Sullivan for sharing it with me and for discussing this topic with me.

18. Sullivan, *The Church We Believe In*, p.79.

19. Ibid. p.70–2.

20. See International Theological Commission, 'Memory and Reconciliation: The Church and Faults of the Past' (December 1999), *Origins* 29/39 (16 May 2000), pp.625–44.

21. Sullivan, *The Church We Believe In*, pp.79–83.

22. Latourelle, *Christ and the Church*, pp.248–9.

23. John Paul II, '*Incarnationis Mysterium*', *Origins* 28/26 (10 December 1998) p.450.

24. See the CDRom *Santa Caterina da Siena Opera Omnia, Testi e Concordanze* (Pistoia: Provincia Romano dei Frati Predicatori Centro Reviste 2002) which I am using here. *Lettera* 233 and *Lettere*, vol.IV, p.5.

25. *Lumen gentium*, 40.

26. See the Code of Canon Law, Canons 573ff. For a study of recent developments regarding the relationship between laity, clergy and those in consecrated life, see Rogelio Garcia Mateo, 'Il rapporto laico-chierico-consacrato secondo le Esortazioni Apostoliche *Christifideles laici, Pastores dabo vobis, Vita consecrata*', *Periodica de Re Canonica* 92 (2003), pp.359–82.

27. Lawrence Cunningham, 'The Universal Call to Holiness: Martyrs of Charity and Witnesses to Truth', in *New Catholic Encyclopaedia* (2000), p.109.

28. Ann W. Astell (ed.), *Lay Sanctity, Medieval and Modern: A Search for Models* (Notre Dame: University of Notre Dame Press, 2000).

29. Ibid., p.19. See my review in *INTAMS* 8, 1 (Spring, 2001), pp.115–6.

30. Michael J. Schultheis, Edward P. DeBerri and Peter J. Henriot, *Our Best Kept Secret. The Rich Heritage of Catholic Social Teaching* (Washington DC: Center of Concern, 1987).

31. This perception of work as a curse is exemplified in Genesis 2:5–25, which 'lies deep within the Western humanity's collective and personal psyches', as we shall explain in the next section. See Edward C.

Sellner, 'Work', in *The New Dictionary of Catholic Spirituality*, ed. Michael Downey, (Collegeville: Michael Glazier, The Liturgical Press, 1993), pp.1044–51; see also D. Dumm, 'Work and Leisure', *American Benedictine Review* 28 (1977), pp.334–50.

32. Barbara Killinger, *Workaholics, The Respectable Addiction* (New York: Simon & Schuster, 1991). As quoted in Harry A. Cronin, 'The Addictions of Clergy and Religious', *Human Development* 16/4 (Winter 1995), p.25.

33. John Paul II, *Laborem Exercens: On Human Work* (1981), n.24.

34. *Gaudium et spes,* 35.

35. US Bishops, *Economic Justice for All*, 32 in *Catholic Social Thought, The Documentary Heritage,* ed. David J. O'Brien and Thomas A. Shannon; Maryknoll (NY: Orbis Books, 1992). Sellner, 'Work', p.1045

36. Pierre Teilhard de Chardin, *Le Milieu Divin* (London: 1967) Fontana, p.64, as quoted in Thomas Corbishley, *The Spirituality of Teilhard de Chardin* (London: Collins, The Fontana Library, 1974), p.111. Cf. also Ursula King, *Christ in All Things* (London: SCM Press, 1997).

37. Gerald L. Stockhausen, 'I'd Love to, but I Don't Have the Time: Jesuits and Leisure', *Studies in the Spirituality of Jesuits* 27/3 (May 1995), p.4.

38. Antony the Great, 13 in *Sayings of the Desert Fathers* (trans. Benedicta Ward: Oxford: Mowbray, 1975), p.3. Thomas Aquinas (*ST* II, II, 168, 2 reply) has a variation on this saying. He attributes it to John the Evangelist instead of to Antony.

39. Stockhausen, 'I'd Love to, But I Don't Have the Time', p.4.

40. Josef Pieper, *Leisure: the Basis of Culture* (New York and Scarborough, Ontario: Mentor, New American Library, 1963), pp.40–1.

41. US Bishops, *Economic Justice for All*, 337 in *Catholic Social Thought,* p.657. See also n.23 on pp.576–7.

42. Pieper, *Leisure: the Basis of Culture*, p.56.

43. John Paul II, Apostolic Letter *Dies Domini* (Vatican City: Libreria Editrice Vaticana, 1998), 15.

44. Ibid. 26. See also *CCC*, 2168–95.

45. John Paul II, *Dies Domini,* 32, see also *CCC,* 2177.

46. US Bishops, *Economic Justice for All*, 23.

47. *SC*, 10.

48. Enzo Bianchi, *Giorno del Signore. Giorno dell'uomo. Per un rinnovamento della domenica* (Casale Monferrato: Edizioni Piemme, 1995), p.9.

49. As quoted in Bianchi, *Giorno del Signore*, p.194.

50. Hugo Rahner, *Homo ludens* (Brescia: Paideia, 1969) has developed this theme without particular reference to lay spirituality. Beginning with the theme of *Deus ludens* (God at play), he moves to speak about the human person at play, the Church at play and finally the celestial dance.

51. Donal Dorr, *Spirituality and Justice* (Dublin: Gill and Macmillian; Maryknoll, NY: Orbis Books, 1985), p1. For a reflection on the link between politics, justice and holiness, see also his *Integral Spirituality* (Dublin: Gill and Macmillian, 1990). See also A. Girodano, 'Politica' *Nuovo dizionario di spiritualità*, pp.1225–41; Leonardo Boff, 'The Need for Political Saints: From a Spirituality of Liberation to the Preactice of Liberation', *Cross Currents* 30 (1980–81), pp.369–75, 384; Philip Sheldrane, *Images of Holiness: Explorations in Contemporary Spirituality* (London: Darton, Longman and Todd, 1987) pp.91–104.

52. US Bishops, *Economic Justice for All*, 25.

53. Paul VI, *A Call to Action, Octagesima Adveniens* (1987), n.4 in *Catholic Social Thought: The Documetary History*, p.266. See also Schultheis, De Berri and Herriot, *Our Best Kept Secret*, pp.14–15.

54. See Lawrence Cunningham, *A Brief History of the Saints* (Oxford: Blackwell Publishing, 2005), p.31.

*'The Cross not only grows in breadth. It has height and its depth. Now we must still regard its height. From above, out of the mystery of God, the hand of the Father reaches down. Thereby movement comes into the image. On the one hand, the divine hand appears to lower the Cross from the height of the eternal in order to bring the world life and reconciliation. But it draws upward at the same time. The descent of God's goodness brings the whole tree, with all of its branches, into the ascent of the Son, into the upward dynamic of his love. The world moves from the Cross upward to the freedom and expanse of the promise of God.'*
Joseph Cardinal Ratzinger (Pope Benedict XVI), *Images of Hope* (San Franncisco: Ignatius Press, 2006), p.76.

Basilica of Saint Clement, Rome
Apse Mosaic, 12th Century
The Empyrean
Reproduced courtesy of the Irish Dominican Fathers.

# 5

# The Expansion Project:
# Holiness in the twenty-first century

'You [dear Friend] asked me what in my opinion will be the
characteristic feature of holiness in the future. Well, in my opinion,
your question cannot be answered. I am no prophet – and I doubt
greatly that the prophets themselves could give you an answer.
... Holiness is the work of the Holy Spirit ... the Spirit is he who
breathes where he will, when he will, as he will. He is liberty,
innovation itself, the eternal and intangible innovation of God.'
Henri de Lubac, *The Church: Paradox and Mystery*
(Staten Island: Ecclesia Press, 1969), p.122.

'... The time has come, at least it seems to us, to discover, to highlight,
to build, not only the "interior castle", but also the "exterior castle".'
Chiara Lubich, from a Speech on the Occasion of the Conferral
of the UELCI Prize (9 March 1995) in *La dottrina spirituale*
(ed. Michel Vandeleene, Milan: Mondadori, 2001), p.74.

'A blur of romance clings to the notions of 'publicans,' 'sinners,' 'the
poor,' 'the people in the marketplace,' 'our neighbor,' as though of course
God should reveal himself, if at all, to these simple people, these Sunday
school watercolour figures, who are so purely themselves in their
tattered robes, who are single in themselves, while we now are various,
complex and full at heart. We are busy. So, I see now, were they. Who
shall ascend into the hill of the Lord? Or who shall stand in his holy
place? There is no one but us. There is no one to send, nor a clean hand,
nor a pure heart on the face of the earth, nor in the earth, but only us, a
generation comforting ourselves with the option that we have come at an
awkward time, that our innocent fathers are all dead ... and our children
busy and troubled, and we ourselves unfit, not yet ready ... But there is
no one but us. There never has been.'
Annie Dillard, 'Holy the firm', in *The Annie Dillard Reader*
(New York: Harper Perennial, 1994), p.445.

In the previous chapters, Christian holiness has been discussed in its personal, ecclesial and social dimensions, revolving around the fundamental transformation of believers in union with Christ. Through Jesus, who is the way, the truth and the life, and in the Spirit, we are drawn into communion with the Father. In light of sacred Scripture and tradition (Chapters 1 and 4), this is a non-negotiable foundation of a Christian perspective on holiness. At the same time, the Holy Spirit, the Spirit of the risen Lord, works in ways beyond our understanding and expectations. 'Holiness is the work of the Holy Spirit', Henri de Lubac reminds us, 'the Spirit is he who breathes where he will, when he will, as he will. He is liberty, innovation itself, the eternal and intangible innovation of God.'[1] In trying to discern some of the designs of holiness (Chapter 2) in God's building project, diverse models of sanctity emerged, each of whom responded to God's call in the circumstances in which they lived and in light of who they were. In a certain sense, their holiness was unique to them. Yet the legacies of their lives, their examples of holiness, have broadened our horizons and enabled us to see some of God's creative ways of inviting us to live out our own call to holiness. Chapter 3 explored the ordinary ways that God draws us into holy living by considering the ordinary daily for this extraordinary dwelling.

The purpose of this concluding chapter is to focus on what it means to live holiness in the complex world that is unfolding around us, a world that requires a new manner of living holiness. Application is fundamental. Critical to the discussion is the point that God is constantly calling us to incarnate the Gospel and not to compromise our potential for holiness. This is the challenge that C. S. Lewis recognized when he wrote that '[God] is building quite a different house from the one you thought of'.[2] By broadening our horizons and cultivating a contemplative gaze, we are able to discern the design of God's expanding building project. Only then will we have the wisdom to see the future blueprints through the eyes of the designer. Then will we perceive God inviting us to construct both an interior and an exterior castle that can only be built with others. The way we live out this holiness will be affected by realities particularly relevant for our age, which include issues such as globalization and contact with people of other religions. Responsibility for the care of God's ever-expanding building project also increases as we consider our social commitment to the vulnerable in society and our environment. The Father's house has many unexplored mansions, and we will be prepared to enter into these new rooms only if we are attentive to the Holy

Spirit, who is described by Hans Urs Von Balthasar as 'the Unknown beyond the Word',[3] and by learning to contemplate God in all things.

## Broadening our horizons

The first requirement for apprehending the designs of God's expansion project is the ability to penetrate beyond appearances. The project requires a wide-angle lens and open vistas. Flannery O'Conner, a twentieth-century American writer from Georgia, whose works focused on humanity's grotesque deformities and head-on collisions with grace, builds her short story 'Revelation' on the surprising way that holiness can manifest itself.

First some necessary background: Ruby Turpin, the protagonist in 'Revelation', is a stout, hardworking, church-going woman, who finds herself in a physician's waiting room. Ruby is there with her husband, Claud, who having been kicked in the shin by their cow, is seeing the doctor. In typical O'Connor fashion, the characters are humorously described in detail. Ruby's ever-observant eye and critical mind assess everyone in the waiting room:

> There is the runny-nose boy asprawl on the couch where she would like to sit herself; his mother, a 'lank-faced woman' whose lips are stained brown by chewing tobacco; his 'thin leathery old' grandmother, wearing a dress like a feed sack; a 'lean stringy old fellow' with his eyes clamped shut; a 'well-dressed gray-haired' lady, her daughter a 'fat girl of eighteen or nineteen' whose face is 'blue with acne' and a nurse with the 'highest stack of yellow hair Mrs. Turpin had ever seen.'[4]

As 'a hillbilly Thomist, who lies awake at night dividing and classifying people with medieval rigor', Mrs Turpin heaves herself into a seat and continues to categorize everybody socially and spiritually.[5] Having scanned and sorted the folks around her, Turpin concludes that she and Claud – holy, righteous, church-going folk – are at the top of the stack, while she put the others where they belonged, in their place far below the two of them.

The conversation turns to hog-raising. In the ensuing discussion, Ruby Turpin's narrow-mindedness and bigotry emerges. The climax occurs when the fat girl with acne, significantly named Mary Grace, who just happens to be a student at a fancy women's college in the North and who has been reading a book titled *Human Development*, begins to glare, leer and groan in protest at Mrs Turpin's tirade. Meanwhile Mrs Turpin continues her narcissistic self-aggrandizing monologue: 'When I think who all I could have been besides myself and what all I got, a little of everything, and a good disposition besides, I just feel like shouting, "'Thank you, Jesus, for making everything the way it is!"' Mary Grace cannot take any more, and she hurls the book at Mrs Turpin while calling her a wart hog. She bluntly tells her to go back to hell where she came from!

The waiting room erupts with activity and the unfortunate girl is hauled away in an ambulance. The Turpins head home, but Ruby is shaken. She eventually finds herself standing alone before the hogpen in her backyard, asking God, 'How, precisely, is she a wart hog? What do she and wart hogs have in common?'[6] Her desire to understand who she was before her Maker was revealed to her in an incredible vision. She saw a vast horde of souls 'rumbling' towards heaven:

> There were whole companies of white trash, clean for the first time in their lives, and bands of black niggers in white robes, and battalions of freaks and lunatics shouting and clapping and leaping like frogs. And bringing up the end of the procession was a tribe of people whom she recognized at once as those who, like herself and Claud, always had a little of everything and the God given wit to use it right. She leaned forward to observe them closer. They were marching behind the others with great dignity, accountable as they had always been for good order and common sense and respectable behaviour. They alone were on key. Yet she could see in their shocked and altered faces that even their virtues were being burned away. She lowered her hands and gripped the rail of the hog pen, her eyes small but fixed unblinkingly on what lay ahead.[7]

In that moment of 'revelation', Ruby Turpin understood her need for God and she faced the future, 'what lay ahead', with a new openness to the Holy One.

### Holiness and Contemplative Living

Openness to the Holy One, so necessary for living holiness, is also enhanced by discovering a more contemplative approach to life – by deliberately becoming aware of the specific realities of existence, by staying mindful of the implications and ramifications of Scripture, theology, basic Catholic social teaching and following through with our lives. In many ways, holiness is a choice that once chosen begs the disciple to practice daily with an active, joyful, purposeful, sensibility. The practise of faithful living demands that we learn to see God in all and all in God.

Throughout human history, individuals have responded to God's call to holiness, despite what appeared to be insurmountable odds. Grace, grit and sweat, all hallmarks of an honest contemplative approach to life, have enabled ordinary men and women to reach out with the compassion of the Christ, to love and serve humanity and their Lord. Grounded in the strong discipline of contemplative living, individuals have joined in God's building project with remarkable results. They have become dwellings where forgiveness, reconciliation and peace prevail. Christ's encounter with the woman caught in adultery (described in Jn 8:1–11) offers a hint of how this can continue to happen, even today. In this passage, Jesus invites the accusers of this woman to a new vision of reality. In an essay titled, *Writing in the Dust. Reflections on 11th September and its Aftermath*, and commenting on John 8, the Archbishop of Canterbury, Rowan Williams, says:

> When the accusation is made [against this woman], Jesus at first makes no reply but writes with his finger on the ground. What on earth is he doing? Commentators have had plenty of suggestions, but there is one meaning that seems to me obvious in the light of what I think we learned that morning [11 September]. He hesitates. He does not draw a line, fix an interpretation, tell the woman who she is and what her fate should be. He allows a moment, a longish moment, in which people are given time to see themselves differently precisely because he refuses to make the sense they want. When he lifts his head, there is both judgement and release.[8]

This hesitation gives the onlookers a chance 'to look again', at themselves and at the woman. As the Nobel-winning Irish poet, Seamus Heaney, notes when referring to this same passage, 'He [Jesus] does something that takes away the obsession of the moment ... People are suddenly gazing at something else and pausing for a moment.'[9] The first thing to do to live holiness today is simply to be open to a contemplative way of life; to look, to see, to ask what is going on. Much of 'applied' holiness depends on simple, personal awareness, reflection and integration with

Scripture. The basic contemplative question is: what is God doing here and how am I called to respond?

Only with a contemplative gaze is it possible to see through distracting appearances and find Christ in others, even if the other is our perceived 'enemy'. The monastic witness of Dom Christian de Chergé, mentioned in Chapter 2, explains what this means in a practical way. He remained loving in the face of death, even when it meant his accepting a shocking and violent death. Holiness in this context implies loving God and others without counting the cost, and refusing to renounce that love and the God who calls. Dom de Chergé wrote:

> For this life lost, totally mine and totally theirs, I thank God, who seems to have willed it entirely for the sake of that JOY in everything and in spite of everything. In this THANK YOU, which is said for everything in my life from now on, I certainly include you, friends of yesterday and today, and you, my friends of this place ... And also you, my last-minute friend, who will not have known what you were doing: Yes I want this THANK YOU and this 'A DIEU' to be for you, too because in God's face I see yours.[10]

De Chergé saw into God's heart and in seeing God's compassion for life, he recognized all of humanity as brothers and sisters, as members of one family. We too can learn to see and incarnate compassion, as did De Chergé. This is our divine assignment. Through prayer and a commitment to follow we begin to perceive others and the world through the lens of a compassionate God. The testament of Dom Christian is subtitled *'Quand un À-Dieu s'envisage'* – 'when a farewell is contemplated', or 'when we have to face an *A-Dieu*'. This is much stronger than the English equivalent, 'farewell': it literally means 'to God'. The word when hyphenated en-visagé can be translated as 'envisaged' or as 'contemplated', but it can also mean something that has received *a visage* or has been given a face (in line with the philosophical thought of Emmanuel Lévinas). So the subtitle can also mean, 'contemplating when God has been given a face'.[11] Dom Christian's contemplation is anticipated at the moment of death and his assassin thus becomes a 'last-minute friend' who is reflected in the face of God. According to Abbot Bernardo Olivera, one might suggest that Dom Christian de Chergé is playing with words here. Dom Christian was a 'true mystic, someone who saw persons and the world as they are in God, even more than a prophet, who sees God in persons and the world. Thus his thought is interpreted better as "'in God's face I see yours".'[12] This begs the question, it is necessary to pause and ask: 'is this not the sort of vision we need to live out the call to holiness today?'

## From the interior castle to the exterior castle

Holiness is God's project. In the mix of divine initiative and human cooperation, the water of grace is blended with the cement of committed discipleship. In turn, the master builder applies this mortar to us, the bricks, 'the living stones', and builds us into a 'spiritual house'. Like all structures, this building is dimensional, having both an exterior and an interior. We are called, chosen by the architect himself, to be so much more than simple cosy cottages lining quiet rural streets in a quaint village. We are living stones and we are being built into a grand edifice where the Triune God desires to dwell in full communion with his people in the thick and thin of tumbling reality.

The Christian East has always been more focused on the three divine Persons than on the one God. Thus its view of holiness is profoundly Trinitarian, which sees the communion of life of the three Persons shared with humankind. The Western view of holiness, being more centred on the one God, needs to be complemented by the richer and more dynamic Eastern sense of varying relationships among the divine Persons. In the West, such Trinitarian diversification is often found as a special grace of deep holiness, as in St Catherine of Siena; the liturgy would, however, teach a Trinitarian life to all Christians. In this, as in many other matters, the Western Church needs to go to school in the East.[13]

Within God's very self is community: a communion of love that is mirrored in the Trinitarian relationship. Since we are created in the image and likeness of God (see Gen. 1:26–27), we live our humanity to the fullest only insofar as we relate to others after the image and likeness of the Trinity. The God who dwells within each of us, who abides in us, also dwells among us and invites us into a relationship with others that mirrors the communion manifest in the Persons of the Holy Trinity. In living our call to holiness in mutual giving, love and availability to those around us, an 'exterior' mansion is being formed – a dwelling that unites us profoundly and inescapably with others. Formed in the image and likeness of the Holy Trinity, the human person says – as in the Lord's Prayer – not me, but us, not my, but ours. Every human community – those who surround us at home, at work, at church, at school – are meant to be transformed by grace into an image or icon of the Trinity.[14]

God's big building project affects all humanity. The Second Vatican Council's pastoral constitution on the Church in the world, *Gaudium et spes*, recognized the communal nature of the human vocation in a world that is 'increasingly one', where people become 'increasingly interdependent'(*GS* 24). This has consequences on how we relate to others:

> Indeed, when the lord Jesus prays to his Father that 'they may all be one ... even as we are one' (Jn 17:21–22), disclosing prospects unattainable to human reason, he indicated a certain similarity between the union of the divine persons and the union of God's children in truth and love. And this similarity indicates that the human, the only creature on earth whom God willed for its own sake, can attain its full identity only in sincere-self giving. (*GS* 24).

Holiness that has its roots in the Holy Trinity is a call to love, to a love that expresses itself more and more in a gift of self to God and to others.

All of this has practical implications for living the call to holiness. Gently placing the challenge before us, Chiara Lubich writes, 'the time has come ... to discover, to highlight, to build not only the interior castle, but the exterior castle'.[15] This means we are invited to recognize God's presence both within us and among us – both personally and communally. It is an invitation to live the call to holiness together, reciprocally, modelling our relationships with one another on the communion of love reflected in the Trinitarian dynamic. Concretely, this spirit of Trinitarian vibrancy must influence the way we interact with those people close to us in our everyday lives, and with those who are beyond our immediate circle.

### Globalization and holiness

Living the call to holiness today includes a genuine concern for the most vulnerable. In Flannery O'Connor's short story, Ruby Turpin's revelation led her to stand before her maker with great humility. It also involved recognizing her fundamental connectedness and solidarity with those around her, including the 'poor' she finds in the doctor's office. They are, in one sense, her 'communion of saints', they are the ones who will lead her to heaven. As it was for Ruby Turpin, so it is for each of us. Ruby's predicament brings up a profound question, namely: who are the poor? It is essential that all would-be saints understand that no-one grows holy out of the riches of self. We are all empty-handed beggars in need of Heaven's alms. Holiness is dependent on dispensed grace. All that we have and all that we are is a gift from our creator. St. Thérèse of Lisieux, echoing St. John of the Cross, wrote, 'In the evening of this life, I shall appear before You with empty hands.'[16] There is nothing any of us beggars can bring before God our creator except our empty, tattered, treasured selves.

This realization becomes urgent in the context of the globalized world in which we live. Globalization,[17] which includes an increased mobility of goods, services, technology and capital throughout the world, literally brings the world into our homes where we are made aware, for example, of the children who die from starvation each day, the ravages of war, and genocide.[18] Instant access to information on natural disasters like tsunamis, hurricanes, floods and earthquakes remind us of the vulnerability of humanity, especially among those who are poor. Information overload – the modern malady of 'up-to-the-minute' current events and the droning chatter surrounding hot topics and timely issues offered by various media – tends to make us less, not more, aware of the magnitude of suffering. Over-awarenesscan leave the informed fatigued, and sadly, but realistically, apathetic. A challenge for Christians is to develop, in the words of Nicholas Lash, a 'global imagination – a sense of solidarity with the whole of humankind – past, present and future'. Globalization requires us to broaden the 'we' from our own family, friends and neighbours to realize that 'who "we" are is nothing less than everyone'.[19] An authentic living of holiness must include this 'we' – the true self in authentic solidarity with all.

In practical terms, responding to the call to holiness cannot be disconnected from a commitment to a more simple way of living and a generous sharing of our resources and talents with others. It also has an effect on our political commitments; for example, in the responsibility to support public policy that takes into account the poor and vulnerable of society. This includes both the poorest of the poor and the hardworking, never-making-ends-meet poor who often fall through the cracks – this group comprises the elderly, the disabled and infirmed, single mothers and their children. While taking initiative to care for abused or abandoned baby girls in China or responding to the HIV epidemic in Africa, one must be careful not to turn an arrogant Turpinish eye towards the less-than-glamorous needy areas and people of Europe and the United

States. In the words of the classic American 1980s bumper sticker, we must 'think globally, act locally'. How we treat others, both the person immediately next door and the flood victim on another continent, is a good way to gauge how we are responding to God's call to holiness. The bottom line is that Jesus' gospel challenge takes on particular poignancy in the context of urgent, very real global needs: 'For I was hungry and you gave me food, I was thirsty and you gave me drink, I was a stranger and you made me welcome' (Mt. 25:35–36).[20] The reality of globalization challenges us to realize that Jesus himself is bidding us to recognize him in our neighbour in London and in Lagos, in New York and in New Delhi, in Turin and in Teheran, and in ourselves.

Jesus is also bidding us to feed the hungry through concrete action, through providing food and supplies to those in need. All acts of compassion done in Jesus' name bless the world and have the power to open spiritually closed doors. The crisis of world famine does not stop with satiating physical hunger. It requires that the bread of life be distributed to the spiritually hungry as well. Hunger pangs rumble around us and within us. The peoples of the earth are hungering both for physical food and spiritual nourishment. The failures of great ideologies, the unhappiness linked with materialism have left a certain void or restlessness in people. This emptiness can lead to both negative as well as positive ends. Negatively, it can turn people towards fundamentalism or a spirituality of the sects. Positively it can open the way for a return to the Holy, to a discovery of that interior space, that interior castle where God dwells.[21] The great temptation is to remedy the ailment with clutter, be it sex, drugs, or frenetic activity. The courage to welcome silence comes only when people are encouraged and reassured by others that God will meet them and their deepest needs in quiet and stillness. Silence is the key to open the door of the contemplative castle that we can become in Christ. This is not just physical silence, but also an interior silence – a sense of tranquillity and serenity. This does not oblige everyone to live a cloistered call, because even in the middle of intense activity, this interior silence opens the door to contemplative living. 'Silence is a way of waiting, a way of watching, and a way of listening to what is going on within and around us,' says John Chyssavgis:

> It is a way of interiority, of stopping and ... of exploring the cellars of the heart and the center of life. It is a way of entering within, so that we do not ultimately go without. Silence is never merely a

cessation of words; that would be too restrictive and too negative a definition of silence. Rather, it is the pause that holds together – indeed, it makes sense of – all the words, spoken and unspoken. Silence is the glue that connects our attitudes and actions. Silence is fullness, not emptiness; it is not an absence, but an awareness of a presence.[22]

Silence will lead us into the interior castle so that we can together be built into an exterior castle where God dwells among his people.[23]

## Christian holiness in the context of world religions

God's ever-expanding building project, our call to holiness, has many rooms that we share in common with people of other religions. We are united in our humanity, in our needs, in our aspirations for a better world. Each of us needs daily bread and basic shelter, security and community. We are all fragile in the face of natural disasters and in the aggressions of war. We all search for meaning and transcendence and the experience of being fully human. People of all religions, people of every philosophical persuasion, share a common humanity. At times, we gather in the same rooms, when, for example, natural disasters draw us to mutual solidarity or when we joyfully celebrate national days. In these rooms, however, we do not set up residence; we do not abide there. At times, we may visit them respectfully when invited, but then it is time to go back to our own space, richer for the encounter, more reflective and filled with wonder, perhaps even awe at the manifestations of holiness we see in others. These signs of holiness can only exist with God's grace, and this grace is, we believe, mysteriously always Christ's.

Recognizing signs of holiness in other religions is not a threat to Christianity: rather, it is a way of acknowledging the Spirit at work in diverse circumstances. The Spirit is present in the world, in our lives, in ways beyond our wildest hopes and expectations. 'In their faithfulness to Christ', Gavin D'Costa notes, 'Christians are obliged to recognize the activity of the Spirit in the world and, through this, deepen their understanding of Christ.'[24] Without a doubt, the Spirit is moving in us, even before we act, working more than we and far better than we. We believe the Holy Spirit is also at work mysteriously in those who are of other religions where we find genuine signs of holiness. We may need to acknowledge honestly that we cannot predict the final design, as we ponder these complex new developments in the building project. At the same time, we enter into dialogue with others convinced that the love of God breaks down barriers that divide humanity.

The Second Vatican Council brought with it a much more positive approach to world religions. Before the Council, theologians mainly sought to point out the inadequacies and flaws in other religions. Now there is an acknowledgement of the riches, in both the Constitution on the Church (*LG* 16) and the Declaration on Non-Christian Religions (Nostra Aetate 2) of the spiritual riches that God has bestowed on the followers of other religions. With this more positive approach, it is now possible to have a dialogue with representatives of these religions not only on ethical matters like justice and peace, but also concerning the transcendent. We can share profoundly about religious experience and examine together the mystical writers of the great traditions. This development in the area of spirituality leaves serious questions for the systematic theologians, who are challenged to show how such holiness is compatible with the unique mediatorship of Christ, how the paschal mystery is shared by those of other religions (see *GS* 22) and how grace is bestowed in, and not despite of, these religions.

When people of other religions visit our homes, hospitality enkindles within us a desire to offer them a generous welcome through sharing our goods, our time and our very selves with them.[25] While we do not impose our ways on them, we also do not feel the need to take on their ways. Recognizing holiness in other religions does not mean trying to smooth over our differences by 'canonizing' good and holy people, like Ghandi, for example. Gavin D'Costa says:

At the level of formal canonisation I do not think ... [this] is at all appropriate. This is not because there are any lack of very holy Hindus, or because the Roman Catholic Church has any problem with affirming that holiness, truth and grace exist outside its visible social boundaries. Vatican II made the latter quite clear. My main objection would be on the grounds that canonization is an intra-ecclesial act retrospectively identifying a person whose life conforms to, but more often extends and sometimes problematises, the under-standing of the orthodox Christian faith in terms of practice, doctrine and liturgy. Such a person is also the object of the cult of veneration, whereby the faithful grow in the Roman Catholic Faith through active communion with that saint ... One point of canonisation, at least as argued in the Second Vatican Council, is to link the earthly church with the heavenly church: Roman Catholic saints are embodiments of the presence of the risen Lord within his Church; their holiness is the extension of the story about God's holiness in the ecclesial body of Christ.[26]

One of the points that D'Costa makes is that in recent years, some scholars assume that holiness and saintliness are 'trans-religious' and 'cross-religious' concepts.[27] D'Costa defines 'trans-religious' as 'a concept of holiness that the researcher creates, or at least assumes as universal, and then finds among many other religions, thereby often running against the self interpretation of the said saint, and their tradition'. A 'cross-religious approach' is described as 'a tradition-specific notion of holiness ... which then finds parallels or mirror-reflections, within other traditions. Karl Rahner supported such a theological history of religion. Though this is more acceptable, it conflicts with the self-description of the valorised saint and his or her community.'[28] Respecting the boundaries associated with a Christian notion of holiness does not deny that genuine signs of holiness exist in other religions.

Chiara Lubich and the Focolare movement's involvement with interreligious dialogue is an example of respecting boundaries while acknowledging genuine holiness in others. The spiritual intuition for a more communal living of the call to holiness, the building together of an 'exterior castle', and an increasing involvement in interreligious dialogue are all part of the Focolare charism. When asked why this involvement in interreligious dialogue has been so rapid and fruitful, Chiara Lubich responds, 'the decisive element and characteristic is love, love poured in our hearts by the Holy Spirit. Love finds a spontaneous and immediate echo in other religions and cultures. And that is why in all there is present the so-called "Golden Rule", that for us is expressed "Do unto others as you would have them do unto you" (Luke 6:31).'[29] This love consists 'in loving without distinction, in loving first without expecting that the other loves us (like the love of God for us)' and in 'being one', that 'is to be all things to all people' (1 Cor. 9:22).[30] To 'be one' with others calls for a self-emptying and a spiritual poverty that finds its roots in Christ crucified and abandoned.[31]

### Holiness and a right relationship with the environment
We are one with each other and all of creation – like it or not, this is the truth. Living the call to holiness ultimately has an effect on every

relationship – with God, others, the physical/natural world, and one's very self. All of creation lives in interdependence on every other aspect of creation. Many articles and books on environmental ethics mention that the word 'ecology' derives from the Greek word *oikos*. Ecology 'explores the "home", the *oikos*, as the matrix of all the relationships of living, where each living thing is at home and has a livelihood.'[32]

In the past, much of Christian spirituality viewed creation with ambivalence. We have sometimes neglected the fact that God's building project also includes the landscape, soil, weather conditions, plant and animal life, and cultural environment in which this dwelling exists. The earth is our home here and now. It is also the much-loved dwelling place of God our Creator and Sustainer. The incarnation is the concrete expression of this reality. Although we are pilgrims and strangers and have no lasting city, nevertheless, we call earth home. It is here Jesus chose to live and bring about our redemption. His relation with the created world was not vague: he was born in Bethlehem, grew up in Nazareth, ministered in Galilee, died and rose from the dead in Jerusalem. He physically lived on very real geographical soil on our precious planet. Because of this, where we are placed in the world is both gift and responsibility. To live contemplatively today, we need, in the words of the Father General of the Jesuits, Peter-Hans Kolvenbach, to take into account the particular in order to respect the universal, as the spirituality of Ignatius of Loyola (1491–1556) suggests:

It is the concrete particular that expresses what God is, Jesus' Father and our Father; and the concrete particular is the only way to know the universal. How can we reduce to a neat sentence this Ignatian vision? In a book published in 1640, an author set himself the task and created this maxim: *Non coerceri a maximo, contineri tamen a minimo, hoc divinum est.* Translating that is not very easy, but the sense is this: 'To be unconstrained by the greatest, to be contained even so in the slightest – this is the divine.'

To put that into our perspectives: To live in the dimension of the universal, yet to labor on the concrete particular, this is the divine. This is the mystery of Christ, because he who is the 'greatest' – above and beyond every conceivable frontier border, the unconstrainable Majesty of God, the divine Majesty that nothing can force or impede, he is found in the 'least' – in the flesh and heart of the Incarnate Word, in a precise place in the Roman empire, in a precise time during human history. In this vision of Christ's mystery, Ignatius adopts a line of conduct: following Christ, to immerse oneself in concrete work according to one's opportunities and one's abilities, but singleheartedly straining towards the infinity of God, who presents in the here and now the wide horizons of his plan of salvation.'[33]

We are made of the same stuff on which we walk and we share our lives with all that has life and gives life. Creation itself teaches us how to open our lives to a more contemplative gaze and live with an informed gentleness and the wisdom of compassion.

It sounds paradoxical, but with this in mind, we must be quick to acknowledge that here 'we have no lasting city' (Heb. 13:13) and we are constantly moving towards our Trinitarian homeland. We are sustained by that Trinitarian love now as God is at work in all things, but we also wait for that time when 'God will be all in all' (1 Cor. 15:28). This is not true only for humans, created in the image and likeness of the Trinity, but for all of creation. The mystery of God's will is that in the fullness of time, all things in heaven and earth will be gathered into that circle of love which is the Trinity.[34] These reflections raise some challenging questions: how do we embrace earth which is home now while clinging to the hope of an eternal home? What does our contemplative reading of today's world, particularly what is happening to the environment, say to us regarding holiness?[35]

The anonymous author of the *Epistle to Diognetus* (V, 1–5) offers a way of answering the question by entering into the dance of creation:

Christians are not distinguished from the rest of humanity by either country, speech or customs. They do not live in cities of their own; they use no particular language, they do not follow an eccentric manner of life ... They reside in their own countries, but only as aliens; they take part in everything as citizens, and endure everything as foreigners. Every foreign land is their home, and every home a foreign land.[36]

The reality for us as Christians is that we are not completely 'at home' on earth. We are always mere pilgrims, 'on the way home but not home yet'.[37] The challenge lies, on the one hand, in respecting and having reverence for God's gift of creation, and joyfully embracing the beauty of the earth. God's 'fingerprints' appear in so many ways on created things, we only need eyes to see. While we are at home, we are also 'strangers' and 'every home [is] a foreign land'. Clinging to the earth without a sense of transcendence is futile. The design of the book cover for *Embracing Earth: Catholic Approaches to Ecology* expresses this well: surrounding an image of Jesus tenderly embracing the world are the words: 'If we seek heaven, the earth will be saved. If we seek only earth, we will lose all.'[38]

In his *Spiritual Exercises*, Ignatius of Loyola offers some practical insights into how the call to holiness is intertwined with a respect for the earth. Underlying the call for a respectful relationship with the totality of creation is the Ignatian conviction that God, the Creator and Lord, is intimately involved in all that is. As Ignatius notes in his 'Contemplation to Attain Love',[39] God 'labors and works for me in all creatures on the face of the earth'. In each particular detail of creation, God is giving, conserving, and conferring life and sensation on them. Joseph Tetlow suggests how this point could be proposed today:

> I let my mind run through all created things: the far reaches of space, our own galaxy, the globe of the earth, imagining how God labors to keep their magnificent order and functioning. Then I enter into living things, perhaps into individual birds or animals and individual persons, imagining how God keeps nerves crackling and bone marrow producing blood, and the like. I might consider a tiny little bug or flower, and imagine how many other living and nonliving things conspired to bring it to life and sustain it.
>
> I consider this and ponder it, letting my heart go out to God. How great God is! How full of life, and how eager to have others exist, particularly other rational creatures. God labors and hopes and keeps sustaining us even when we destroy.[40]

Ignatius knew the importance of contact with nature for Christian spirituality. He intimates that awe and wonder at the beauty of creation lead to an experience of the invisible God who created them. All reality is sacramental. For Ignatius, creation is not just a past event, but even now God's creative action is calling each person and all things out of chaos into a universal hymn of praise.[41]

Ignatius' 'Contemplation to Attain Love,' his final meditation in the *Spiritual Exercises*, shows how God is at work in all of creation. It also opens one up to the possibility of a profound experience of union with the Triune God in and through the world.[42] Ignatius begins by noting that 'love ought to manifest itself in deeds more than in words'.[43] Ignatius does not have a romantic or sentimental notion of love: though love involves mutual sharing and communication, it is primarily an action. In Spanish, the difference is between '*amor*' and '*caridad*'. Ignatius chooses '*amor*' to emphasize this dimension of action. The lover and the beloved mutually give to one another.

It is in this context that Ignatius invites us to ask for an 'interior knowledge of the many blessings received', and to 'recall the blessings of creation and redemption'. Ignatius asks us not only to ponder the gifts, but also to recognize that the Divine Lover gives not only gifts, but gives himself. For Ignatius, all is gift, all that we have and all that we are – indeed 'the whole universe' is gift. This elicits a desire in us to beg for the grace: 'That I may in all things love and serve the Divine Majesty'.[45]

Ignatius's own personal enlightenment regarding the connection between the Trinity, creation, the incarnation and the call to holiness finds its roots in his 'Manresa' experience at the River Cardoner in 1522 where, with 'great clarity', he came to understand 'many things, both spiritual matters and matters of faith and of scholarship'.[46] The impact of this moment is hard to underestimate – it was for Ignatius similar to Moses' encounter with God at the burning bush, or Paul's Damascus road experience.[47] One of his closest companions, Jerónimo Nadal, explained what happened to Ignatius:

> Then God began to teach him as a schoolteacher teaches a child ... There he received a penetrating knowledge of the Persons of the Trinity and of the Divine Essence. Even more, he received not only a clear intelligence, but an interior vision of how God created the world, of how the Word became flesh.[48]

Careful analysis of Ignatius's experience shows that fundamentally he came to perceive an interconnection and harmony between all things. Quite simply, he understood that all creatures came from God and would find their ultimate reintegration in him.[49] Adolf Haas masterfully shows the link between Ignatian Trinitarian mysticism and creation:

> In all creatures there is already a trace of the Trinity, but in all rational beings there is more – an image of the Most Holy Trinity.

This aspect seems important to me because it carries on the spiritual motif which had already begun in Loyola, when Ignatius found the greatest consolation in the contemplation of the heavens and the stars. This religious contemplation of creation is now unconsciously deepened in Manresa through Trinitarian understanding. Ignatius now, through his supernaturally elevated understanding and his heart inflamed by God's love, recognizes the traces, analogies and images of the Most Holy Trinity in all God's creatures. Here lies one of the essential sources of the Ignatian principle of seeking and finding God in all things. A characteristic feature of the spiritual Gestalt of St. Ignatius also becomes more clearly visible here: the overflow of interior grace into a cosmic relation to all things.[50]

## Holiness and doxological living

Ignatius recognized that our lives are fundamentally doxological: we were created to praise, reverence and serve God,[51] and this has practical implications on how we live out our call to holiness, and specifically how we relate to all of creation. Conscious of such boundless love received, we are invited to return love patterned on God's way of proceeding. As Ignatius says in the 'Contemplation to Attain Love':

> I will ponder with deep affection how much God our Lord has done for me, and how much he has given me of what he possesses, and consequently how much, he, the same Lord, desires to give me even his very self, in accordance with his divine design.
>
> Then I will reflect on myself, and consider what I on my part ought in all reason and justice to offer and give to his Divine Majesty, namely, all my possessions, and myself along with them.[52]

Aware that ultimately we cannot give anything to God save what we have received as gift, Ignatius prays:

> Take, Lord, and receive all my liberty, my memory, my understanding, and all my will – all that I have and possess. You, Lord, have given all that to me. I now give it back to you, O Lord. All of it is yours. Dispose of it according to your will. Give me your love and your grace, for that is enough for me.[53]

In the second point of the 'Contemplation to Attain Love', there is a gradual crescendo as Ignatius considers how God dwells in the elements, in plants, in animals, in humans. Finally, he concludes: 'I will consider ... how ... he dwells also in myself, giving me existence, life, sensation, and intelligence; and even further, making me his temple, since I am created as a likeness and image of his Divine Majesty.'[54] Moving from the universal to the individual, Ignatius brings out the personal implications of this meditation for us: 'Then I will reflect upon myself'. The closest we can come to reflecting a perfect image of the Trinity is through self-gift, and Ignatius encourages no less than this.

In the 'Contemplation to Attain Love,' Ignatius warns us not to take for granted the gifts that have been given. At the same time, though, there is a marked difference between humanity's limited power, justice, goodness, mercy and other gifts, and that of God. This does not mean that Ignatius underestimates the gifts in themselves. William Peters explains the Ignatian intent behind this point:

> The attention given to oneself, and, in general, to created things, is far from being a device for ascending far above them, presumably even forgetting all about them as soon as possible, in order to arrive at the contemplation of God's goodness, justice, and so forth. On no account must matters be reversed in this exercise. It is essentially a question of enjoying the light and enjoying the water, but it is pointed out that the light and waters have a source.[55]

In order to live in harmony and order with God and all of creation, one must always return to the source.[56] Ignatius reminds us that 'all gifts descend from above'. Just as the 'rays of light descend from the sun, or the rain from their source',[57] so all the blessings and gifts which we have received come from God. The purpose of this last point, in the words of Gerard Manley Hopkins, is to recognize that everything and everyone is 'charged with the grandeur of God'.[58]

The 'Contemplation to Attain Love' is no mere conclusion to the *Spiritual Exercises*, rather it is a new way of praying and being and living out the call to holiness. It brings us closer to Ignatius's own experience at the River Cardoner, where he saw all things coming out of and reintegrated into the Triune God. Growing out of this foundational experience, Ignatius began to contemplate God in all things, especially towards the end of his life. Nadal reports:

This contemplation of the Trinity was often given to him, but in an altogether unique way during the last years of his pilgrimage.

This manner of praying was granted to Father Ignatius ... and also this further grace, that in all things and actions and conversations he experienced and contemplated the presence of God and had a lively feeling for spiritual reality – being contemplative in his very action (*simul in actione contemplativus*). His own favorite way of putting it was: God must be found in all things.[59]

Ignatius's experience of finding God in all things had its roots in discovering the ultimate value or horizon of his life, which was to praise, reverence, and serve his Creator. As we discover this horizon of ultimate value in our own lives, we will live our call to holiness in light of this reality – our everyday experience, our work, our family responsibilities, our political and social commitments. In simpler terms, we might say that the experience of finding God in all things, another way of expressing the call to live Christian holiness, has its roots in 'being in love with God'. As the Jesuit philosopher and theologian Bernard Lonergan (1904–84) says, 'Such being in love has its antecedents, its causes, its conditions, its occasions. But once it has blossomed forth and as long as it lasts, it takes over. It is the first principle. From it flow one's desires and fears, one's joys and sorrows, one's discernment of values, one's decisions and deeds.'[60] Lonergan explains that 'Being in love with God, as experienced, is being in love in an unrestricted fashion. All love is self-surrender, but being in love with God is being in love without limits or qualifications or conditions or reservations.'[61]

Pedro Arrupe, S. J. (1907–91), a former Father General of the Society of Jesus, expresses in a poetic way Lonergan's point:

Nothing is more practical than
finding God, that is, than falling in love
in a quite absolute, final way.

What you are in love with,
what seizes your imagination,
will affect everything.
It will decide
what will get you out of bed in the morning,
what you will do with your evenings,

how you spend your weekends,
what you read, who you know,
what breaks your heart,
and what amazes you with joy and gratitude.

Fall in love, stay in love,
and it will decide everything.[62]

The call to holiness begins with a fundamental experience of God's love that then flows into every dimension of life. It made a difference in the lives of those who have gone before us, and it will continue to make a difference in our lives today.

## Conclusion

God's building project, our call to holiness, has a context. This context is the whole sweep of the divine plan from all eternity, a plan that embraces the whole universe and leads to eternity. This vision, expressed poetically in the Letter to Ephesians 1:3-14 (*passim*) is a fitting conclusion both to this chapter and to this whole book.

Blessed be the God and Father of our Lord Jesus Christ, who has blessed us in Christ with every spiritual blessing in the heavenly places, just as he chose us in Christ before the foundation of the world to be holy and blameless before him in love. He destined us for adoption as his children through Jesus Christ, according to the good pleasure of his will, to the praise of his glorious grace that is freely bestowed on us in the Beloved. In him we have redemption through his blood, the forgiveness of our trespasses, according to the riches of his grace that he lavished on us. With all wisdom and insight he has made known to us the mystery of his will, according to his good pleasure that he set forth in Christ, as a plan for the full-ness of time, to gather up all things in him, things in heaven and things on earth.

Holiness, as understood here, allows us to be inserted into the *plērôma* (fullness) that is being formed in Jesus Christ. This cosmic vision sheds new light on what we had perceived originally as a modest building proj-ect. The Master Designer's plans are far beyond anything we could have hoped for. And our response to God's dwelling, the interior and exterior castle, this work in progress, is to say, 'Now to him who by the power at work within us is able to accomplish abundantly far more than we can ask or imagine, to him be glory in the church and in Christ Jesus to all generations, forever and ever. Amen' (Eph. 3:20).

## Notes

1. Henri de Lubac, *The Church: Paradox and Mystery* (Staten Island: Ecclesia Press, 1969), p.122.

2. Clive Staples Lewis, *Mere Christianity* (San Francisco: HarperSan Francisco, 2001), pp.205–6.

3. Hans Urs Von Balthasar, *'The Unknown Lying Beyond the Word', 3 Creator Spirit* (San Francisco: Ignatius, 1993), pp.105–16.

4. Paul Elie, *The Life You Save May be Your Own: An American Pilgrimage* (New York: Farrar, Straus and Giroux, 2003), pp.351–52. Elie offers a superb summary of O'Connor's characters.

5. Ibid. p.352.

6. Ibid. p.353.

7. Flannery O'Connor, 'Revelation', in *The Complete Stories* (New York: The Noonday Press, 1990, 32nd printing), pp.508–9.

8. Rowan Williams, *Writing in the Dust. Reflections on 11th September and Its Aftermath* (London: Hodder and Stoughton, 2002), pp.80–1.

9. Seamus Heaney, 'The Art of Poetry' (interview), *The Paris Review* 144 (1997), pp.114–15, as quoted in William Isaacs, *Dialogue and the Art of Thinking Together* (New York: Currency/Doubleday, 1999) p.140.

10. Bernardo Olivera, *How Far to Follow? The Martyrs of Atlas* (Kalamazoo, MI: Cistercian Publications, 1997), p.129.

11. Armand Veilleux, 'Community, Church and the Contemplative Life', in *The Gethsemane Encounter. A Dialogue on the Spiritual Life by Buddhist and Christian Monastics*, (eds Donald Mitchell and James Wiseman: New York: Continuum, 1999), p.133.

12. Olivera, *How Far to Follow?*, pp.36–7.

13. For a reflection on holiness in the East, see Andrew Louth, 'Holiness and the Vision of God in the Eastern Fathers', in *Holiness Past and Present* (ed. Stephen C. Barton: London: T&T Clark, 2003), pp.217–38; Tomas Spidlik, *The Spirituality of the Christian East* (Kalamazoo: Cistercian Publications, 1986).

14. Kallistos of Diokleia (Timothy Ware), 'The Human Person as an Icon of the Trinity,' *Sobornost* 8 (1986), pp.6–23.

15. Chiara Lubich, from a *Speech on the Occasion of the Conferral of the*

*UELCI Prize* (9 March 1995) in *La dottrina spirituale* (ed. Michel Vandeleene: Milan: Mondadori, 2001), p.74. She sees the work of Mary as an exterior castle where Christ is present and illumines every part of it, from the centre to the periphery. Cf. Chiara Lubich, 'La spiritualità collettiva e i suoi strumenti', in *Unità e carismi* 5 (1995), 3-4, p.19 as quoted in the excellent article by Jesús Castellano Cervera, 'Dal "castello interiore" al "castello esteriore"' in *Unità e carismi*, 2 (March/April, 2005), pp.10–16. I am grateful to Dr Teresa Gonçalez for this reference.

16. Thérèse of Lisieux, *Prière* 6 in *Œuvres completes* (Paris: Les Éditions du Cerf et Desclée De Brouwer, 1996), p.963. According to p.1448, n.14, she is quoting *Maxim* 70 of John of the Cross. The English translation is 'Act of Oblation to Merciful Love', in *Story of a Soul. The Autobiography of St. Thérèse of Lisieux (*ed. John Clarke: Washington: ICS Publications, 1996), p.277.

17. The bibliography on globalization is vast. One short and challenging discussion on its impact on Christianity is Robert Schreiter, 'Preaching the Gospel in the Twenty-first Century', 11 July 2001, as found in www.dominicains.ca\providence\English/documents\ shreiter.

18. Cf. Kevin Culligan, 'The Darkest Night: Carmelite Spirituality in the Twenty-first Century', *Spiritual Life* 51 (Spring 2005) pp.21–38, especially p.25.

19. Nicholas Lash, *Holiness, Speech and Silence. Reflections on the Question of God* (Burlington VT: Ashgate, 2004), p.26.

20. This passage is taken from the *New Jerusalem Bible* (New York: Doubleday, 1985).

21. See Jean Vermette, *Il XXI secolo sara mistica o non sarà* (Roma Morena: Edizioni OCD, 2005), pp.6–7.

22. John Chryssavgis, *In the Heart of the Desert. The Spirituality of the Desert Fathers and Mothers* (Bloomington IN.: World Wisdom, 2003).

23. This theme has been developed particularly by Chiara Lubich and members of the Focolari movement. For an overview of her spirituality, see Chiara Lubich, *La dottrina spirituale* edited by Michel Umdeleene (Milan: Mondadori, 2001). One publication of her conferences actually has the title 'Constructing an Exterior Castle': see Chiara Lubich, *Costruendo il castello esteriore* (Rome: Città nuova, 2002). See also the essay by Jesùs Castellano Cervera, 'Una spiritualità che unisce il vertice del divino e dell'umano', in *La Dottrina spirituale*, pp.27–34.

24. Gavin d'Costa, 'Christ, The Trinity and Religious Pluralism', in *Christian Uniqueness Reconsidered* (ed. Gavin d'Costa: Maryknoll: Orbis Books, 1990), p.25.

25. See *Rule of Saint Benedict,* 53, which is dedicated to the welcoming of guests in a monastery. There is much wisdom in the monastic tradition that also can be applied to interreligious dialogue. See Pierre-François Béthune, *By Faith and Hospitality: The Monastic Tradition as a Model for Interreligious Encounter* (Herefordshire: Gracewing, 2002).

26. Gavin D'Costa, 'The Communion of Saints and Other Religions: On Saintly Wives in Hinduism and Catholicism', in *Holiness Past and Present* (London: T&T Clark, 2003), p.423. For two thoughtful, though somewhat different approaches to what is proposed here, see Lawrence Cunningham, *A Brief History of Saints* (Oxford: Blackwell Publishing, 2005), especially Chapter Six on 'The Saints, World Religions, and the Future'. Also see Elizabeth Johnson, *Friends of God and Prophets. A Feminist Theological Reading of the Communion of Saints* (New York: Continuum, 1999), especially pp.219ff.

27. For example, see John Stratton Hawley (ed.), *Saints and Virtues* (Berkeley: University of California Press, 1987). Some of the titles in this book give an idea of the direction he is going in: 'Prophet and Saint: The Two Exemplars of Islam'; 'Morality beyond Morality in the Lives of Three Hindu Saints'; 'Saint Ghandi.' Some examples of this approach can be found in the writings of Rudolf Otto, William James, John Hick and, more recently, Edith Wyschogrod, *Saints and Postmodernism. Revisioning Moral Philosophy* (Chicago: University of Chicago Press, 1990).

28. D'Costa, 'Saints and Other Religions', in Barton, *Holiness Past and Present,* p.423.

29. Ibid., *La dottrina spirituale,* p.379.

30. Ibid. p.380.

31. Ibid. pp.380–1.

32. Tony Kelly, *An Expanding Theology: Faith in a World of Connections* (Newtown: E.J. Dwyer, 1993), pp.23–4.

33. Peter-Hans Kolvenbach, 'Ignatius of Loyola: Experience of Christ', *CIS, Review of Ignatian Spirituality* 86 (1997) pp.31–2.

34. Bruno Forte, *The Trinity as History.* Translated from the 3rd Italian edition, *La Trinità come storia,* by Paul Rotondi (New York: Alba House, 1989), pp.222. Forte is quoting J. Moltmann, *Trinità e regno di Dio La dottrina Su Dio* (Brescia: Queriniana, 1983), p.212.

35. See Donna Orsuto, 'Catholic Spirituality and the Environment. St Ignatius of Loyola: A Case Study', *Studies in Spirituality* 9 (1999), pp.140–57. This section is a reworking of this article.

36. This passage was quoted by Marcello Semeraro, *Con la Chiesa nel mondo: il laico nella teologia nel la magistero* (Rome: Edizioni Vivere In, 1991), p.35, n17. See also Christopher O'Donnell, 'Diognetus, Epistle to' in *Ecclesia, A Theological Encyclopedia of the Church* (Collegeville: Liturgical Press, 1996), pp.131–2.

37. Forte, *The Trinity as History*, p.228.

38. Albert Lachance and John E. Carroll (eds), *Embracing Earth. Catholic Approaches to Ecology* (New York: Orbis, 1994).

39. Ignatius of Loyola, *Spiritual Exercises,* in *Ignatius of Loyola. The Spiritual Exercises and Selected Works* (Mahush: Paulist Press, 1991).

40. Joseph Tetlow, *Choosing Christ in the World. Directing the Spiritual Exercises of St. Ignatius According to Annotations Eighteen and Nineteen* (St. Louis: The Institute of Jesuit Sources, 1989), p.173.

41. Joseph Tetlow, 'The Fundamentum: Creation in the Principle and Foundation' *Studies of Jesuit Spirituality* 21 (September 1989), p.24.

42. See also David Lonsdale, *Eyes to See. Ears to Hear* (London: Darton, Longman, and Todd, 1990), especially pp.45–62 on 'The World and the Trinity'.

43. Ignatius of Loyola, *Spiritual Exercises*, 230.

44. William Peters, *The Spiritual Exercises of St. Ignatius, Exposition and Interpretation* (Rome: Centrum Ignatianum Spiritualitatis, 1980), p.158.

45. Ignatius of Loyola, *Spiritual Exercises*, 233.

46. *A Pilgrim's Testament. The Memoirs of Ignatius of Loyola* (transcribed by Luis Gonçalves da Camara; trans. Parmananda R. Divarkar: Rome: PUG, 1983), pp.31–2, para. 30. He briefly describes the River Cardoner experience on pp.29–31, paras. 28–30.

47. Pedro Arrupe, 'The Trinitarian Inspiration of the Ignatian Charism', in *The Trinity in the Ignatian Charism* (Rome: Centrum Ignatianum Spiritualitatis, 1985), p.19, para. 18.

48. Jerónimo Nadal, *Dialogi pro Societate* (1563), n.8 in *Fontes narrativi de S. Ignatio de Loyola et de Societatis Iesu initiis* II, 408, as quoted by Arrupe, 'The Trinitarian Inspiration', p.17, para. 16.

49. See Pedro Leturia, 'Génesis de los Ejercicios de s. Ignacio y su influjo en la fundación de la Compañía de Jesùs (1521-1540)', *Acta Historica*

*Societatis Iesu* (1941), p.32 as quoted by Pedro Arrupe, 'The Trinitarian Inspiration', p.18, para. 17.

50. Adolf Haas, 'The Foundations of Ignatian Mysticism in Loyola and Manresa', *The Trinity in the Ignatian Charism,* p.175. This is part of Haas' introduction to the German translation and edition of Ignatius's *Spiritual Diary.*

51. See John O'Donnell, 'Faith in God the Creator', *Gregorianum*, 78, 2 (1997), pp.324–5.

52. Ignatius of Loyola, *Spiritual Exercises*, 234.

53. Ibid. 234.

54. Ibid. 235.

55. Peters, *The Spiritual Exercises of St Ignatius*, p.168.

56. Ibid. p.166.

57. Ignatius of Loyola, *Spiritual Exercises*, 237.

58. Gerard Manley Hopkins, *Poems and Prose* (selected and ed. W. H. Gardner: Middlesex: Penguin Books, 1972), p.27.

59. Jerome Nadal, *Annot. in Examen*, c IV (*Mon. Nadal* V, 162–3) as quoted in Herbert Alphonso, *Placed with Christ the Son: Glimpses into the Spirituality of the Jesuit Constitutions* (Anand: Gujarat Sahitya Prakash, 1993), p.39.

60. Bernard Lonergan, *Method in Theology* (Toronto: University of Toronto Press for the Lonergan Research Institute, 1971), p.105.

61. Lonergan, *Method*, pp.105–6.

62. This passage is attributed to Fr Pedro Arrupe, S. J. I tired, without success, to track down the reference in print. According to Herbert Alphonso, S. J. the former director of the Ignatian Spirituality Centre (CIS), Father Arrupe said these words at the Ignatian Course of February 1981 when he spoke on the topic 'Rooted and Grounded in Love' (for the English version of this profound lecture see *Acta Romana* 1981, pp.472–504). Significantly, this was Fr Arrupe's final public lecture before he suffered a stroke on 7 August 1981.

# Postcript

The interior of St. Clement's Basilica in Rome always demands attention. A few weeks ago, after participating in an early-morning celebration of the Eucharist, its extraordinary twelfth-century mosaic caught and held my attention in a fresh sort of way. Even though I frequent this church almost daily and am perhaps a bit overly familiar with the amazing artistry evident in each carefully placed piece of precious stone (or *tesserae*), the mosaic always leaves me marvelling. On this particular morning, its tree of life cross, with the branches winding throughout the apse just above the altar, elicited a strong response of awe and gratitude within me. Enfolded within the branches, as mentioned in Chapter 1, are saints, doctors of the Church and ordinary folks going about their daily tasks.

The mosaic intricately illustrates the significance of the cross of Christ and the sacrificial, life-giving nature of his love. It holds before us the eucharistic challenge to live 'through Him, with Him and in Him. In the unity of the Holy Spirit'. Along with the sacrificial challenge and example of loving service, the mosaic serves to remind us that we are interconnected with one another. Across the globe, involved in a variety of vocations and tasks, we are united to one another as in the living vine. This particular morning I noticed in the strong branches winding out from the central focus of the cross, the hand of the Father just above Christ crucified from whom came streams of waters – living water pouring forth from the cross. All this seemed to sum up our discussion of holiness.

Holiness is the result of costly love, Trinitarian love poured out, given without measure, given without merit. Christ, in the words of St. Catherine of Siena, is 'madly in love' (*pazzo d'amore*) with us, and his death on the cross is proof of this magnificent gift. Holiness is about receiving this gift and then allowing the life-giving power of Christ's love to flow into our lives so that we can freely give ourselves to God and to others. It means allowing this Trinitarian love, manifest in Christ crucified, to penetrate our lives and transform us into the image and likeness of the divine lover.

Imagining a contemporary rendering of the mosaic, I see it entwining my aunt, lovingly caring for my infirm uncle. She would probably think it odd if I told her she manifests the holy to me, that she is a witness to the compassion of a loving God. Life is not easy for her or her family. Daily, she goes through her routine, tending to family needs and life's demands. Daily, she places her trust in God and abides in his care and finds herself entwined in Christ's strong love in the midst of challenges, confusion and pain. Her costly love is joined with that of Christ. In those same branches springing forth from the cross of Christ, there are students studying in the library, grappling with the demands of academics although their hearts are restless with the desire to reach out with practical compassion and serve the family of God. I imagine politicians and diplomats wanting to build the kingdom of God – good people who commit themselves to their secular calling, having taken the time to inform and renew their conscience each morning in prayer and Scripture reading. The vine embraces us all, including those whose lives are difficult – those to whom the wide scope of life is truncated. In those tendrils I envision my sister, who at fifty-five knows incredible physical suffering and confinement. As she rests in the arbour of God's love, she recognizes the hand of providence in the simple, barely perceptible things that make up daily life. Faith has trained her, faith is sustaining her. By faith, she recognizes the sap is flowing through the vine and into her soul. In her affliction, holiness and peace have met. Grace working through her is generative in simple ministry. Although limited, she is able to practise an everyday, simple, easily overlooked type of holiness. Through her prayer and in her reaching out to others in her volunteer efforts at the care facility where she resides, by placing telephone calls and in sharing her smile, she is able to both manifest and recognize the love of God flowing from the cross and through the ever-living vine. Arlene is living transforming, self-giving love, and in the living, she is becoming increasingly Christ-like, increasingly holy. Her life is gift – a gift to her loving Lord, a gift to those who love her, and most especially a gift to me. It is to her that I dedicate this book.

*Feast of All Saints*
*1 November 2005*
*Rome*

# Index